Jack C. Richards & Chuck Sandy

Passages

Third Edition

Student's Book

1

CAMBRIDGE
UNIVERSITY PRESS

CAMBRIDGE
UNIVERSITY PRESS

32 Avenue of the Americas, New York, NY 10013-2473, USA

Cambridge University Press is part of the University of Cambridge.

It furthers the University's mission by disseminating knowledge in the pursuit of education, learning and research at the highest international levels of excellence.

www.cambridge.org
Information on this title: www.cambridge.org/9781107627697

© Cambridge University Press 2015

First published 1998
Second edition 2008

Printed in Hong Kong, China, by Golden Cup Printing Company Limited

A catalog record for this publication is available from the British Library.

ISBN 978-1-107-62705-5 Student's Book 1
ISBN 978-1-107-62701-7 Student's Book 1A
ISBN 978-1-107-62706-2 Student's Book 1B
ISBN 978-1-107-62725-3 Workbook 1
ISBN 978-1-107-62718-5 Workbook 1A
ISBN 978-1-107-62720-8 Workbook 1B
ISBN 978-1-107-62768-0 Teacher's Edition 1 with Assessment Audio CD/CD-ROM
ISBN 978-1-107-62754-3 Class Audio 1 CDs
ISBN 978-1-107-62769-7 Full Contact 1
ISBN 978-1-107-62771-0 Full Contact 1A
ISBN 978-1-107-62772-7 Full Contact 1B
ISBN 978-1-107-62762-8 DVD 1
ISBN 978-1-107-66626-9 Presentation Plus 1

Additional resources for this publication at www.cambridge.org/passages

Cambridge University Press has no responsibility for the persistence or accuracy of URLs for external or third-party Internet Web sites referred to in this publication and does not guarantee that any content on such Web sites is, or will remain, accurate or appropriate. Information regarding prices, travel timetables, and other factual information given in this work is correct at the time of first printing but Cambridge University Press does not guarantee the accuracy of such information thereafter.

Art direction, book design, layout services, and photo research: Q2A / Bill Smith
Audio production: John Marshall Media
Video production: Steadman Productions

Authors' Acknowledgments

A great number of people contributed to the development of *Passages Third Edition*. Particular thanks are owed to the following reviewers and institutions, as their insights and suggestions have helped define the content and format of the third edition:

Paulo A. Machado, Rio de Janeiro, Brazil; Simone C. Wanguestel, Niterói, Brazil; Athiná Arcadinos Leite, **ACBEU**, Salvador, Brazil; Lauren Osowski, **Adult Learning Center**, Nashua, NH, USA; Brenda Victoria, **AIF System**, Santiago, Dominican Republic; Alicia Mitchell-Boncquet, **ALPS Language School**, Seattle, WA, USA; Scott C. Welsh, **Arizona State University**, Tempe, AZ, USA; Silvia Corrêa, **Associação Alumni**, São Paulo, Brazil; Henrick Oprea, **Atlantic Idiomas**, Brasília, Brazil; Márcia Lima, **B.A. English School**, Goiânia, Brazil; Carlos Andrés Mejía Gómez, **BNC Centro Colombo Americano Pereira**, Pereira, Colombia; Tanja Jakimoska, **Brava Training**, Rio de Janeiro, Brazil; Paulo Henrique Gomes de Abreu, **Britannia International English**, Rio de Janeiro, Brazil; Gema Kuri Rodríguez, **Business & English**, Puebla, Mexico; Isabela Villas Boas, **Casa Thomas Jefferson**, Brasília, Brazil; Inara Lúcia Castillo Couto, **CEL-LEP**, São Paulo, Brazil; Ana Cristina Hebling Meira, **Centro Cultural Brasil-Estados Unidos**, Campinas, Brazil; Juliana Costa da Silva, **Centro de Cultura Anglo Americana**, Rio de Janeiro, Brazil; Heriberto Díaz Vázquez, **Centro de Investigación y Docencia Económicas**, Mexico City, Mexico; D. L. Dorantes-Salas, **Centro de Investigaciones Biológicas del Noroeste**, La Paz, Mexico; Elizabeth Carolina Llatas Castillo, **Centro Peruano Americano El Cultural**, Trujillo-La Libertad, Peru; Márcia M. A. de Brito, **Chance Language Center**, Rio de Janeiro, Brazil; Rosalinda Heredia, **Colegio Motolinia**, San Juan del Río, Mexico; Maria Regina Pereira Filgueiras, **College Language Center**, Londrina, Brazil; Lino Mendoza Rodriguez, **Compummunicate**, Izúcar de Matamoros, Mexico; Maria Lucia Sciamarelli, **Cultura Inglesa**, Campinas, Brazil; Elisabete Thess, **Cultura Inglesa**, Petrópolis, Brazil; Catarina M. B. Pontes Kruppa, **Cultura Inglesa**, São Paulo, Brazil; Sheila Lima, **Curso Oxford**, Rio de Janeiro, Brazil; Elaine Florencio, Beth Vasconcelos, **English House Corporate**, Rio de Janeiro, Brazil; Vasti Rodrigues e Silva, **Fox Idiomas**, Rio de Janeiro, Brazil; Ricardo Ramos Miguel Cézar, Walter Júnior Ribeiro Silva, **Friends Language Center**, Itapaci, Brazil; Márcia Maria Pedrosa Sá Freire de Souza, **IBEU**, Rio de Janeiro, Brazil; Jerusa Rafael, **IBEUV**, Vitória, Brazil; Lilianne de Souza Oliveira, **ICBEU**, Manaus, Brazil; Liviane Santana Paulino de Carvalho, **ICBEU**, São Luís, Brazil; Manuel Marrufo Vásquez, **iempac Instituto de Enseñanza del Idioma Ingles**, Tequila, Mexico; Nora Aquino, **Instituto de Ciencias y Humanidades Tabasco**, Villahermosa, Mexico; Andrea Grimaldo, **Instituto Laurens**, Monterrey, Mexico; Cenk Aykut, Staci Jenkins, Kristen Okada, **Interactive College of Technology**, Chamblee, GA, USA; Imeen Manahan-Vasquez, Zuania Serrano, **Interactive Learning Systems**, Pasadena, TX, USA; Nicholas J. Jackson, **Jackson English School**, Uruapan, Mexico; Marc L. Cummings, **Jefferson Community and Technical College**, Louisville, KY, USA; Solange Nery Veloso, **Nery e Filho Idiomas**, Rio de Janeiro, Brazil; Tomas Sparano Martins, **Phil Young's English School**, Curitiba, Brazil; Paulo Cezar Lira Torres, **PRIME Language Center**, Vitória, Brazil; Angie Vasconcellos, **Robin English School**, Petrópolis, Brazil; Barbara Raifsnider, **San Diego Community College District**, San Diego, CA, USA; James Drury de Matos Fonseca, **SENAC**, Fortaleza, Brazil; Manoel Fialho da Silva Neto, **SENAC**, Recife, Brazil; Marilyn Ponder, **Tecnológico de Monterrey**, Irapuato, Mexico; Linda M. Holden, **The College of Lake County**, Grayslake, IL, USA; Janaína da Silva Cardoso, **UERJ**, Rio de Janeiro, Brazil; Gustavo Reges Ferreira, Sandlei Moraes de Oliveira, **UFES**, Vitória, Brazil; Nancy Alarcón Mendoza, **UNAM, Facultad de Estudios Superiores Zaragoza**, Mexico City, Mexico; Rosa Awilda López Fernández, **UNAPEC**, Santo Domingo, Dominican Republic; Vera Lúcia Ratide, **Unilínguas**, São Leopoldo, Brazil; Elsa Yolanda Cruz Maldonado, **Universidad Autónoma de Chiapas**, Tapachula, Mexico; Deida Perea, **Universidad Autónoma de Ciudad Juárez**, Ciudad Juárez, Mexico; Gabriela Ladrón de Guevara de León, **Universidad Autónoma de la Ciudad de México**, Mexico City, Mexico; Juan Manuel Ardila Prada, **Universidad Autónoma de Occidente**, Cali, Colombia; Lizzete G. Acosta Cruz, **Universidad Autónoma de Zacatecas**, Fresnillo, Mexico; Ary Guel, Fausto Noriega, Areli Martínez Suaste, **Universidad Autónoma de Zacatecas**, Zacatecas, Mexico; Gabriela Cortés Sánchez, **Universidad Autónoma Metropolitana Azcapotzalco**, Mexico City, Mexico; Secundino Isabeles Flores, Guillermo Guadalupe Duran Garcia, Maria Magdalena Cass Zubiria, **Universidad de Colima**, Colima, Mexico; Alejandro Rodríguez Sánchez, **Universidad del Golfo de México Norte**, Orizaba, Mexico; Fabiola Meneses Argüello, **Universidad La Salle Cancún**, Cancún, Mexico; Claudia Isabel Fierro Castillo, **Universidad Politécnica de Chiapas**, Tuxtla Gutierrez, Mexico; Eduardo Aguirre Rodríguez, M.A. Carolina Labastida Villa, **Universidad Politécnica de Quintana Roo**, Cancún, Mexico; Gabriela de Jesús Aubry González, **Universidad TecMilenio Campus Veracruz**, Boca del Rio, Mexico; Frank Ramírez Marín, **Universidad Veracruzana**, Boca del Río, Mexico.

Additional thanks are owed to Alex Tilbury for revising the Self-assessment charts, Paul MacIntyre for revising the Grammar Plus section, and Karen Kawaguchi for writing the Vocabulary Plus section.

Welcome to **Passages!**

Congratulations! You have learned the basics; now it's time to raise your English to a whole new level.

Your journey through each unit of *Passages Third Edition* will include a range of activities that will **progressively expand your language ability** in a variety of contexts, including formal and informal communication.

Along the way, you will encounter frequent communication reviews and progress checks that will **systematically consolidate your learning**, while **additional grammar and vocabulary practice** is available whenever you need it in the Grammar Plus and Vocabulary Plus sections in the back of this book.

RAISING YOUR ENGLISH TO A WHOLE NEW LEVEL
Unique features to boost your English proficiency!

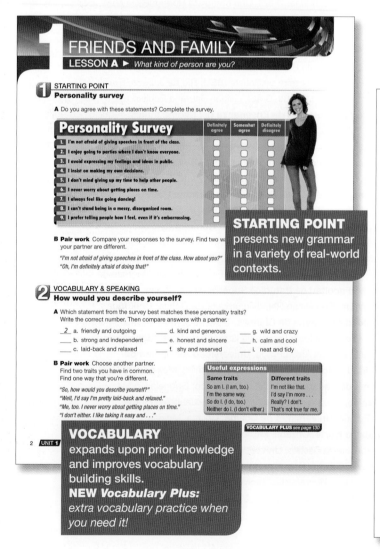

STARTING POINT presents new grammar in a variety of real-world contexts.

VOCABULARY expands upon prior knowledge and improves vocabulary building skills.
NEW Vocabulary Plus: extra vocabulary practice when you need it!

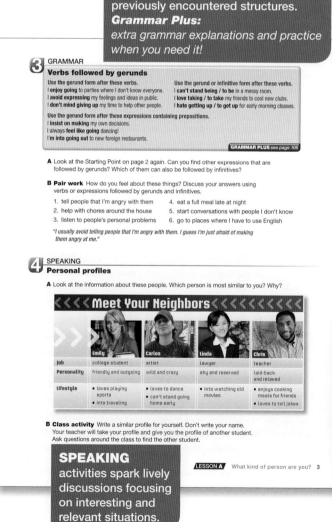

GRAMMAR is explored in context and builds on previously encountered structures.
Grammar Plus: extra grammar explanations and practice when you need it!

SPEAKING activities spark lively discussions focusing on interesting and relevant situations.

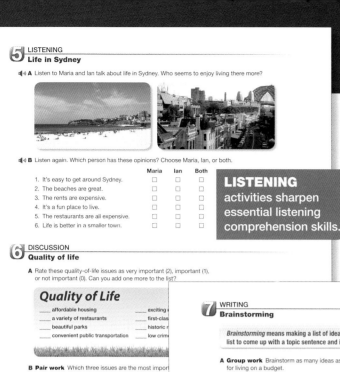

5 LISTENING
Life in Sydney

🔊 **A** Listen to Maria and Ian talk about life in Sydney. Who seems to enjoy living there more?

🔊 **B** Listen again. Which person has these opinions? Choose Maria, Ian, or both.

	Maria	Ian	Both
1. It's easy to get around Sydney.	☐	☐	☐
2. The beaches are great.	☐	☐	☐
3. The rents are expensive.	☐	☐	☐
4. It's a fun place to live.	☐	☐	☐
5. The restaurants are all expensive.	☐	☐	☐
6. Life is better in a smaller town.	☐	☐	☐

6 DISCUSSION
Quality of life

A Rate these quality-of-life issues as very important (2), important (1), or not important (0). Can you add one more to the list?

Quality of Life

____ affordable housing
____ a variety of restaurants
____ beautiful parks
____ convenient public transportation
____ exciting
____ first-clas
____ historic n
____ low crim

B Pair work Which three issues are the most impor
considering where to live? Explain why.

*"I guess affordable housing and exciting nightlife are the m
find a place I could afford that was near someplace fun."*

*"I know what you mean. But for me, I guess low crime rates
I want to live somewhere where I feel safe. I don't mind if .*

C Class activity Share your answers with your clas
mentioned most often?

24 **UNIT 3** Exploring new cities

LISTENING activities sharpen essential listening comprehension skills.

Passages Third Edition is a two-level course that will open the door to communicating with greater fluency and proficiency, with:

- **more sophisticated** real-world grammar and vocabulary,
- **thought-provoking** discussions and academic writing activities,
- **more challenging** listening and reading comprehension topics.

READING passages drawn from authentic sources promote critical thinking and analysis.

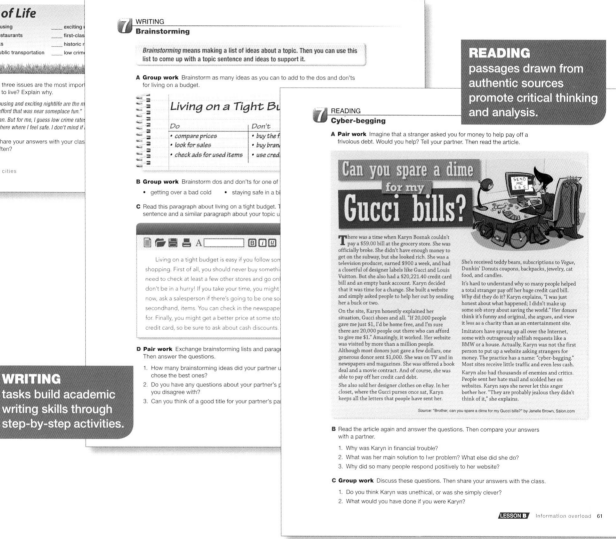

7 WRITING
Brainstorming

Brainstorming means making a list of ideas about a topic. Then you can use this list to come up with a topic sentence and ideas to support it.

A Group work Brainstorm as many ideas as you can to add to the dos and don'ts for living on a budget.

Living on a Tight Bu

Do	Don't
• compare prices	• buy the f
• look for sales	• buy bran
• check ads for used items	• use cred

B Group work Brainstorm dos and don'ts for one of

- getting over a bad cold
- staying safe in a bi

C Read this paragraph about living on a tight budget. T
sentence and a similar paragraph about your topic u

📄 📂 📋 🖨 A [____] 🅱️/🆄

Living on a tight budget is easy if you follow som
shopping. First of all, you should never buy somethi
need to check at least a few other stores and go on
don't be in a hurry! If you take your time, you might
now, ask a salesperson if there's going to be one so
secondhand, items. You can check in the newspape
for. Finally, you might get a better price at some sto
credit card, so be sure to ask about cash discounts.

D Pair work Exchange brainstorming lists and paragi
Then answer the questions.

1. How many brainstorming ideas did your partner u
chose the best ones?
2. Do you have any questions about your partner's p
you disagree with?
3. Can you think of a good title for your partner's pai

WRITING tasks build academic writing skills through step-by-step activities.

7 READING
Cyber-begging

A Pair work Imagine that a stranger asked you for money to help pay off a frivolous debt. Would you help? Tell your partner. Then read the article.

Can you spare a dime for my Gucci bills?

There was a time when Karyn Bosnak couldn't pay a $59.00 bill at the grocery store. She was officially broke. She didn't have enough money to get on the subway, but she looked rich. She was a television producer, earned $900 a week, and had a closetful of designer labels like Gucci and Louis Vuitton. But she also had a $20,221.40 credit card bill and an empty bank account. Karyn decided that it was time for a change. She built a website and simply asked people to help her out by sending her a buck or two.

On the site, Karyn honestly explained her situation, Gucci shoes and all. "If 20,000 people gave me just $1, I'd be home free, and I'm sure there are 20,000 people out there who can afford to give me $1." Amazingly, it worked. Her website was visited by more than a million people. Although most donors just gave a few dollars, one generous donor sent $1,000. She was on TV and in newspapers and magazines. She was offered a book deal and a movie contract. And of course, she was able to pay off her credit card bill.

She also sold her designer clothes on eBay. In her closet, where the Gucci purses once sat, Karyn keeps all the letters that people have sent her.

She's received teddy bears, subscriptions to *Vogue*, Dunkin' Donuts coupons, backpacks, jewelry, cat food, and candles.

It's hard to understand why so many people helped a total stranger pay off her huge credit card bill. Why did they do it? Karyn explains, "I was just honest about what happened; I didn't make up some sob story about saving the world." Her donors think it's funny and original, she argues, and view it less as a charity than as an entertainment site.

Imitators have sprung up all over the Internet, some with outrageously selfish requests like a BMW or a house. Actually, Karyn was not the first person to put up a website asking strangers for money. The practice has a name: "cyber-begging." Most sites receive little traffic and even less cash.

Karyn also had thousands of enemies and critics. People sent her hate mail and scolded her on websites. Karyn says she never let this anger bother her. "They are probably jealous they didn't think of it," she explains.

Source: "Brother, can you spare a dime for my Gucci bills?" by Janelle Brown, Salon.com

B Read the article again and answer the questions. Then compare your answers with a partner.

1. Why was Karyn in financial trouble?
2. What was her main solution to her problem? What else did she do?
3. Why did so many people respond positively to her website?

C Group work Discuss these questions. Then share your answers with the class.

1. Do you think Karyn was unethical, or was she simply clever?
2. What would you have done if you were Karyn?

LESSON B Information overload **61**

KEEP MOVING UP!
More support is always available – when and where you need it!

The **WORKBOOK** provides extensive practice of grammar and vocabulary as well as additional reading and writing activities.

The **ONLINE WORKBOOK** – a digital version of the Workbook – enables your teacher to provide instant feedback on your work.

The *PASSAGES* **ONLINE VOCABULARY ACCELERATOR** increases the speed and ease of learning new vocabulary through powerful and innovative digital learning techniques.

Plan of **BOOK 1**

SPEAKING	LISTENING	WRITING	READING
■ Finding out what personality traits you have in common with your classmates ■ Comparing personal profiles ■ Talking about how you have changed or how you would like to change ■ Comparing families	■ Two people describe how they have changed ■ Two people compare similarities and differences between their families ■ A young man describes his recent family reunion	■ Identifying the topic sentence in a paragraph ■ Writing a paragraph about your most positive or negative quality	■ "From Circle of Friends to Modern Tribe": A group of friends can function as a family
■ Talking about past mistakes ■ Comparing reactions to a news story ■ Discussing what might have caused three mysterious events ■ Making guesses about unusual questions ■ Comparing opinions about a real-life unexplained event	■ A man talks about a bad decision he made ■ Three people talk about how they dealt with their problems ■ Two people talk about everyday mysteries	■ Brainstorming topic sentences and supporting ideas ■ Writing a paragraph with dos and don'ts	■ "Amnesia Spoils Newlyweds' Bliss": A man loses his memory after his wedding
■ Explaining why you'd like to visit a particular city ■ Choosing the right city for a particular purpose ■ Deciding which city is best to live in ■ Describing your hometown ■ Discussing quality-of-life issues	■ A TV show introduces two exciting cities ■ Two foreign students explain what they like about their host city ■ Two Sydney residents talk about the city	■ Organizing ideas with a mind map ■ Writing a paragraph about a place you know	■ "Rivals with a Lot in Common": The rivalry between two major Australian cities
■ Discussing personal energy levels ■ Talking about how to deal with stress ■ Giving advice on sleep and energy levels ■ Talking about sleeping habits ■ Interpreting dreams	■ Three people describe methods they use to lower stress ■ Two people describe their dreams and try to interpret them	■ Choosing the best topic sentence ■ Writing a paragraph giving advice on good habits	■ "To Sleep or Not to Sleep?": People are sleeping fewer hours than ever before
■ Discussing conversational styles ■ Discussing awkward social situations ■ Determining appropriate topics for small talk ■ Comparing who you confide in ■ Recounting an interesting conversation	■ People make small talk at parties ■ Two people tell some interesting news	■ Making an outline ■ Writing about a cultural rule	■ "Cell Phone Personality Types": What kind of cell phone user are you?
■ Determining if a story is true or false ■ Presenting a recent news story ■ Discussing how you follow the news ■ Telling stories about uncomfortable situations	■ A radio news broadcast ■ Two people describe complicated experiences ■ An actor describes some embarrassing moments	■ Putting events in chronological order ■ Writing a narrative paragraph	■ "It Happened to Me!": Two comical personal anecdotes

SPEAKING	LISTENING	WRITING	READING
■ Talking about Internet trends ■ Debating whether social networking is a positive or negative influence ■ Giving opinions on modern information technology ■ Discussing potential future technologies	■ Three people talk about social networking ■ A news report describes health problems caused by technology	■ Writing a product or service review	■ "Can you spare a dime for my Gucci bills?": A woman uses the Internet to get money to pay off a frivolous debt
■ Discussing jobs that require creativity ■ Taking a creativity quiz ■ Suggesting new uses for everyday items ■ Talking about creative thinking habits ■ Choosing the inventions that have had the greatest impact on modern life ■ Explaining why new products are invented	■ Three employees explain how their jobs are creative ■ Two descriptions of important business and product ideas	■ Choosing when to begin a new paragraph ■ Writing a composition about a creative or unique person	■ "The Man Who Taught the World to Sing": A profile of the man who invented karaoke
■ Talking about what is typical ■ Discussing what makes you typical or not ■ Discussing the effect of major life changes ■ Giving advice in a role play	■ Three people discuss how they're unique or typical ■ Three people describe how they solved a problem	■ Identifying supporting statements ■ Writing a paragraph with supporting statements	■ "Painting and Problem Solving: Four Lessons": How problem solving and the dynamics of painting are alike
■ Discussing how to handle irritating situations ■ Comparing styles of complaining ■ Role-playing complaints ■ Describing how difficult situations make you feel ■ Stating consumer complaints	■ Two people describe irritating situations ■ A man uses an automated phone menu	■ Writing a message of complaint	■ "Dave Carroll Airs a Complaint": A musician posts music videos to complain about an airline
■ Discussing the results of a survey on ethical behavior ■ Comparing what you would do about different ethical dilemmas ■ Discussing your experiences with unreliable people or services ■ Talking about values that are important to you ■ Explaining what you'd choose if you were given three wishes	■ Two people describe being confronted by an ethical dilemma ■ Three people talk about the values that are most important to them	■ Writing a thesis statement ■ Writing a four-paragraph composition about a happy memory or a regret	■ "New York Honors a Hero": How a construction worker became a hero
■ Describing the benefits and challenges of living abroad ■ Comparing customs between Canada and your country ■ Sharing bad travel experiences ■ Planning a trip with your group	■ Three people talk about their experiences living abroad ■ Two people describe travel mishaps	■ Writing conclusions ■ Writing a composition about living or traveling abroad	■ "Get Yourself Lost": The best way to experience a foreign destination

1 FRIENDS AND FAMILY

LESSON A ▶ *What kind of person are you?*

 STARTING POINT
Personality survey

A Do you agree with these statements? Complete the survey.

Personality Survey	Definitely agree	Somewhat agree	Definitely disagree
1. I'm not afraid of giving speeches in front of the class.	☐	☐	☐
2. I enjoy going to parties where I don't know everyone.	☐	☐	☐
3. I avoid expressing my feelings and ideas in public.	☐	☐	☐
4. I insist on making my own decisions.	☐	☐	☐
5. I don't mind giving up my time to help other people.	☐	☐	☐
6. I never worry about getting places on time.	☐	☐	☐
7. I always feel like going dancing!	☐	☐	☐
8. I can't stand being in a messy, disorganized room.	☐	☐	☐
9. I prefer telling people how I feel, even if it's embarrassing.	☐	☐	☐

B Pair work Compare your responses to the survey. Find two ways you and your partner are different.

"I'm not afraid of giving speeches in front of the class. How about you?"
"Oh, I'm definitely afraid of doing that!"

VOCABULARY & SPEAKING
How would you describe yourself?

A Which statement from the survey best matches these personality traits? Write the correct number. Then compare answers with a partner.

_2_ a. friendly and outgoing   ___ d. kind and generous   ___ g. wild and crazy

___ b. strong and independent   ___ e. honest and sincere   ___ h. calm and cool

___ c. laid-back and relaxed   ___ f. shy and reserved   ___ i. neat and tidy

B Pair work Choose another partner. Find two traits you have in common. Find one way that you're different.

"So, how would you describe yourself?"
"Well, I'd say I'm pretty laid-back and relaxed."
"Me, too. I never worry about getting places on time."
"I don't either. I like taking it easy and . . ."

Useful expressions	
Same traits	**Different traits**
So am I. (I am, too.)	I'm not like that.
I'm the same way.	I'd say I'm more . . .
So do I. (I do, too.)	Really? I don't.
Neither do I. (I don't either.)	That's not true for me.

VOCABULARY PLUS *see page 130*

GRAMMAR

Verbs followed by gerunds

Use the gerund form after these verbs.
I **enjoy going** to parties where I don't know everyone.
I **avoid expressing** my feelings and ideas in public.
I **don't mind giving up** my time to help other people.

Use the gerund or infinitive form after these verbs.
I **can't stand being / to be** in a messy room.
I **love taking / to take** my friends to cool new clubs.
I **hate getting up / to get up** for early morning classes.

Use the gerund form after these expressions containing prepositions.
I **insist on making** my own decisions.
I always **feel like going** dancing!
I'm **into going out** to new foreign restaurants.

GRAMMAR PLUS see page 106

A Look at the Starting Point on page 2 again. Can you find other expressions that are followed by gerunds? Which of them can also be followed by infinitives?

B Pair work How do you feel about these things? Discuss your answers using verbs or expressions followed by gerunds and infinitives.

1. tell people that I'm angry with them
2. help with chores around the house
3. listen to people's personal problems
4. eat a full meal late at night
5. start conversations with people I don't know
6. go to places where I have to use English

"I usually avoid telling people that I'm angry with them. I guess I'm just afraid of making them angry at me."

SPEAKING

Personal profiles

A Look at the information about these people. Which person is most similar to you? Why?

<<<< Meet Your Neighbors <<<<<<<<<<<

	Emily	Carlos	Linda	Chris
Job	college student	artist	lawyer	teacher
Personality	friendly and outgoing	wild and crazy	shy and reserved	laid-back and relaxed
Lifestyle	• loves playing sports • into traveling	• loves to dance • can't stand going home early	• into watching old movies	• enjoys cooking meals for friends • loves to tell jokes

B Class activity Write a similar profile for yourself. Don't write your name. Your teacher will take your profile and give you the profile of another student. Ask questions around the class to find the other student.

5 LISTENING
Changes

◀)) **A** Listen to Marcos and Heather talk about how they have changed over the last five years. How did they change? Complete the chart with the expressions from the box.

kind and generous	friendly and outgoing	shy and reserved	wild and crazy

	used to be . . .	has become . . .
Marcos		
Heather		

◀)) **B** Listen again. Choose the person you think would be more likely to do each of these things this weekend.

	Marcos	Heather
1. stay out late at a big party	☐	☐
2. stay at home and watch TV	☐	☐
3. help someone with a personal problem	☐	☐
4. invite a friend to a funny movie	☐	☐

6 DISCUSSION
How have you changed?

A How have you changed over the last five years? What do you want to change now? Complete the chart.

	How I've changed	How I'd like to change
Habits		
Personality		
Likes and dislikes		

B **Pair work** Compare your charts.
Ask follow-up questions.

"I used to watch a lot of TV, but now I don't."
"Really? What made you change?"
"Well, I was afraid of getting out of shape. So I . . ."

Useful expressions	
Describing how you've changed	**Describing how you'd like to change**
I used to . . . , but now I . . .	I'd like to be more . . .
I think I've become more . . .	I'm interested in . . .

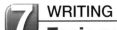

WRITING
Topic sentences

> The main idea is usually found in the first sentence of the paragraph. This sentence is called the topic sentence.

A Read these paragraphs about people's best and worst qualities. Underline the topic sentence in each paragraph.

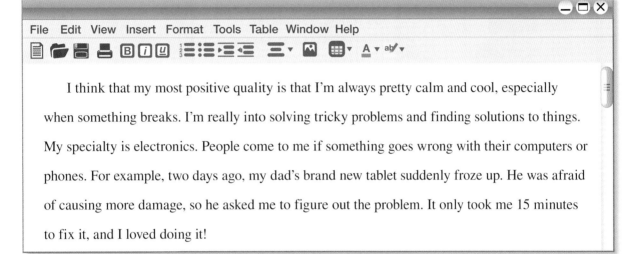

File   Edit   View   Insert   Format   Tools   Table   Window   Help

I think that my most positive quality is that I'm always pretty calm and cool, especially when something breaks. I'm really into solving tricky problems and finding solutions to things. My specialty is electronics. People come to me if something goes wrong with their computers or phones. For example, two days ago, my dad's brand new tablet suddenly froze up. He was afraid of causing more damage, so he asked me to figure out the problem. It only took me 15 minutes to fix it, and I loved doing it!

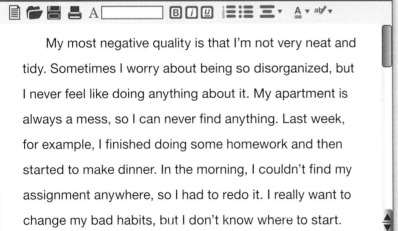

My most negative quality is that I'm not very neat and tidy. Sometimes I worry about being so disorganized, but I never feel like doing anything about it. My apartment is always a mess, so I can never find anything. Last week, for example, I finished doing some homework and then started to make dinner. In the morning, I couldn't find my assignment anywhere, so I had to redo it. I really want to change my bad habits, but I don't know where to start.

B Think about your own personal qualities. Make a list. Then decide which quality is the most positive and which is the most negative. Circle each one.

C Write a paragraph about either your most positive or your most negative quality. Make sure your paragraph has only one main idea.

D Pair work Exchange paragraphs with a partner. Then answer the questions.

1. What is your partner's topic sentence? Underline it.
2. What examples does your partner give to support the topic sentence?
3. What do you find most interesting about your partner's paragraph?

1 **STARTING POINT**
Different types of families

A Look at the families in the pictures. What's different about each type of family?

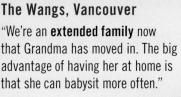
What's Your Family Like?

The Wangs, Vancouver

"We're an **extended family** now that Grandma has moved in. The big advantage of having her at home is that she can babysit more often."

The Watsons, Sydney

"My wife and I both work now, and the extra money is great. The only trouble with being a **two-income family** is we don't spend as much time together."

The Patels, London

"We're a typical **nuclear family** – it's just my sister, my parents, and me. The only bad thing about living in our house is there's only one bathroom!"

B Pair work What are some more advantages and disadvantages of each type of family in part A? Compare ideas.

"In a nuclear family, you might not see your grandparents every day. That's a disadvantage."

2 **LISTENING & SPEAKING**
How are their families different?

🔊 **A** Listen to Paul and Andrea talk about their families. What kind of family did each person grow up in? How have their families changed?

🔊 **B** Listen again. Match the people on the left with the phrases on the right.

1. Andrea _b_   a. has two daughters.
2. Andrea's husband ____   b. doesn't know her in-laws very well.
3. Andrea's sister-in-law ____ c. has three brothers.
4. Paul's sister ____   d. is looking forward to seeing the family.
5. Paul ____   e. will be cooking for 12 people.
6. Paul's mother ____   f. is a law student.

C Pair work Is your family similar to Paul's or Andrea's? How is it similar? How is it different?

GRAMMAR

Noun clauses after *be*

A noun clause is a part of a sentence with a subject and a predicate that functions as a noun. *That* is optional in noun clauses after *be*. Also notice the prepositions followed by gerunds in the first part of the sentences.

The only trouble **with** being a two-income family is **(that) we don't spend as much time together.**
The big advantage **of** having Grandma at home is **(that) she can babysit more often.**

GRAMMAR PLUS *see page 107*

A Look at the Starting Point on page 6 again. Can you find the noun clause in the last paragraph? Which preposition is used in the first part of the sentence?

B Combine the sentences. Then compare answers with a partner.

1. I'm the youngest in the family. The nice thing is I get a lot of attention.
   The nice thing about being the youngest in the family is that I get a lot of attention.
2. I have a younger sister. The trouble is she always wants to borrow my clothes.
3. I'm away at college. The bad part is that I miss my family.
4. I work at night. The worst thing is I can't have dinner with my family.
5. I'm the oldest in the family. One bad thing is that I always have to babysit.

C Complete the sentences with your own ideas. Then compare answers with a partner.

1. An advantage of being a twin is . . .
   that you always have someone to hang out with.
2. A problem with being an only child is . . .
3. One benefit of being the oldest is . . .
4. A big disadvantage of having an older sibling is . . .
5. The best thing about having a big family is . . .

DISCUSSION

Family matters

A Choose at least three questions you'd like to talk about with your group.

- ☐ What's the best thing about spending time with your family? What's the worst thing?
- ☐ What's one advantage of having a close family?
- ☐ What are some rules that people have to follow in your family?
- ☐ What's a benefit of having strict parents?
- ☐ Are you most likely to confide in a parent, a sibling, or a friend?
- ☐ Do you believe mothers and fathers should do the same chores?
- ☐ What are the advantages and disadvantages of having a two-income family?

B Group work Discuss the questions you chose in part A. Ask follow-up questions and make sure everyone in your group participates.

5 VOCABULARY
Compound family terms

A Match the family members on the left with the definitions on the right.

1. Your great-aunt is ____
2. Your granddaughter is ____
3. Your sister-in-law is ____
4. Your great-grandmother is ____

a. your father's or mother's grandmother.
b. your mother's or father's aunt.
c. your son's or daughter's daughter.
d. your wife's or husband's sister, or your brother's wife.

B Pair work Which of the family members in the box can be combined with a prefix or suffix in the chart? Complete the chart with a partner. What does each term mean?

aunt	daughter	mother	niece	son
brother	father	nephew	sister	uncle

great-	grand-	great-grand-	-in-law
aunt	*daughter*	*mother*	*sister*

"Your great-nephew is your brother's or sister's grandson."

VOCABULARY PLUS *see page 130*

6 LISTENING
Family reunion

 A Listen to Victor tell a friend about his family reunion. What were they celebrating at the reunion?

B Listen again. In addition to Victor, who else was at the reunion? Select the people mentioned.

☐ 1. his grandfather
☐ 2. his uncle's cousin
☐ 3. his brother
☐ 4. his sister-in-law
☐ 5. his niece
☐ 6. his son
☐ 7. his mother-in-law
☐ 8. his cousin
☐ 9. friends of the family

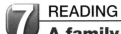

A family of friends

A Group work Do you tend to rely more on friends or family for help and advice? Why? Discuss with your group.

From Circle of Friends to Modern Tribe

Who celebrates birthdays and holidays with you? Who do you call when a crisis hits or when good luck strikes? If your answer is "my friends," you may have a "tribe."

When Ethan Watters took stock of his life a few years ago, the San Francisco writer realized that he was more dependent on friends than family, who lived hundreds of miles away.

"My friends were the centerpiece of my social life," he says. "They had taken on all the responsibilities that family members typically tackle – connecting me to the city, being a matchmaker, and helping me find jobs and places to live."

This circle of friends had become a tribe, which started when a group of artists, writers, and photographers began meeting for dinner every Tuesday night. Before long, they had begun functioning as a family of choice.

Watters grew to believe that non-family members forming close-knit social networks was a growing trend in the United States, and he wrote a book about it called *Urban Tribes: Are Friends the New Family?*

Modern tribes like Watters's often grow out of a shared interest or experience, but not every group of friends becomes a tribe.

The shift from "circle of friends" to tribe happens when members begin to treat each other like family – offering support without expectation of repayment; sheltering each other from gossip, stress, and attack; and looking out for everyone's overall well-being in life, work, and relationships.

Modern tribes often have a regular meeting place, annual parties, and group trips. Shared rites and rituals create a tribal story. "The members of the group may change," Watters says, "but the story of that group has central elements that remain. It gives the group a history."

Every tribe usually has an individual or core group that tends to its growth and survival. These tribal leaders are the ones who get everyone together on a regular basis and make the phone calls that get members excited about upcoming events.

Like families, tribes have a way of shaping their members: Individuals feel more confident, secure, loved, and stable. Even if your own family is close-knit, you may benefit from cultivating a family-like circle of friends. "The love and support we get from one," Watters says, "does not take away from the love and support we get from another."

Source: "My Tribe," by Erin Peterson, Experience Life

B Read the article and answer the questions. Then compare answers with a partner.

1. In what ways does Watters's circle of friends function as a family?
2. According to the article, what are some differences between a tribe and a family?
3. How does a group of friends become a tribe?

C Group work Discuss these questions. Then share your answers with the class.

1. What are some advantages and disadvantages of relying on friends for family-like support?
2. Do you consider yourself a member of a modern tribe? Why or why not?

2 MISTAKES AND MYSTERIES

LESSON A ▶ *Life lessons*

1 STARTING POINT
Learning the hard way

A Read about these people's problems. What mistake did each person make?

What Did I Get Myself Into?
Three mistakes that led to big messes

I was supposed to be studying for a math test this weekend, but my friends made me go to the beach with them instead. I mean, I didn't have to go with them, but I did. Now the test is in two hours, and I'm totally unprepared. I should have stayed home and studied!
— **Alicia, Tepic, Mexico**

In high school, I had to wear a uniform, so I didn't have a lot of fashionable clothes. When I started college, I thought I needed to have more, so I wasted a lot of money on trendy outfits. But I really shouldn't have done it. Now I'm broke!
— **Kenichi, Osaka, Japan**

We weren't supposed to cook in our dorm rooms, but I had a microwave anyway. The cafeteria was right next door, so I really didn't need to have it. Anyway, I got caught making popcorn last week, and the school took the microwave away.
— **Melanie, Toronto, Canada**

B Pair work What should each person do differently in the future? Compare ideas.

"I don't think Alicia should listen to her friends in the future."
"Yeah, I agree. She shouldn't let them influence her like that."

2 LISTENING
I'll never do that again!

A Listen to Frank talk about a bad decision he made. What was his decision? Why was it a bad one?

B Listen again. Are these statements true or false? Choose the correct answer.

	True	False
1. Frank and his neighbor were good friends.	☐	☐
2. Frank knew he was allergic to cats.	☐	☐
3. Frank marked his calendar to remember to feed the cat.	☐	☐
4. Frank forgot what time his train was going to leave.	☐	☐
5. Frank remembered to feed the cat on Saturday.	☐	☐

3 GRAMMAR

Past modals and phrasal modals of obligation

Should have, was supposed to, had to, and *needed to* all describe obligations in the past, although they have slightly different uses.

I **should have** stayed home and studied! *(It was a good idea, but I didn't do it.)*
I **was supposed to** be studying this weekend. *(It was expected, but I didn't do it.)*
I **had to** wear a uniform. *(We were forced to do this.)*
I **didn't have to** go with my friends, but I did. *(There was no obligation.)*
I thought I **needed to** have more clothes. *(I thought this was necessary.)*

GRAMMAR PLUS *see page 108*

A Look at the Starting Point on page 10 again. Can you find other examples of past modals and phrasal modals of obligation? What does each one mean?

B Choose the answer that is true for each sentence. Then compare answers with a partner.

1. I shouldn't have invited them.
   - ☐ a. I didn't invite them.
   - ☐ b. I invited them.

2. That was a secret! You weren't supposed to tell anyone!
   - ☐ a. You didn't tell anyone.
   - ☐ b. You told someone.

3. We didn't have to study for the test.
   - ☐ a. We forgot to study.
   - ☐ b. We were prepared for the test.

4. I know Jane didn't like my cooking, but she didn't need to be so rude about it.
   - ☐ a. Jane was rude to me.
   - ☐ b. Jane wasn't rude to me.

C Complete the sentences with information about yourself. Then compare answers with a partner.

1. After I started high school, I had to . . .
   study a lot harder.
2. I made someone angry once because I wasn't supposed to . . .
3. I wasted a lot of money once because I thought I needed to . . .
4. When I had the opportunity, I should have . . .

4 DISCUSSION

Past experiences

A Look at the survey and choose the items that are true for you.

Have you ever . . .

- ☐ enjoyed doing something you weren't supposed to do?
- ☐ not done something you should have done?
- ☐ done something foolish that you didn't need to do?
- ☐ had to follow a rule you didn't like?
- ☐ had to enforce a rule you didn't like?

B Pair work Discuss your answers. Ask follow-up questions.

"Have you ever enjoyed doing something you weren't supposed to do?"
"Sure. At my old job, I wasn't supposed to take a long lunch, but I took long lunches at the park, anyway. How about you?"

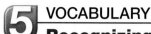

5 VOCABULARY
Recognizing problems

A These verbs are often used to talk about problems. Use the verbs to replace the boldfaced words and phrases in the sentences.

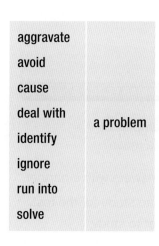

aggravate	
avoid	
cause	
deal with	a problem
identify	
ignore	
run into	
solve	

1. My friend **never does anything about** his problems.
   My friend always ignores his problems.
2. Maria can look at a broken bicycle and **find** the problem right away.
3. My sister is never afraid to **try to take care of** a difficult problem.
4. Dan always **makes** his problems **worse**.
5. Ruby always follows the recipe closely to **prevent** problems when she cooks.
6. Michael always **unexpectedly encounters** problems when he tries to fix things.
7. Carla is great at **completely fixing** any kind of problem at work.
8. Al is the kind of student who always **makes** problems for teachers.

B Pair work Tell your partner about people you know who are similar to the people in the sentences in part A.

"My cousin always ignores her problems. Her car is always making strange noises, but she never does anything about it."

VOCABULARY PLUS *see page 131*

6 LISTENING
Dealing with problems

 A Listen to Ray (*R*), Felipe (*F*), and Jennifer (*J*) talk about a problem that they each had. What did each person finally do about the problem? Write the correct letter.

____ ignored it   ____ dealt with it   ____ aggravated it

 B Listen again. Briefly describe each person's problem.

Ray: _____

Felipe: _____

Jennifer: _____

7 WRITING
Brainstorming

> *Brainstorming* means making a list of ideas about a topic. Then you can use this list to come up with a topic sentence and ideas to support it.

A Group work Brainstorm as many ideas as you can to add to the dos and don'ts for living on a budget.

Living on a Tight Budget

Do	Don't
• compare prices	• buy the first thing you see
• look for sales	• buy brand names
• check ads for used items	• use credit cards

B Group work Brainstorm dos and don'ts for one of these topics. Write your ideas.

- getting over a bad cold
- staying safe in a big city
- preparing for entrance exams

C Read this paragraph about living on a tight budget. Then write a topic sentence and a similar paragraph about your topic using your ideas.

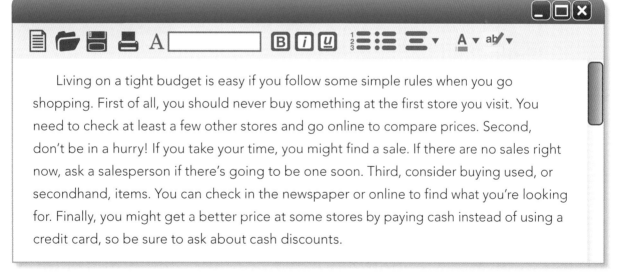

Living on a tight budget is easy if you follow some simple rules when you go shopping. First of all, you should never buy something at the first store you visit. You need to check at least a few other stores and go online to compare prices. Second, don't be in a hurry! If you take your time, you might find a sale. If there are no sales right now, ask a salesperson if there's going to be one soon. Third, consider buying used, or secondhand, items. You can check in the newspaper or online to find what you're looking for. Finally, you might get a better price at some stores by paying cash instead of using a credit card, so be sure to ask about cash discounts.

D Pair work Exchange brainstorming lists and paragraphs with a partner. Then answer the questions.

1. How many brainstorming ideas did your partner use? Do you think he or she chose the best ones?

2. Do you have any questions about your partner's paragraph? Is there anything you disagree with?

3. Can you think of a good title for your partner's paragraph? Explain your choice.

1 STARTING POINT
A mysterious artist

A Read the article and the comments on the right. Whose comments do you agree with?

The Mystery of BANKSY

Banksy is a British graffiti artist who has become famous around the world for two things: his controversial work and the mystery surrounding him. Usually working in disguise or at night, Banksy has managed to keep his identity secret and both his fans and detractors alert. Any clues to his identity always make the news.

In 2010, *Time* magazine featured Banksy as one of the 100 most influential people of the year. Readers hoping to finally see his face must have been pretty disappointed when they saw the picture of Banksy — with a paper bag over his head.

In 2011, when a movie by Banksy was nominated for an Oscar, his graffiti appeared on buildings and signs around Los Angeles. (People thought he could have been trying to get publicity for the movie.) At that time, a passerby photographed a man busy taking photos of the graffiti. It may have been Banksy documenting his own work, but nobody is sure.

In 2013, a website claimed Banksy had been arrested and his identity finally revealed. However, the claims were later discovered to be false. It's not clear who was behind the hoax, but one thing was certain: Banksy's secret was still safe.

Reader Comments

CafeLife: People should stop trying to find out who Banksy is. It's a waste of time.

Hye_Jung: The magazine readers shouldn't have expected Banksy to reveal his identity just because of an article.

Paul2001: I'm certain Banksy must have wanted to win that Oscar. But would he have shown his face at the award ceremony?

ArtFan: Banksy does return to photograph his art, so it might have been him taking the pictures. He should be more careful.

Zorro565: Banksy shouldn't have painted on other people's property. That's illegal.

WebWatcher: That website hoax might have been planned by Banksy himself. What a joke.

More >>

B Pair work Compare your reactions to the article.

"The people who worked on his movie might know who Banksy is."
"Well, maybe, but I'm sure his family must know he is the mysterious artist."

GRAMMAR

Modals with multiple uses

To express degrees of certainty, use *must (not)*, *can't*, *could (not)*, *might (not)*, or *may (not)*.
I'm certain Banksy **must have wanted** to win that Oscar.
People thought he **could have been trying** to get publicity for the movie.
That website hoax **might have been planned** by Banksy himself.

To express obligation, advice, or opinions, use *should (not)*. Do not use *must (not) have* for obligations, advice, or opinions about the past.
Banksy **shouldn't have painted** on other people's property. *(obligation)*
He **should be** more careful. *(advice)*
The magazine readers **shouldn't have expected** Banksy to reveal his identity just because of an article. *(opinion)*

Also notice how these modals are used in the passive and continuous.

GRAMMAR PLUS *see page 109*

A Look at the Starting Point on page 14 again. What does each modal express? Which one is used in the passive?

B Use modals to write reactions to these situations. Then compare answers with a partner.

1. You and your friend planned to meet, but your friend never arrived.
   He might have been busy at work, but he should have called to tell me.

2. You loaned your classmate a lot of money last week, but she still hasn't repaid you.

3. You feel sick after a big fish dinner.

4. You receive flowers from a secret admirer.

5. You haven't received any phone calls or text messages in a week.

6. Your boss promised to promote you, but it still hasn't happened.

 DISCUSSION

What's the explanation?

A Read these headlines about strange events. How would you explain them?

MYSTERY SOUND IRRITATES VILLAGE

 Each night from midnight to 4 A.M., a mysterious humming sound keeps the 300 residents of Woodland, England, awake. There are no factories or large roads nearby, and so far nobody can explain the sound.

 **River Runs Red**

Shocked residents watched in disbelief last week as the river running through their city turned a deep red color. Some people rushed to save a bottle of the colored water while they had the chance.

 **Colored Honey Puzzles Farmers**

In a French region famous for its honey, bees have been producing it in shades of blue and green. Farmers say the honey is unsellable, and they are investigating the cause.

B Group work Discuss your explanations. Do you agree?

"Airplanes flying overhead could have caused the noise in that village."
"I'm not so sure. I think someone may have been making the sound on purpose as a prank."

Useful expressions
Disagreeing
I don't know.
I'm not so sure.
Well, maybe, but . . .
I know what you mean, but . . .

4 VOCABULARY & SPEAKING
Verbs of belief

A Put these verbs of belief in the correct columns. Discuss your answers with a partner.

| assume | be positive | bet | figure | have a hunch | suppose |
| be certain | be sure | doubt | guess | know for a fact | suspect |

Certain	Not certain
	assume

B Group work Use the verbs of belief to discuss these questions.

1. Why do giraffes have long necks?
2. Why do some buildings not have a thirteenth floor?
3. Is there life on other planets?
4. Why doesn't a haircut hurt?
5. Why do some people fall in love at first sight?
6. What color is an insect's blood?

"Why do giraffes have long necks?"

"I'm not sure, but I assume they have long necks to eat the leaves at the tops of trees."

"Yeah, I bet that's the reason why."

VOCABULARY PLUS *see page 131*

5 LISTENING & SPEAKING
Solving mysteries

 A Listen to Sheila and Adam discussing some myths and mysteries researched by the TV show *Solving Mysteries*. Choose the ones discovered to be true.

☐ 1. Using a cell phone can cause a fire at a gas station.
☐ 2. Talking to plants for a short time will help them grow better.
☐ 3. A person can break a glass using just his or her voice.
☐ 4. Yawning is contagious.

B Listen again. What ideas did Sheila and Adam originally have? Answer the questions.

1. How did Sheila think that cell phones could cause fires?

   _____

2. Why did Adam doubt that talking to plants could help them grow?

   _____

3. Why did Sheila have trouble believing voices could break a glass?

   _____

4. Why didn't Adam believe that yawning could be contagious?

   _____

C Group work Brainstorm other mysteries you might like to have *Solving Mysteries* investigate for you. Can anyone in the group explain the mysteries?

Do I know you?

A Group work What does *amnesia* mean? What are some things that might cause amnesia? Discuss with your group.

Amnesia Spoils Newlyweds' Bliss

What if the person you married forgot who you were? For one Texas couple, marriage became a blind date when the groom came down with amnesia days after their wedding.

Amy and Sean McNulty's wedding day started well, but ended with a shock. One of Sean's good friends was in a serious car accident after the wedding and ended up in a coma. Nevertheless, Amy and Sean decided to make their honeymoon trip according to plans.

At the airport, Sean realized he'd left his wallet in their car. He said to Amy, "I'll be right back." But he didn't return.

Amy contacted the police, who found Sean wandering near a motel three days later. He was confused and covered in bug bites. He had no idea who he was or who Amy was. Sean could not remember any personal details from his life, not even his mother.

Amy was now married to a man who viewed her as a stranger. "I wondered, you know, is he going to remember me? How is our relationship going to, you know, form?" said Amy.

This was a big change after a six-year courtship and plenty of shared memories.

When Sean got out of the hospital, Amy had to give him a tour of their home. Although he had a room devoted to music, he couldn't even remember what it meant to hear music.

Psychiatrist Dr. Daniel Brown says Sean's amnesia might have been caused by a series of stressful moments, like his friend's car accident. According to Dr. Brown, Sean's brain didn't connect with his identity anymore. "He doesn't know who Sean McNulty is and has no personal memories or autobiographical memories to account for who he might be."

Dr. Brown explained that amnesia was like forgetting the name of a file you stored on your computer. "You know it's there but you can't find it," said Brown. "His memory is like that. He still has the file."

Fortunately, better times soon arrived. The day before their first anniversary, Sean's memories flooded back in an instant. He soon remembered everything, including their wedding. "I remember shoving cake in her face," said Sean. "It was great."

Sean views the experience as a chance to confirm he picked the right bride. "I got to see how much she loves me," said Sean. "We have a much stronger and closer bond from the experience. I couldn't have found a better woman to spend my life with."

Source: "Amnesia Spoils Newlyweds' Bliss," ABC News

B Read the article. Are these statements true or false? Choose the correct answer.

	True	False
1. Sean's amnesia began after he was in a car accident.	☐	☐
2. Sean and Amy didn't know each other well before they got married.	☐	☐
3. Sean shoved cake in Amy's face when he remembered who she was.	☐	☐
4. The amnesia might have been caused by stress.	☐	☐

C Group work Discuss these questions. Then share your answers with the class.

1. What would you have done if you had been in Amy's position?
2. What would be some of the problems you'd face if you ever forgot everything?

3 EXPLORING NEW CITIES
LESSON A ▶ *Popular destinations*

1 STARTING POINT
Cities of the world

A Read about these cities. Which city would you most like to visit?

BARCELONA

Barcelona is famous for museums, nightlife, and seafood – and for the architect Antoni Gaudí, who designed several of the city's most distinctive buildings. Most restaurants here stay open until midnight, when many locals are still enjoying dinner.

BEIJING

Beijing has many popular tourist attractions, which include the Summer Palace and the Forbidden City. Tourists who come here for the first time are amazed by the crowds, the busy streets, and the constantly changing skyline.

SEOUL

Seoul is well known for its spicy food and its shopping areas, where you can find everything from antique pottery to custom-made clothing. The Myeong-dong area has dozens of shops that sell the latest fashions.

SYDNEY

The place where most tourists go first in Sydney is the famous Opera House, but this Australian city also has great restaurants and museums. The spring and fall are the seasons when most people come to visit.

B Pair work Tell your partner about a city you know.

"I know Vancouver. It's got the ocean on one side and mountains on the other. It's really beautiful, but it's expensive . . . "

2 LISTENING
Where in the world . . . ?

🔊 **A** Listen to Diana and Matt talk about two cities. Who is talking about Athens and who is talking about Seoul?

🔊 **B** Listen again. Who mentions these topics, Diana (*D*) or Matt (*M*)? Write the correct letter.

____ 1. founded 3,000 years ago	____ 4. a river	____ 7. traffic
____ 2. delicious spicy food	____ 5. a subway system	____ 8. street vendors
____ 3. beautiful beaches	____ 6. monuments	____ 9. nightlife

3 GRAMMAR
Defining and non-defining relative clauses

A defining relative clause defines or gives essential information about a noun.
The Myeong-dong area has dozens of shops **that sell the latest fashions**.
The spring and fall are the seasons **when most people come to visit**.

A non-defining relative clause gives optional information about a noun and cannot begin
with the pronoun *that*. Notice the use of commas.
Most restaurants here stay open until midnight, **when many locals are still enjoying dinner**.
Beijing has many popular tourist attractions, **which include the Summer Palace and the Forbidden City**.

GRAMMAR PLUS *see page 110*

A Look at the Starting Point on page 18 again. Can you find more relative clauses?

B Underline the relative clauses in the sentences and add commas where
necessary. Write *D* for a defining and *ND* for a non-defining relative clause.

_ND_ 1. Bangkok, which is the capital of Thailand, has many
     excellent restaurants and markets.

____ 2. Over one million people come to Pamplona in July when
     the festival of San Fermín takes place in this Spanish city.

____ 3. Aden is an ancient port city that is located in southern Yemen.

____ 4. Bogotá which is situated on a high plateau in central
     Colombia has frequently changing weather.

____ 5. Montreal is a sophisticated city where some of the best
     cuisine in Canada is found.

____ 6. São Paulo which is the biggest city in Brazil is one of the
     world's most populated cities.

C Join the sentences using non-defining relative clauses. Then compare answers.

1. Gaudí designed Barcelona's Park Güell. You can see fabulous sculptures there.
2. Seoul's name comes from the ancient word *seorabeol*. *Seorabeol* means "capital."
3. The center of Beijing is Tiananmen Square. It is the world's largest public square.
4. A great time to visit Seoul is in the fall. This is when Koreans celebrate the
   Chuseok festival.
5. Fast-food restaurants are already fairly common in China. They are increasing
   in number each year.
6. Australia's first European settlers came to Sydney in the late 1700s. They were
   originally from Great Britain.

4 SPEAKING
A great place to visit

A Which of the cities on page 18 would you like to visit? Write three sentences
explaining your reasons. Use relative clauses where appropriate.

Barcelona is a city that I'd like to visit because . . .

B Pair work Tell your partner which city you'd like to visit and why.

5 VOCABULARY
What makes a city?

A Are these features of cities more important to tourists or to residents?
Put the words in the correct columns. Add ideas of your own.

| climate | crime rate | green spaces | job market | neighborhoods | shopping |
| cost of living | cuisine | hotels | landmarks | nightlife | transportation system |

Important to tourists	Important to residents	Important to both

B Pair work Use the features from part A to talk about your city. Give examples
and add extra information.

*"Salvador is famous all over Brazil for its cuisine. Acarajé is one of the most popular foods,
and it's really delicious. It's a deep-fried cake that's made from mashed beans."*

VOCABULARY PLUS *see page 132*

6 LISTENING
What's the city like?

 A Listen to Carlos and Vicki talk about San Francisco. Who seems to like the city better?

B Listen again. Choose the city features that Carlos and Vicki mention.

- ☐ 1. climate
- ☐ 2. architecture
- ☐ 3. shopping
- ☐ 4. customs
- ☐ 5. hotels
- ☐ 6. job market
- ☐ 7. landmarks
- ☐ 8. nightlife
- ☐ 9. cuisine

7 DISCUSSION
Perfect places

A Answer the questions with your own ideas.

What is...

1. a good city for budget travelers? _____
2. a good city for a honeymoon? _____
3. a place that would make a great family vacation spot? _____
4. a city where you'd like to live for a few years? _____
5. a good city to go to school in? _____
6. a place that you would never want to visit? _____

B Pair work Discuss your answers.

*"I think New York is a good place
for budget travelers."*

*"I'm not sure I agree. New York is
incredibly expensive."*

*"That's true, but there are lots of
cheap fast-food restaurants . . ."*

Useful expressions	
Agreeing with an opinion	**Disagreeing with an opinion**
I think you're right.	I'm not sure I agree.
I'm with you.	Maybe, but don't you think . . . ?
That's true.	Really?
I think so, too.	I know what you mean, but . . .

C Group work Join another pair and try to agree on one answer for each question.

WRITING
Organizing ideas with a mind map

Making a mind map is a good way of organizing your brainstorming ideas. Mind maps help you map out the supporting details about your topic.

A Look at the phrases in the box about Cuzco, Peru. Choose the main idea and write it in the center of the mind map. Then write the supporting details around it.

a mix of history and culture   great shopping   something for everyone
beautiful architecture   nice hotels   wonderful restaurants

B Read the paragraph about Cuzco. Underline the ideas from the mind map in the paragraph.

Cuzco has something for everyone. It's one of the oldest cities in the Americas, and it was once the capital of the Inca empire. Today, Cuzco is Peru's tourist capital because of its unique mix of history and culture. People who are interested in architecture will love the nearby Inca ruins of Machu Picchu and the palace of Inca Roca. Cuzco has many places to stay, which range from first-class hotels to cozy inns. There are also many cafés and restaurants where you can eat delicious local dishes or international cuisine. Also, Cuzco has great markets where you can shop for local arts and crafts. When you visit Cuzco, you should try to experience all it has to offer.

C Choose a place you know and make your own mind map. Be sure the main idea is general and the map contains several supporting ideas.

D Write a paragraph based on the ideas in your mind map.

E **Pair work** Exchange paragraphs with a partner. Then answer the questions.

1. Are there enough supporting details? Are there any details you'd like your partner to add?
2. Does the content of the paragraph reflect the ideas in the mind map?
3. Would you like to visit the place your partner wrote about? Why or why not?

1 STARTING POINT
City search

A Complete the descriptions with the sentences below. Then compare answers.

> **This exciting large city** with bustling streets is a great place to live. Most evenings you can choose from a movie, a concert, or even a museum. (1) _____ There are lots of jobs here, and the average salary is about $4,000 per month. (2) _____ Our efficient new subway system can get you anywhere you want to go. (3) _____

> **This is a picturesque little resort town** with year-round outdoor activities. There's something to do in all four seasons. But there's not much action here at night. (4) _____ There are many quaint little stores and boutiques in this beautiful town. (5) _____ Apartments are affordable, too. You can get a great place for about $1,000 a month, and average monthly salaries are about $2,500. (6) _____

a. However, housing costs are high. A nice apartment is about $2,500 per month.

b. So, even though our streets are safe, the evenings can be dull.

c. But be careful – in spite of all the late-night activity, the crime rate is high.

d. On the other hand, it can sometimes be difficult to find a job.

e. Although it's fast, clean, and cheap, it's pretty crowded during rush hour. Nevertheless, it's becoming one of the most popular ways for people to get to work.

f. Despite the attractive location, the prices of houses are surprisingly reasonable.

B Pair work Which place do you think has more to offer – the city or the town?

2 VOCABULARY
Compound terms for towns

A These compound terms describe different types of towns. How would you define each one?

border town	college town	mountain town	resort town	suburban town
coastal town	industrial town	port town	rural town	tourist town

A border town is near a border with another state or country.

B Pair work Which of the terms best describes your hometown? Which best describes the town where you'd like to live someday? Compare ideas.

VOCABULARY PLUS *see page 132*

GRAMMAR

Order of modifiers

When two or more modifiers occur in a sentence, they usually follow this order.

	Quality	Size	Age	Type	Noun	Descriptive phrase
this	exciting	large			city	with bustling streets
a	picturesque	little		resort	town	with year-round outdoor activities
a	run-down		old	port	town	that has seen better days

GRAMMAR PLUS *see page 111*

A Look at the Starting Point on page 22 again. Can you find more sentences that have two or more modifiers?

B Write descriptions of places you know. Then compare answers with a partner.

1. a nearby city or town that you frequently visit
   Middleton is a typical suburban town with a good shopping mall.
2. a place you'd like to visit one day
3. a place tourists to your country want to see
4. a place you enjoy visiting, but wouldn't want to live in

GRAMMAR

Connecting contrasting ideas

You can use these words and phrases to connect contrasting ideas.

despite	although	however	on the other hand
in spite of	even though	nevertheless	

GRAMMAR PLUS *see page 111*

A Look at the Starting Point on page 22 again. What words and phrases connect the contrasting ideas?

B Choose the words that are true for you. Then complete the sentences.

1. Although I would / wouldn't like to live in this town forever, . . .
   Although I would like to live in this town forever, I'll have to move if rents go up.
2. There are *not many / a lot of* things I like about this town. However, . . .
3. Even though finding an apartment is *easy / difficult* in this town, . . .
4. Despite the high cost of living in this city, there are *a number of / no* . . .
5. The *spring / summer / fall / winter* here is very nice. On the other hand, . . .
6. Most places in this town close *early / late*. In spite of that, . . .
7. The areas around this town are mainly *rural / suburban / urban*. Nevertheless, . . .

C Pair work Discuss your answers. Ask and answer follow-up questions.

"Although I'd like to live in this town forever, I'll have to move if rents go up."
"Really? Where would you move?"
"I'm not sure. I hope someplace cheaper, but still near here."

5 LISTENING
Life in Sydney

🔊 **A** Listen to Maria and Ian talk about life in Sydney. Who seems to enjoy living there more?

🔊 **B** Listen again. Which person has these opinions? Choose Maria, Ian, or both.

	Maria	Ian	Both
1. It's easy to get around Sydney.	☐	☐	☐
2. The beaches are great.	☐	☐	☐
3. The rents are expensive.	☐	☐	☐
4. It's a fun place to live.	☐	☐	☐
5. The restaurants are all expensive.	☐	☐	☐
6. Life is better in a smaller town.	☐	☐	☐

6 DISCUSSION
Quality of life

A Rate these quality-of-life issues as very important (2), important (1), or not important (0). Can you add one more to the list?

Quality of Life

____ affordable housing   ____ exciting nightlife   ____ pleasant weather

____ a variety of restaurants   ____ first-class health care   ____ varied retail shops

____ beautiful parks   ____ historic neighborhoods   ____ wireless hot spots

____ convenient public transportation   ____ low crime rates   ____ _____

B Pair work Which three issues are the most important to you personally when considering where to live? Explain why.

"I guess affordable housing and exciting nightlife are the most important to me. I'd love to find a place I could afford that was near someplace fun."

"I know what you mean. But for me, I guess low crime rates are probably the most important. I want to live somewhere where I feel safe. I don't mind if it's a little boring."

C Class activity Share your answers with your classmates. Which issues were mentioned most often?

Melbourne versus Sydney

A Pair work What do you know about the Australian cities of Melbourne and Sydney? Tell your partner. Then read the article.

RIVALS with a lot IN COMMON

What's the truth behind the rivalry between **Melbourne** and **Sydney**?

According to Melbournians, they live in a paradise where ideas are discussed, the arts are celebrated, and life is beautiful. Sydneysiders claim to live in the same kind of place – only better. Nobody can agree on how the rivalry between Sydney and Melbourne started, but it's been going on for as long as anyone can remember.

If you believe the stereotypes that fuel this rivalry, Melbourne is just a quaint coastal city with nothing to do unless you're into indie music festivals and a slow-paced lifestyle, while Sydney is an expensive, unfriendly place with a focus on business and no place to park. If you believe what Melbournians and Sydneysiders say, the cities don't have much in common except that they're both Australian cities whose residents love where they live.

In reality, Sydney is a warm, beautiful city with lots of green, cross-harbor ferries, and world-class beaches, while Melbourne's right-in-the-city beaches are near colorful neighborhoods where there are plenty of things to do for entertainment.

Melbourne

Both Melbourne and Sydney have fabulous restaurants featuring cuisine from just about anywhere in the world, and both offer nightlife possibilities with something for everyone. In addition, both cities feature a year-round schedule of art and music festivals, as well as other cultural events catering to every taste. And their excellent public transportation systems help you get around easily.

It's true that Melbourne tends to have less rain than Sydney and that Sydney's average temperatures are higher, but it's wonderfully pleasant in either place. And while the cost-of-living is a little lower in Melbourne and salaries are higher in Sydney, prices in both really are quite comparable.

So, what's the rivalry all about? It probably comes down to civic pride. Residents of both of these world-class cities are rightly proud of where they live, and though there are differences, the differences are not really all that extreme. If you're not convinced, visit both and see for yourself.

Sydney

B Read the article again. Are these statements true (*T*), false (*F*), or is the information not given (*NG*) in the article? Write the correct letters.

_____ 1. The rivalry between Sydney and Melbourne is a recent development.

_____ 2. Life in Sydney, like in Melbourne, can also be slow.

_____ 3. It's hard to get anywhere in Melbourne or Sydney without a car.

_____ 4. It costs slightly less to live in Melbourne than it does in Sydney.

C Group work Discuss these questions. Then share your answers with the class.

1. Why do you think people in Melbourne and Sydney tend to focus on the differences between the two cities rather than on the similarities?

2. Are there any cities in your country that have a rivalry? How are the cities similar and different? Is the rivalry based on stereotypes or on facts?

SELF-ASSESSMENT

How well can you do these things? Choose the best answer.

I can . . .	Very well	OK	A little
▸ Express personal likes and dislikes and give relevant explanations (Ex. 1)	☐	☐	☐
▸ Make and evaluate recommendations to improve a city in a problem-solving discussion (Ex. 2)	☐	☐	☐
▸ Understand anecdotes and say how the speakers feel about past mistakes (Ex. 3)	☐	☐	☐
▸ Describe past mistakes in my life (Ex. 3)	☐	☐	☐
▸ Give a presentation about "must-see" places in my city and explain my choices (Ex. 4)	☐	☐	☐

Now do the corresponding exercises. Was your assessment correct?

1 DISCUSSION
Likes and dislikes

A Look at these items. Can you think of a personal example for each one?

1. something you're into / not into doing by yourself
2. the kind of music you feel like listening to when you're in a bad mood
3. something you like doing when you're stressed out
4. a household chore you don't mind / can't stand doing
5. something you avoid doing, if possible

B Pair work Discuss your answers with a partner.

"I'm really into going to art galleries by myself. That way I can spend as much time as I want."

"Oh, I'm just the opposite. I don't really like going to galleries alone. It's nice to share the experience with someone."

2 DISCUSSION
The people's action committee

A Pair work You are members of an action group that has been asked to suggest improvements for your city. Make a list of changes you think should be made.

"We think the city shouldn't allow cars in the downtown area on weekends. It would be nice to be able to walk around without worrying about traffic."

B Group work Compare your recommendations in groups. Choose the four most interesting recommendations and share them with the class.

> **Useful expressions**
>
> **Making recommendations**
> The city should provide . . .
> The city ought to . . . because . . .
> Wouldn't it be nice if . . . ?
> It would make a lot of sense to . . .

3 LISTENING & SPEAKING
Who's sorry now?

◀)) **A** Listen to a radio show called *Who's Sorry Now?*
What is the focus of the show? Choose the correct answer.

- ☐ a. people's roommates in college
- ☐ b. things that people should or should
  not have done in the past
- ☐ c. family vacations

◀)) **B** Listen again. Are these statements true or false? Choose the correct answer.

	True	False
1. Mark made the manager think that Luke didn't want the job.	☐	☐
2. Mark said he should feel terrible, but he doesn't.	☐	☐
3. Anna buried her brother's harmonica in the desert.	☐	☐
4. Anna said she should have bought her brother a drum set.	☐	☐
5. Luke didn't tell his roommate that he knew about the call.	☐	☐
6. Luke thinks he should have told his roommate he knew about the call.	☐	☐

C Pair work Have you ever made a mistake like the ones on the radio show?
Would you consider calling a show like *Who's Sorry Now?* to talk about it?

"Have you ever made a mistake like the ones on the radio show?"

*"Well, when I was in college, I used to make up excuses so that I could avoid going to
French class. I should have gone. I really wish I could speak French now."*

"Would you call up a show like Who's Sorry Now?*"*

"I don't know. Maybe it would be fun. What about you?"

4 DISCUSSION
Welcome to my city!

A What are three places in your city that
people would enjoy visiting? Make a list.

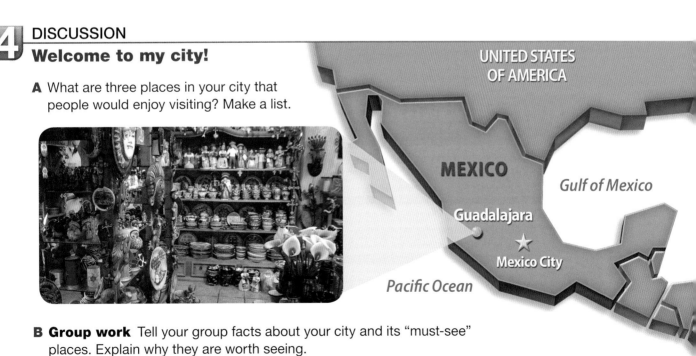

B Group work Tell your group facts about your city and its "must-see"
places. Explain why they are worth seeing.

*"Guadalajara, which is the second largest city in Mexico, has a lot of great markets.
The Libertad Market is fantastic. It's a market every tourist should see because . . ."*

EARLY BIRDS AND NIGHT OWLS

LESSON A ▶ It's about time!

1 STARTING POINT

What's your best time of day?

A Read these statements. How would you define the boldfaced words?

Teresa, South Africa

As soon as I get up in the morning, I race off to the gym. After I finish my workout, I head to the office. I always get there before any of my colleagues arrive. I suppose I'm a **morning person**.

Caio, Brazil

Ever since I was a kid, I've had trouble getting up early, so I guess I'm a **late riser**. Until I've had my coffee, I'm such a grouch. I'm not very approachable right after I wake up!

Mieko, Japan

I'm a **power napper**. While I take my lunch break at work, I often sneak a five-minute nap at my desk. After I have a little sleep, I feel great the rest of the day.

Richard, U.S.

I don't get much done until it gets to be late afternoon. Then I usually get a spurt of energy. I can concentrate best after everyone else has gone to bed. I'd say I'm a real **night owl**.

B Group work Which of the people in part A are you most similar to? Why?

2 DISCUSSION

The time is right.

A Pair work Read this information. Do you agree with the advice given? Why or why not?

When the Mind and Body Are at Their Best

 Get on social networking sites between **8:00 and 9:00** A.M., when people tend to post more positive messages.

 Whenever you need to study for a test, do it in the **late morning**, when most adults perform their best.

 Whenever you have to work with numbers, plan to do it around **noon**, when thinking power is at its peak.

 Energy levels drop between **1:00 and 4:00** P.M., and sleepiness is at its peak around **2:00** P.M. This is a good time for a short nap.

 Exercise between **4:00 and 7:00** P.M., when physical strength is at its greatest and risk of injury is at its lowest.

 People can be most creative when they are less focused. Therefore, morning people are most creative in the evening, and night owls are most creative in the morning.

B Pair work Do you prefer to do these things in the morning, the afternoon, the evening, or at night? Why? Compare answers.

1. exercise   2. listen to music   3. study   4. speak English

3 GRAMMAR

Reduced time clauses

Notice how these clauses show time relationships. **If the subject is the same in both clauses of the sentence, time clauses with** *(right) before*, *(right) after*, and *while* **can be reduced.**
After I finish / **After** finishing my workout, I head to the office.
While I take / **While** taking my lunch break at work, I often sneak a five-minute nap.
I'm not very approachable **right after** I wake up / **right after** waking up!

However, other time clauses cannot usually be reduced.
Ever since I was a kid, I've had trouble getting up early.
As soon as I get up in the morning, I race off to the gym.
Until I've had my coffee, I'm such a grouch.
Whenever you have to work with numbers, plan to do it around noon.
I've been a night person **from the moment** I started college.

GRAMMAR PLUS *see page 112*

A Look at the Starting Point on page 28 again. Can you find more time clauses? Which one can be reduced?

B Pair work Complete the sentences with information about yourself. Then discuss your answers with a partner.

1. While working on a really difficult task, . . .
2. I don't feel awake in the morning until . . .
3. Whenever I have trouble sleeping, . . .
4. I can never concentrate after . . .
5. From the moment I wake up in the morning, . . .
6. As soon as I start to feel sleepy in the evening, . . .
7. Ever since I was young, . . .

"While working on a really difficult task, I have to stretch every 30 minutes."

4 VOCABULARY & SPEAKING

Energy and sleep

A Match the phrasal verb in the question with the correct definition.

1. Do you ever **burn out** from too much work? ____   a. become calm
2. How do you **calm down** after an argument? ____   b. get more energy
3. How do you **chill out** after a rough day? ____   c. go to bed
4. Do you ever **doze off** for a few minutes in public? ____   d. lose all your energy
5. How do you **perk up** when you feel sleepy? ____   e. fall asleep for a short time
6. Do you **race off** as soon as class is over? ____   f. take it easy
7. How often do you **sleep over** at a friend's? ____   g. stay for the night
8. What time do you **turn in** on the weekend? ____   h. go quickly

B Pair work Discuss the questions in part A. Ask follow-up questions.

"Whenever I feel like I'm going to burn out, I go for a bike ride to relax."
"That sounds like a good idea. Where do you like to ride?"

VOCABULARY PLUS *see page 133*

5 LISTENING & SPEAKING
Chilling out

A Stress can cause fatigue and a lack of energy. Select the things you do to cope with stress. Can you add other suggestions to the list?

- ☐ call a friend
- ☐ do yoga
- ☐ exercise vigorously
- ☐ get a massage
- ☐ listen to music
- ☐ take a hot bath
- ☐ vent your feelings
- ☐ _____
- ☐ _____

B Listen to Sean (*S*), Lisa (*L*), and Victor (*V*) talk about stress. What is the main cause of stress for each person? Write the correct letter.

____ too little time   ____ too much traffic   ____ too many responsibilities

C Listen again. What solution has each person found? Complete the chart.

	Solution
1. Sean	
2. Lisa	
3. Victor	

6 ROLE PLAY
I need some advice.

A Look at the problems below. Have you ever had problems like these? What other problems do people have with sleep and energy levels?

CALLER 1
I've been working day and night on an important project. It's going well, but I'm feeling so worn out. I'm worried about my health.

CALLER 2
I get so nervous before I have to give a presentation that I can't sleep the night before, and then I'm not at my best.

CALLER 3
I always put off studying until the night before a test. I stay up all night studying, but after that, I still don't do very well.

CALLER 4
Whenever my friends call or text me late at night, we chat for hours and hours. The next day, I can't keep my eyes open!

B Pair work Imagine you have one of the problems in part A. Take turns asking for and giving advice.

"I have a real problem. I've been working a lot on this project, and I'm so worn out. I'm worried about my health."

"So, how late do you usually work during the week?"

"I usually stay until 9:00 P.M. or so."

"Have you ever thought of telling someone that you need a little help?"

> **Useful expressions**
>
> **Giving advice**
> Have you ever thought of (going) . . . ?
> You might want to . . .
> It might not be a bad idea to . . .
> The way I see it, you ought to . . .

WRITING
Effective topic sentences

> Effective topic sentences are neither too general nor too specific. A topic sentence is supported by the other sentences in the paragraph.

A Read the paragraph. Then choose the best topic sentence from the list.

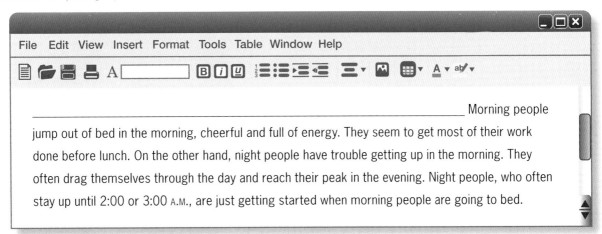

File   Edit   View   Insert   Format   Tools   Table   Window   Help

_____ Morning people jump out of bed in the morning, cheerful and full of energy. They seem to get most of their work done before lunch. On the other hand, night people have trouble getting up in the morning. They often drag themselves through the day and reach their peak in the evening. Night people, who often stay up until 2:00 or 3:00 A.M., are just getting started when morning people are going to bed.

a. Early morning is a bad time of day for most people.
b. Morning people and night people live very different lives.
c. Working at night is hard for morning people.
d. Night people get enough sleep even though they go to bed late.

B Read the paragraph and complete the topic sentence. Then compare answers with a partner.

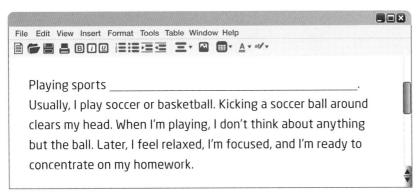

File   Edit   View   Insert   Format   Tools   Table   Window   Help

Playing sports _____.
Usually, I play soccer or basketball. Kicking a soccer ball around clears my head. When I'm playing, I don't think about anything but the ball. Later, I feel relaxed, I'm focused, and I'm ready to concentrate on my homework.

C Choose one of these topics or your own idea. Then write a paragraph with a topic sentence.

- the best way to stay healthy
- an effective study plan
- earning extra money

D Pair work Take turns reading your paragraphs out loud, but don't read the topic sentence. Can you guess what your partner's topic sentence is?

LESSON B ▶ *Tossing and turning*

 STARTING POINT
A good night's sleep

A Read the statements about sleep habits. Choose the statements that are true for you.

☐ I sometimes lie awake at night, even if I'm really tired.

☐ I'm lucky I can get by on six hours of sleep, considering that most people need eight.

☐ I'm a light sleeper, so any little noise wakes me up unless I'm really tired.

☐ I can manage on five hours of sleep, as long as I take a nap during the day.

☐ Unless I get a good night's sleep, I can easily fall asleep at school, at work, or even on the bus.

☐ I always set two alarm clocks just in case one of them doesn't go off.

☐ I only wake up early if I have somewhere to be in the morning.

☐ I never have any trouble sleeping.

☐ I'm exhausted every morning, even if I slept great all night.

B Pair work Compare your answers. Which statements are true for you?

"I definitely lie awake at night, even if I'm really tired. I can't help it. I replay everything that happened during the day."

"You're not the only one. I do the same thing, especially when I'm feeling stressed."

 VOCABULARY
Expressions related to sleep

A Put these expressions about sleep in the correct columns. Then compare answers.

be fast asleep	be wide awake	feel drowsy	nod off	take a power nap
be sound asleep	drift off	have a sleepless night	sleep like a log	toss and turn

Having trouble sleeping	Falling asleep	Sleeping a short time	Sleeping deeply
			be fast asleep

B Pair work Use the expressions in part A to discuss your sleep habits and suggestions about sleeping better.

"Do you ever take a power nap during the day?"

"Not really. Whenever I try to take a nap, I end up sleeping until the next morning. But let me ask you something. What do you do when you feel drowsy after lunch?"

VOCABULARY PLUS see page 133

GRAMMAR

Clauses stating reasons and conditions

Even if introduces a condition that does not influence the main clause.
I sometimes lie awake at night, **even if** I'm really tired.

Considering that introduces causes and reasons that explain the main clause.
I'm lucky I can get by on six hours of sleep, **considering that** most people need eight.

As long as introduces a condition on which the main clause depends.
I can manage on five hours of sleep, **as long as** I take a nap during the day.

Unless introduces something that must happen in order to avoid a consequence.
Unless I get a good night's sleep, I can easily fall asleep at school, at work, or even on the bus.

(Just) in case introduces an undesirable circumstance that needs to be taken into account.
I always set two alarm clocks **(just) in case** one of them doesn't go off.

Only if or *only . . . if* introduces a condition that must be met for the main clause to be true.
I **only** wake up early **if** I have somewhere to be in the morning.
I wake up early **only if** I have somewhere to be in the morning.

GRAMMAR PLUS *see page 113*

A Look at the Starting Point on page 32 again. Can you find more clauses stating reasons and conditions?

B Match the clauses to make sentences. Then compare answers with a partner.

1. Drivers can fall asleep on the highway ____
2. Power naps at work are a good idea, ____
3. Some people set two morning alarms ____
4. I was surprisingly alert at work, ____
5. Night owls hate to wake up early, ____
6. I drink hot milk before bed only ____

a. if I've been having trouble sleeping.
b. even if it's a beautiful morning.
c. unless they rest before long trips.
d. as long as you have your boss's OK.
e. considering that I didn't sleep at all last night.
f. in case they sleep through one.

C Complete the sentences with information about yourself. Then compare answers with a partner.

1. Unless I have enough sleep at night, . . .
   I can't think very clearly in the morning.
2. I usually wake up on time,
   as long as . . .
3. I fall asleep pretty quickly at night,
   considering that . . .
4. I always have a boring book on
   my night table just in case . . .
5. Even if I'm extremely stressed out,
   I never . . .
6. I only leave a light on if . . .

4 LISTENING & SPEAKING
I had the wildest dream.

 A Listen to Kate and Sérgio talk about their recurring dreams. Whose dream do you think is scarier?

B Listen again. What is each person's dream? What do they think the dreams mean? Complete the chart.

	Dream	Meaning
Kate		
Sérgio		

C Pair work What do you think their dreams mean? Do you ever have similar dreams?

5 DISCUSSION
The meaning of dreams

A Read the information. Match the dreams with their possible meanings.

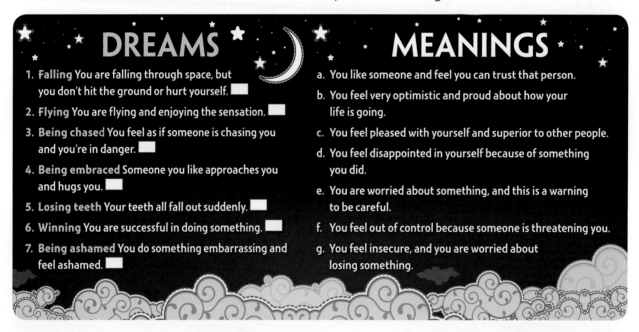

DREAMS

1. **Falling** You are falling through space, but you don't hit the ground or hurt yourself. ☐
2. **Flying** You are flying and enjoying the sensation. ☐
3. **Being chased** You feel as if someone is chasing you and you're in danger. ☐
4. **Being embraced** Someone you like approaches you and hugs you. ☐
5. **Losing teeth** Your teeth all fall out suddenly. ☐
6. **Winning** You are successful in doing something. ☐
7. **Being ashamed** You do something embarrassing and feel ashamed. ☐

MEANINGS

a. You like someone and feel you can trust that person.
b. You feel very optimistic and proud about how your life is going.
c. You feel pleased with yourself and superior to other people.
d. You feel disappointed in yourself because of something you did.
e. You are worried about something, and this is a warning to be careful.
f. You feel out of control because someone is threatening you.
g. You feel insecure, and you are worried about losing something.

B Pair work Read these accounts of unusual dreams. What do you think they mean?

"Suddenly I found myself on stage in a school play and realized that I didn't know my lines. . . ."

"I was in a hot-air balloon above a big park. When I looked down, I was amazed to see hundreds of people on the ground pointing up at me. . . ."

"I was in a strange country and didn't know how I'd gotten there. I asked a man for help, and he held up a sign in a language I'd never seen before. . . ."

> **Useful expressions**
> **Interpreting meaning**
> I think that means . . .
> It sounds like . . .
> The (balloon) probably stands for . . .
> It might symbolize . . .

C Group work Finish each of the dreams. Take turns adding sentences.

To sleep or not to sleep?

A Group work How many hours do you think people should sleep? Why?
Discuss with your group. Then read the article.

To Sleep or Not to Sleep?

In the days before electricity, people didn't worry much about sleep. They usually went to bed a couple of hours after sunset and woke at sunrise. Even if they stayed up, there wasn't much to do in those days after the sun went down. But then came the electric lightbulb. And now we have the Internet, smartphones, stores that are open 24/7, and longer hours at work. How much can we sleep? How much should we sleep?

Like it or not, many of us are sleeping less on average. In 1910, most Americans slept nine hours a night. That dropped to seven hours by 2001. In 2009, a study by the National Sleep Foundation found that the average American got only 6.7 hours of sleep. The news is even worse for people who work the night shift. They sleep an average of just five hours.

Are we sleeping enough? Not if you believe in the old formula of eight hours of rest, eight hours of work, and eight hours of play. On the other hand, Neil Stanley, a British scientist who studies sleep, believes people's sleep needs vary. Some people need as many as 11 hours, but others need as few as three. How much do you really need? "To find out," he says, "simply sleep until you wake naturally, without the aid of an alarm clock. Feel rested? That's your sleep need."

Meanwhile, other scientists and pharmaceutical researchers are searching for new ways to keep us awake longer and prevent us from nodding off. A group of scientists is studying a gene found in some fruit flies that lets them get by on one-third the usual amount of sleep. Other researchers are developing chemicals that are more powerful than caffeine, the chemical found in coffee and tea. One experimental drug, CX717, kept laboratory monkeys working happily and accurately for 36 hours. Future breakthroughs may allow people to stay wide awake for several days straight.

The implications of this research are huge. On the one hand, this could lead to a world where we work longer and longer hours with less and less sleep. On the other hand, if we needed less sleep, we would have more free time for travel, sports, personal goals, and family.

To sleep or not to sleep – that may soon be the question.

B Read the article again. Then answer the questions.

1. What scientific research is mentioned in the article? What surprised you the most? What surprised you the least?

2. How much sleep does Neil Stanley think a person needs? Why?

3. What effects did the experimental drug mentioned in the article have on laboratory animals?

C Group work Discuss these questions. Then share your answers with the class.

1. Do you think you get enough sleep? What things keep you from getting more?

2. What do you think would happen if scientists found ways to let people stay awake longer? Would people be happier? Explain your answers.

5 COMMUNICATION

LESSON A ► *Making conversation*

1 STARTING POINT

Types of people you might meet

A Read about six different types of people you sometimes meet on social occasions. Match the descriptions with the pictures.

1 It's a good idea to try out different topics to get a conversation going, and the **conversation starter** does just that. ▭

2 Talking about your accomplishments too much is often considered rude, but that doesn't stop the **braggart**. ▭

3 Saying nice things about others is customary for the **complimenter**. ▭

4 It's rude to ignore your conversation partner, but the **wandering mind** does it anyway. ▭

5 Talking about topics that interest you is fun. Unfortunately, the **bore** is interesting to no one else. ▭

6 It's usually considered impolite to interrupt people, but the **interrupter** is always jumping into the conversation out of turn. ▭

a Excuse me, let me say . . .

b Hi. Are you enjoying the party?

c I really enjoyed . . .

d I'm absolutely the best tennis player .

e That's a great tie!

f So then I blah, blah, blah . . .

B Pair work Do you know any people like the six types above? What is it like to have a conversation with them?

"My best friend is kind of an interrupter. She's really nice, but I guess she just gets excited about the conversation and wants to jump in. It can be very annoying."

2 GRAMMAR

Infinitive and gerund phrases

It + *be* + adjective/noun + infinitive phrase is often used to comment on behavior.
These sentences can also be restated with gerund phrases.

It's rude to ignore your conversation partner.   **Ignoring** your conversation partner **is rude**.

It's a good idea to try out different topics.   **Trying out** different topics **is a good idea**.

The word *considered* may also follow *be* in this kind of sentence.

It's considered impolite to interrupt people.   **Interrupting** people **is considered impolite**.

These sentences can also include the phrase *for* + person/pronoun.

It's customary for the complimenter to say nice things about others.   Saying nice things about others **is customary for the complimenter**.

> **GRAMMAR PLUS** *see page 114*

A Look at the Starting Point on page 36 again. Can you find more sentences that begin with gerunds? Try to change them into sentences beginning with *it's*.

B Rewrite the sentences using infinitive or gerund phrases. Then compare answers with a partner.

1. It's inappropriate to talk about politics at work or school.
   Talking about politics at work or school is inappropriate.
2. Using certain gestures is impolite in some foreign countries.
3. Asking someone's age is often considered rude.
4. It's not unusual in the U.S. to address a professor by his or her first name.
5. Hugging friends when you greet them is customary in many cultures.
6. Asking strangers if they're married is inappropriate in some countries.

3 VOCABULARY & SPEAKING

What's appropriate?

A Are these words and phrases positive (+), negative (–), or neutral (~)?
Write the correct symbol next to each word.

____ 1. a compliment	____ 4. bad form	____ 7. offensive	____ 10. strange
____ 2. an insult	____ 5. inappropriate	____ 8. polite	____ 11. typical
____ 3. appropriate	____ 6. normal	____ 9. rude	____ 12. unusual

B Group work How do you feel about these things? Discuss these situations using the words and phrases in part A.

1. You kiss people on the cheek when you meet them.
2. You and your classmates interrupt the teacher.
3. You stand very close to people when you talk to them.
4. You and your parents talk honestly and openly.
5. Your best friend calls you after 11:00 P.M.
6. You start a conversation with a stranger on a bus or subway.

"It's unusual for me to kiss people I meet on the cheek."

> **VOCABULARY PLUS** *see page 134*

4 ROLE PLAY
Making small talk

A Small talk is light conversation, often between people who don't know each other. Select the topics that are appropriate for small talk in your culture.

What's **Safe** *for* **Small Talk?**

☐ Children and family ☐ Health problems ☐ Salaries
☐ Current affairs ☐ Hobbies ☐ Sports
☐ Entertainment ☐ Marital status ☐ The weather

B Group work Imagine you are at a party. Start a conversation with one person, keep it going for one minute, and bring it to a close. Then find a new partner and repeat.

"Hi. How's it going?"

"Pretty good. Hey, did you see that soccer game last night?"

"I did! It's amazing to see our team play so well."

"I know! Hey, I should get going, but I'll call you later."

Useful expressions	
Conversation openers	**Conversation closers**
How's it going?	See you later.
Can you believe this weather? It's (awful)!	Sorry, I've got to run. Talk to you soon.
That's a great (jacket).	It was great to meet you.
Do you know many people here?	I should get going. I'll call you later.

5 LISTENING
Party talk

 **A** Listen to three conversations at different parties. Who is speaking in each one?

1. a. a mother and her son
   b. a teacher and her student
   c. a woman and her son's friend

2. a. two young students
   b. two older friends
   c. a father and his son

3. a. two cooks
   b. two wives
   c. two classmates

 **B** Listen again. What closing phrase is used to end each conversation?

1. _____ 2. _____ 3. _____

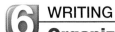

WRITING

Organizing ideas with an outline

> Making an outline is a good way to organize your ideas before you write.
> An outline is usually written in reduced sentences or in notes and provides
> a general plan to follow when you write.

A Read the paragraph about a cultural rule in Japan. Then complete the outline
below with information from the paragraph. What additional information is
included in the paragraph but not in the outline?

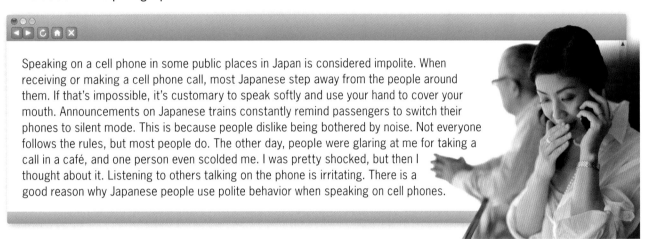

Speaking on a cell phone in some public places in Japan is considered impolite. When
receiving or making a cell phone call, most Japanese step away from the people around
them. If that's impossible, it's customary to speak softly and use your hand to cover your
mouth. Announcements on Japanese trains constantly remind passengers to switch their
phones to silent mode. This is because people dislike being bothered by noise. Not everyone
follows the rules, but most people do. The other day, people were glaring at me for taking a
call in a café, and one person even scolded me. I was pretty shocked, but then I
thought about it. Listening to others talking on the phone is irritating. There is a
good reason why Japanese people use polite behavior when speaking on cell phones.

A. Topic sentence

  Speaking on a cell phone in some public places in Japan **is impolite**_____.

B. Supporting sentences

  • Recommended behavior:

   _____ *or speak softly and cover mouth*

  • General example:

   Train announcements remind passengers – put phone on silent

  • Personal example:

   People glaring for taking a call in _____

C. Concluding sentence

  There is a good reason why Japanese people _____.

B Pair work Write an outline about a cultural rule from your country.
Then exchange outlines and answer the questions.

  1. Is the outline in a logical order?

  2. Does the outline provide enough information? Is there anything else you would include?

C Pair work Use your outline to write a paragraph about the cultural rule.
Then exchange paragraphs and answer the questions.

  1. Does the paragraph follow the outline?

  2. Is the cultural rule clear? What suggestions do you have to make it clearer?

LESSON B ► *It's personal.*

Eavesdroppers

A Read each person's statement. What do you think they should do about each situation?

I Wish I Hadn't Heard That!

Luis, 23, Mexico City

"On the bus to work, I heard my boss's voice behind me. I think he was talking to the office manager on his cell phone. He was telling her that it would be a bad day at work. He explained that they were going to lay off my entire department!"

Rebecca, 25, Vancouver

"I overheard my roommate and her friend gossiping about me when I got home. I asked them what they were saying, but they claimed they hadn't been talking about me. I knew that wasn't true. It really hurt my feelings."

Pam, 18, Portland

"Last week, I overheard my little brother on his cell phone. He was warning his friend not to say anything. So of course I listened. He said he was getting a terrible grade in math this year! And he said it was a big secret, too. In fact, my parents still don't know the truth."

B Group work Have you ever heard someone talking about you? What did you do?

2 DISCUSSION

Who can you confide in?

A Read the information in the chart. Would you rank each person in the same way?

Who do you tell first?

We asked a group of young adults to rate each person in the chart according to when they would tell that person different types of personal news (1 = tell first, 4 = tell last). This is what they said.

Who would you tell . . .	Family member	Spouse	Close friend	Colleague
good news?	2	1	3	4
bad/tragic news?	1	2	3	4
gossip?	4	3	2	1
personal information?	3	2	1	4

Source: Interviews with people between the ages of 22 and 35

B Pair work Why would you tell something to one person and not to another? Discuss your reasons.

"I would usually talk about a personal problem with my close friends rather than my colleagues because my friends already know most of my secrets."

Reported speech

Statements	Reported statements
"It**'s** a big secret."	He said (that) it **was** a big secret.
"I**'m getting** a terrible grade."	He said (that) he **was getting** a terrible grade.
"They **got** engaged."	He said (that) they **had gotten** engaged.
"We **weren't talking** about you."	They claimed (that) they **hadn't been talking** about me.
"She**'s been** absent since Tuesday."	He said (that) she **had been** absent since Tuesday.
"We **had never been** there before."	She said (that) they **had never been** there before.
"I**'ll meet** you at the café."	He said (that) he **would meet** me at the café.

Questions	Reported questions
"**Did** you **know** about the layoffs?"	I asked him if he **had known** about the layoffs.
"What **are** you **saying**?"	I asked them what they **were saying**.

Commands	Reported commands
"**Don't say** anything!"	He warned his friend **not to say** anything.

General truths	Reported general truths
"The sun **rises** in the east."	She said (that) the sun **rises** in the east. (*No change in tense.*)

GRAMMAR PLUS *see page 115*

A Look at the Starting Point on page 40 again. Can you find more examples of reported speech?

B Rewrite the sentences using reported speech. Then compare answers with a partner.

1. "I'm not surprised at all."   She told me _____.
2. "Have you heard the news?"   He asked me _____.
3. "There's a bank down the street."   She said _____.
4. "Why aren't you talking?"   She asked me _____.
5. "Give him a call!"   He told me _____.
6. "We're getting married!"   She told me _____.
7. "Was the movie scary?"   The children asked me _____.
8. "We didn't take the 8:00 train."   They told me _____.

C **Pair work** Imagine that you have overheard this conversation. Take turns reporting each line of the conversation.

Ryan: I heard some interesting news. Do you know Amanda Jenkins?
Lara: I know what she looks like, but I've never met her.
Ryan: Well, she's going to study for a year in Australia.
Lara: How can she afford that?
Ryan: She got a scholarship that will take care of all her expenses.
Lara: I think that's great. When is she leaving?
Ryan: I don't know . . .

"Ryan told Lara that he'd heard some interesting news. He . . ."

4 VOCABULARY & SPEAKING
Tell me what he said.

A Put these expressions for reported speech in the correct columns.

He claimed that . . .	He promised to . . .	He told me that . . .	He advised me to . . .
He asked me to . . .	He wanted to know . . .	He told me to . . .	He encouraged me to . . .
He warned me not to . . .	He explained that . . .	He asked me . . .	He wondered . . .

Statements	Commands or advice	Questions
He claimed that . . .		

B Pair work Tell a partner about a conversation you recently had. What was said? Use one of these topics or your own idea.

- an argument you had with a friend
- a time you asked someone for a big favor
- some exciting news a friend told you
- an apology you made or received

"My roommate claimed I had borrowed her sweater without asking, but I explained that . . ."

VOCABULARY PLUS see page 134

5 LISTENING
Tell me all about it!

A Listen to Nicole's and Tony's news. Choose the correct pictures.

1. Nicole

a. ☐

b. ☐

2. Tony

a. ☐

b. ☐

B Listen again. Choose the best answers.

1. Nicole's sister met her boyfriend . . .
   - ☐ a. in the fall.
   - ☐ b. yesterday.
   - ☐ c. over four years ago.

2. Nicole's sister is probably . . .
   - ☐ a. not afraid to be different.
   - ☐ b. very traditional.
   - ☐ c. shy.

3. How are things at the design studio?
   - ☐ a. There isn't enough work.
   - ☐ b. Things are picking up.
   - ☐ c. Everything's about the same.

4. Tony has been working at the studio . . .
   - ☐ a. longer than most other workers.
   - ☐ b. less time than most other workers.
   - ☐ c. as long as most other workers.

6 READING
Mobile mania

A Read the article. These headings are missing from the text. Put them in the correct place.

The Generic Ring	The Distracted Driver	The Useless Call Maker
The I-Talk-Anywhere	The Shouter	The Corporate Big Shot

CELL PHONE PERSONALITY TYPES

In her travels, "Telephone Doctor" Nancy Friedman has noticed a variety of "cell phone personalities." Which of these types have you seen around?

1. *The Shouter*

Talking three times louder than necessary is characteristic of this offensive cell phone user. He seems to think everyone has a hearing impairment. Doesn't he know the phone already amplifies his voice?

2.

This pompous fellow makes all his business calls in public places while standing in the middle of a crowded room. He conducts big business deals right there in front of us, but we're not impressed.

3.

This exasperating person makes trivial phone calls, one after another, after another. On airplanes, you'll overhear her saying ridiculous things like, "Hi, we haven't left yet," or "Hi, we just landed. OK, see you in a minute."

4.

Making and taking calls anytime, anywhere is the trademark of this infuriating person. She'll chat in restaurants, at movie theaters, and even at funerals. When her cell phone rings, she looks at you and says insincerely, "Oh, sorry about that."

5.

Drive or use the phone – don't do both at the same time. This can be dangerous. It's really scary to see a delivery truck in the rearview mirror with a distracted driver on a phone behind the wheel.

6.

These are the people who haven't bothered to personalize their ring tone. One phone rings and 10 people check to see if it's theirs. Hang on, I think that's my phone!

Source: "What Type of Cell Phone User Are You?"
by Nancy Friedman, www.telephonedoctor.com

B Group work Does the article describe any cell phone users you know or have seen? What bad cell phone manners have you seen recently?

1 STARTING POINT
Weird news

A Read the news articles. Match each headline with the correct article.

a

CELL PHONE *OPENS* CAR DOOR

b

SEA LION
Paints for Her Supper

c

SURFING DOG
Upstages Rivals

1 The police have been called to a surfing contest in Brazil because a dog has been stealing all the attention. The dog became the main attraction at Praia da Tiririca in Bahia during the Surf World Championship. The dog and his owner surfed together on the same surfboard between the competitions. Police said, "They've called us to remove the pair because they've been getting more attention than the actual contest." The dog's owner said, "I've always surfed with my dog. He's always loved it. Sometimes I think he's a better surfer than I am!"

2 Maggie, a California sea lion at the Pittsburgh Zoo, has been amazing visitors by painting for her supper. She has created dozens of paintings. Her trainer said, "I started teaching her to paint last year, and she caught on quickly." Maggie spent three months learning to hold the paintbrush in her mouth and to touch it to the canvas. Adding the paint was the next step. Maggie earned a fish for every successful brushstroke. The trainer has saved all the paintings. She'll probably sell them to raise money to help animals.

3

A shopper in Michigan saved time and money after her husband helped her unlock her car from 10 miles away. After a day at the mall, the woman went out to her car, but couldn't find her keys. When she saw them still in the ignition, she called home and said, "I've locked my keys in the car. I've never done that before. I don't know what to do." Following her husband's instructions, she held her cell phone about a foot from the car door, while her husband held the spare car remote near his phone and pressed the unlock button. The door unlocked. She said, "I've totally stopped worrying about my keys now."

B Pair work One of the news stories isn't true. Which one do you think it is?
(For the answer, see page 142.)

"I think story number one has got to be false. I just don't believe that a dog could surf. Story number two is also pretty amazing, but I have a feeling it's true."

GRAMMAR

Present perfect vs. simple past

Use the present perfect to report a recent event without giving a specific time reference.
I've locked my keys in the car.

Use the simple past to report an event with a specific time reference.
After a day at the mall, the woman **went out** to her car.
I **started** teaching her to paint **last year**.

GRAMMAR PLUS see page 116

A Look at the first story on page 44 again. Can you find more examples of the present perfect and the simple past? Why is each tense used?

B Complete the news story with the present perfect or simple past form of the verbs in parentheses. Then compare answers with a partner.

A group of thieves (1) _**has stolen**_ (steal) the Dragon's Eye ruby from the Grand Gallery. Last night at about 1:00 A.M., the alarm (2) _____ (go off). Police (3) _____ (rush) to the building immediately, but they (4) _____ (be) too late. Right after learning of the robbery, the mayor (5) _____ (set up) a telephone hotline for information about the theft. Three people (6) _____ (call) so far, but the police are still looking for further information. They believe it is probable that the thieves (7) _____ (leave) the city. The curator of the Grand Gallery (8) _____ (offer) a $50,000 reward for information leading to the capture of the thieves.

GRAMMAR

Present perfect vs. present perfect continuous

Use the present perfect continuous to describe temporary situations and actions that are not yet completed. The present perfect describes permanent situations and recently completed actions.
A dog **has been stealing** all the attention. *(temporary situation)*
I've always **surfed** with my dog. *(permanent situation)*
Maggie **has been amazing** visitors by painting for her supper. *(not yet completed action)*
I've locked my keys in the car. *(recently completed action)*

Use the present perfect with the passive or with stative verbs such as *be*, *love*, and *have*.
He's always **loved** it.

GRAMMAR PLUS see page 116

A Look at the first story on page 44 again. Can you find another example of the present perfect continuous? Why is this form used?

B Complete the sentences with the present perfect or present perfect continuous form of the verbs in parentheses. Then compare answers with a partner.

1. Many residents _**have been**_ (be) homeless ever since last month's storm and _____ (stay) with relatives while their homes are being repaired.

2. Although crews _____ (repair) the subway signals all week, they still _____ (not solve) the problem of long delays.

3. Police _____ (guard) the stores that the thieves _____ (not rob) yet.

4. Some organizations _____ (provide) free meals to residents, and will continue to do so all week.

4 VOCABULARY & SPEAKING
It's in the news.

A How would you define each of these news events?

epidemic	hijacking	natural disaster	rebellion	robbery
famine	kidnapping	political crisis	recession	scandal

"A natural disaster is something like a volcanic eruption, a flood, or an earthquake."

B Pair work Tell your partner about some news stories you've recently heard. Use the words in part A.

"I saw something about a big scandal on the news this morning."
"Really? What was it?"
"Well, it said that a politician had been arrested for taking bribes."

VOCABULARY PLUS *see page 135*

5 LISTENING
Broadcast news

🔊 **A** Listen to an early morning news broadcast. What is each story about? Write the correct number.

____ a natural disaster   ____ a scandal   ____ an unusual family event   ____ an epidemic

🔊 **B** Listen again. Are the statements true or false? Choose the correct answer. Then correct the false statements to make them true.

	True	False
1. More people are suffering from TB than ever before.	☐	☐
2. Standard TB drugs are ineffective in about one-fourth of cases.	☐	☐
3. The painting *Sunflowers* was purchased by a large company.	☐	☐
4. The high price paid for the painting caused a scandal.	☐	☐
5. The hurricane has trapped some people in their homes.	☐	☐
6. Tourism in the area hit by the hurricane will not be affected.	☐	☐
7. The mother left the house to give her children freedom.	☐	☐
8. The children used food to get their mom down from the tree.	☐	☐

6 SPEAKING
Speaking of the news

A Pair work Discuss the questions. Ask follow-up questions and add extra information.

1. How closely do you follow the news? What kinds of stories interest you?
2. What do you think was the most important news story in the last few years?
3. Do you think stories about sports or celebrities count as "real news"?

B Group work Compare your answers with another pair. How are your opinions about the news different?

Narratives

> A narrative is usually organized in chronological order and uses a variety of verb tenses.

A Number the events in this news story in the correct order. Then write a title for the article.

Title: _____

_____ As he was punching the shark, it began to release its grip on his leg.

_____ When the stunned shark finally let go, Anderson swam to shore, dragging his badly wounded leg behind him.

_____ He was pulling himself up on the rocks when another surfer came to his aid and called an ambulance.

_____ Anderson's leg was bleeding badly when emergency workers arrived, so they took him to a local hospital, where he was kept overnight for observation.

_____ In an interview shortly after Brian came home, his wife, also a surfer, said she knew her husband would surf again. However, she didn't know if she wanted her son to ever go back in the water!

_____ Doctors released Anderson the next day, and he spent the afternoon at home with his wife and son.

__1__ Brian Anderson was surfing at a popular spot south of Seaside, Oregon, on December 24, when he felt something was grabbing his leg.

__2__ Realizing it was a shark, he punched it repeatedly in the nose so it would loosen its grip.

_____ Anderson said he did this automatically because he'd heard on a TV show that sharks' noses are sensitive.

B Write a brief news story about a recent event. Use the simple past, present perfect, and present perfect continuous to show the order of events.

C Group work Take turns reading your stories. Ask follow-up questions. Who has the most interesting story? Why?

LESSON B ▶ *Storytelling*

1 STARTING POINT
What happened?

A Pair work Read the stories. What do you think happened? Choose two
stories and complete them by filling in the gaps indicated by 〰▶.

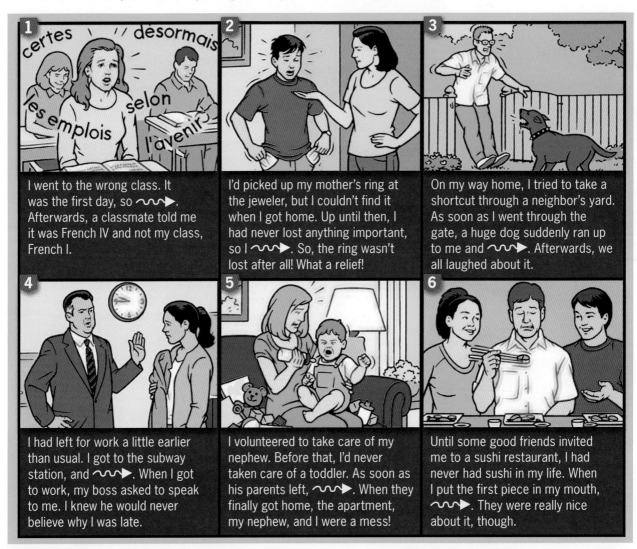

1
I went to the wrong class. It was the first day, so 〰▶. Afterwards, a classmate told me it was French IV and not my class, French I.

2
I'd picked up my mother's ring at the jeweler, but I couldn't find it when I got home. Up until then, I had never lost anything important, so I 〰▶. So, the ring wasn't lost after all! What a relief!

3
On my way home, I tried to take a shortcut through a neighbor's yard. As soon as I went through the gate, a huge dog suddenly ran up to me and 〰▶. Afterwards, we all laughed about it.

4
I had left for work a little earlier than usual. I got to the subway station, and 〰▶. When I got to work, my boss asked to speak to me. I knew he would never believe why I was late.

5
I volunteered to take care of my nephew. Before that, I'd never taken care of a toddler. As soon as his parents left, 〰▶. When they finally got home, the apartment, my nephew, and I were a mess!

6
Until some good friends invited me to a sushi restaurant, I had never had sushi in my life. When I put the first piece in my mouth, 〰▶. They were really nice about it, though.

B Group work Take turns sharing your stories. Have you had similar experiences?

2 LISTENING
How did it all end?

🔊 **A** Listen to two stories from the Starting Point. Which stories are they?

🔊 **B** Listen again. Choose the correct ending of each story.

1. ☐ a. He found the ring in his pocket.
   ☐ b. The jeweler had the ring.
   ☐ c. His mother found the ring.

2. ☐ a. The conductor helped her.
   ☐ b. A passenger helped her.
   ☐ c. The door finally opened.

Adverbs with the simple past and past perfect

Use these adverbs with the simple past to describe something that happened at a later time.
Afterwards, / **Later,** / **The next day**, we all **laughed** about it.

Use these adverbs with the simple past to describe two things that happened at the same time.
When / **As soon as** / **The moment** I **got** to work, my boss **asked** to speak to me.

Use these adverbs with the past perfect to describe something that was true or that happened
before another event in the past.
Up until then, / **Before that,** / **Until that time**, I **had** never **lost** anything important.

GRAMMAR PLUS *see page 117*

A Look at the Starting Point on page 48 again. Can you find the adverbs from the
grammar box? Which verb tenses are used after them?

B Write two sentences for these situations using the adverbs from the grammar box.
Then compare answers with a partner.

1. My apartment was robbed last week.
   *Up until then, I had never had
   anything stolen. The moment it
   happened, I called the police.*

2. I moved into my own apartment
   this summer.

3. I failed my driving test last week.

4. I really enjoyed my trip to Singapore
   last month.

5. I was nervous about going to the dentist.

6. I knew I shouldn't have lent my friend my
   new laptop.

C Match the sentences with the illustrations. Then compare answers with a partner.

_b_ 1. This morning, I was on my way
   to work.

___ 2. Last night, I was telling a joke at
   a dinner party.

___ 3. I was backing my car out of
   the garage. I crashed into my
   neighbor's car.

___ 4. I got to the punch line. I knocked over
   a glass of water with my hand.

___ 5. She had never parked in front of
   my driveway.

___ 6. I noticed everyone laughing. I wasn't
   sure if they were laughing at the joke
   or at me.

D Pair work Take turns telling the stories for each picture. Use adverbs to show
the order of events.

*"This morning, I was on my way to work. I was backing my car out of the garage when
I crashed into my neighbor's car. I couldn't believe it! Until then, she had . . ."*

4 LISTENING
Embarrassing moments

A Listen to an interview with actor Dan Carville. What jobs does he talk about?

1. _____   2. _____   3. _____

B Listen again. Answer the questions.

1. Why did Dan lose his job at the department store?
2. Why didn't Dan last long as a painter?
3. Why was Dan fired from his job as a taxi driver?
4. How seriously do you think Dan took these jobs?

5 VOCABULARY & SPEAKING
Creating a story

A These phrases are used to tell a story. Put them in the correct columns.

I'll never forget the time . . .	Meanwhile . . .	To make a long story short . . .
The thing you have to know is . . .	And in the end . . .	I've got to tell you about . . .
It all started when . . .	That reminds me of when . . .	The other thing is . . .
What happened was . . .	The next thing we knew . . .	So finally . . .
I forgot to mention that . . .	So later on . . .	

Beginning a story	Continuing a story	Going back in a story	Ending a story
I'll never forget the time . . .			

B **Pair work** Tell a story about yourself. Use these story ideas and the phrases in part A. Ask follow-up questions.

STORY IDEAS

▶ You tried something for the first time.
▶ You did something really exciting.
▶ You forgot something important.
▶ You had a surprising experience.
▶ You met an unusual person.

"I'll never forget the first time I cooked a big dinner by myself. I had always helped my mother cook, so I thought it would be easy."
"Why were you cooking a big dinner?"
"Well, I had invited all my friends over, and . . ."

C **Group work** Share your story with another pair of students. Then choose one of the stories and tell it to the class.

VOCABULARY PLUS *see page 135*

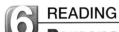

READING
6 Personal anecdotes

A Pair work Look at the titles of the anecdotes. What do you think each one is about? Read the anecdotes to check your answers.

IT HAPPENED TO ME!
(or my friend . . . or a friend of a friend . . .)

Babysitter's Blues

I'll never forget the time last winter when I was babysitting these two kids for the first time. It was about 7:30 at night. Their mom had asked me to make them a pizza for dinner. It had been in the oven for about 15 minutes when suddenly I heard a noise outside, and the dog started barking. As soon as I opened the door and stepped outside, the kids slammed and locked it behind me. It was winter, and I stood outside freezing while they rolled around on the floor laughing hysterically. Meanwhile, the kitchen started getting smoky, and the smoke detector started buzzing. They didn't know what to do, so they let me back in. The pizza was burnt to a crisp. I didn't say anything. But, as we sat around the kitchen table having a bowl of cold cereal instead of their favorite, pizza, I could tell they regretted what they'd done. Anyway, to make a long story short, I babysit them all the time now, and guess what. I haven't had any problems since that first night.

– Amy Fernandez, Boston

A Bad Holiday

Have I learned any lessons the hard way? I sure have! What happened was I wanted a Monday off from work. Tuesday was a national holiday, and I thought a four-day weekend would be just perfect. I asked my boss, and he said no. At that company, all employees got their birthday off, so I asked if we could pretend that the Monday was my birthday. He said no. I woke up on the Monday morning feeling a little defiant, so I called in sick. I told them I got a terrible sunburn on the weekend. Later on, I realized that I had no color at all because I hadn't been out in the sun. So my friends and I went to the beach and stayed there all day. When I woke up the next morning, I had the worst sunburn of my life. I even had to go to the hospital! In the end, I learned a valuable lesson – I can't get away with anything!

– Rita Wagner, San Diego

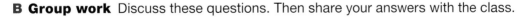

B Group work Discuss these questions. Then share your answers with the class.

1. Why do you think Amy hasn't had any more problems?
2. What would you have done if you were Rita?
3. Which anecdote did you find more amusing? Why?

C Group work Choose one of the topics below, or one of your own, and tell your group an anecdote. Who had the most interesting anecdote? Whose was the funniest?

- celebrity encounters
- food experiences
- school days
- strange coincidences
- childhood memories
- mistaken identity
- speaking English
- travel stories

COMMUNICATION REVIEW

UNITS 4–6

 SELF-ASSESSMENT

How well can you do these things? Choose the best answer.

I can . . .	Very well	OK	A little
▸ Describe how I deal with everyday problems (Ex. 1)	☐	☐	☐
▸ Describe a conversation I've heard or participated in (Ex. 2)	☐	☐	☐
▸ Understand the main points of an academic presentation about stress (Ex. 3)	☐	☐	☐
▸ Evaluate suggestions in a discussion about ways to deal with stress (Ex. 3)	☐	☐	☐
▸ Tell an interesting anecdote from my life (Ex. 4)	☐	☐	☐

Now do the corresponding exercises. Was your assessment correct?

1 SPEAKING
Calm down, chill out.

A What do you do in these situations?

1. Tomorrow is a big day – you have a job interview or an exam. You are worried that you won't sleep well.

2. You've been lying in bed for hours and can't get to sleep. You can't stop thinking about what you have to do tomorrow.

3. You feel angry about something a friend did.

4. You have been studying or working, and you need to take a break.

B Pair work Compare your answers with a partner. Are any of your solutions the same?

"Whenever I have something important the following day, I make sure I get some exercise so that I'll nod off as soon as I lie down."

2 SPEAKING
Guess what I heard!

A Read these situations. Can you think of a personal example for each one?

1. You overheard someone say something really funny.

2. Someone told you a big secret.

3. You realized something important.

B Pair work Discuss your answers with a partner.

"I was on the subway, and I overheard this guy tell his friend that he'd gotten into the bathtub the night before and realized he was still wearing his socks! I just burst out laughing."

🔊 **A** Listen to Dr. Phillips talking about stress. What is the main topic of his presentation? Choose the correct answer.

☐ a. the stress of living on a tight budget

☐ b. college students and stress

☐ c. stress and nutrition

🔊 **B** Listen again. Choose the causes of stress that are mentioned.

☐ 1. not having enough money   ☐ 3. noisy roommates   ☐ 5. not enough studying

☐ 2. jobs   ☐ 4. too much studying   ☐ 6. missing family

C Pair work Look at the causes of stress you chose and these suggestions for ways to deal with stress. Which do you think is the best suggestion? Why?

Ways to Deal with Stress

- Find a physical activity you enjoy and make time for it.
- Organize your time.
- Make time to relax.
- Eat breakfast. Don't drink too much coffee.
- Have a sense of humor.

"When you feel like you've got too much work, I think it's really important to sit down and organize your time. If you do, you'll feel more in control."

4

SPEAKING
Tell me a story.

A Pair work Tell your partner about a time when one of these things happened to you. Ask and answer follow-up questions so that you will be able to retell your partner's story. Take notes.

- You met someone fascinating.
- You did something that took a lot of courage.
- Something made you laugh hysterically.

B Group work Join another pair and tell your partner's story.

"Maria once met a famous marathon runner at a café. It was pretty crowded, and she had just sat down at the last free table. The next thing she knew, the runner walked up to her and . . ."

THE INFORMATION AGE

LESSON A ▶ *A weird, wired world*

1 STARTING POINT
Internet trends

A Look at these Internet trends. Choose the ones that affect you.

Internet Trends

NOW...

- ☐ Music fans have been given access to nearly unlimited music libraries in "the cloud."
- ☐ Increasingly, information about Internet users is being collected for marketing purposes.
- ☐ Many traditional textbooks have been replaced by online versions.
- ☐ With the development of new online tools, more employees are being allowed to work remotely for part of their workweek.

IN THE FUTURE...

- ☐ Most store purchases will be made by using a mobile device linked to an online account. Cash or credit cards will rarely be used.
- ☐ More and more doctor's examinations are likely going to be done over the Internet.
- ☐ More candidates for employment will be identified, interviewed, and hired online.
- ☐ The Internet is going to be subjected to a greater number of hacker attacks due to the increasing amount of personal information stored online.

B Pair work What did people do before these trends appeared?

"People used to buy CDs, and they put them in CD players to listen to them."

2 VOCABULARY
Technology buzzwords

A Match the terms on the left with the definitions on the right.

1. download ____
2. app ____
3. post ____
4. blog ____
5. Wi-Fi ____
6. the cloud ____
7. podcast ____
8. spyware ____
9. text ____
10. virus ____

a. wireless connection to the Internet
b. a radio or TV show downloadable from the Internet
c. transfer files to your computer or smartphone
d. harmful software that attacks computers or phones
e. send a short typed message from a cell phone
f. put something on the Internet for others to see
g. software that secretly records your online activity
h. a program often used on mobile devices
i. large, remote information storage areas on the Internet
j. an online journal or newsletter, usually of personal opinions

B Pair work Which of these technologies do you have experience with? When do you use them? Why?

"I've been downloading music and videos for years. And if I'm too busy to watch TV, I download podcasts of interesting shows to my smartphone. It's great!"

VOCABULARY PLUS *see page 136*

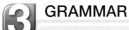

GRAMMAR

Passive of present continuous, present perfect, future

Use the passive for actions where the emphasis is on the object of the action.

Use the passive of the present continuous for ongoing actions.
More employees **are being allowed** to work remotely for part of their workweek.

Use the passive of the present perfect for recently completed actions.
Music fans **have been given** access to nearly unlimited music libraries in "the cloud."

Use *will* + passive or *be going to* + passive for actions that will begin in the future.
Most store purchases **will be made** by using a mobile device linked to an online account.
More and more doctor's examinations **are** likely **going to be done** over the Internet.

GRAMMAR PLUS *see page 118*

A Look at the Starting Point on page 54 again. Can you find more examples of each passive?

B Complete the sentences with the correct passive form of the verb in parentheses. Sometimes more than one answer is possible.

1. Thousands of computers already ___*have been infected*___ (infect) by spyware.

2. Currently, the cloud _____ (utilize) by a large number of businesses.

3. Thousands of blogs _____ (start) on all sorts of topics every day.

4. In coming years, even more fun game apps _____ (develop) for the youth market.

5. Nowadays, teen Internet use _____ (monitor) by concerned parents.

6. These days, podcasts _____ (download) by people of all ages.

7. Many computer viruses _____ (create) by teenagers.

8. In the future, Wi-Fi _____ (make) available in most public places.

LISTENING

Social networking: Different opinions

A Listen to three people's opinions about social networking. What do they mainly use it for?

1. _____   2. _____   3. _____

B Listen again. Choose the correct answers to complete the sentences.

1. Michael believes that social networking at work . . .
   - ☐ a. should be restricted.
   - ☐ b. makes workers happier.

2. In the case of children, Lisa believes that social networking . . .
   - ☐ a. teaches social skills.
   - ☐ b. is potentially harmful.

3. Daniel is careful about what he uploads or posts so people won't . . .
   - ☐ a. steal his work.
   - ☐ b. form a bad opinion of him.

5 VOCABULARY
Connecting ideas formally

A These expressions connect ideas in different ways. Put them in the correct columns. Sometimes more than one answer is possible.

additionally	as a result	for instance	in fact	nevertheless	similarly
as a matter of fact	for example	furthermore	likewise	on the other hand	therefore

Add information	Compare or contrast	Emphasize	Give an example	Show a result
additionally				

B Choose the appropriate connector to complete the sentences.

1. Tom loves technology; *similarly / for example*, he has the latest cell phone.

2. Many airports offer inexpensive Wi-Fi; *nevertheless / in fact*, at some it's even free.

3. Many of my friends' computers have been damaged by viruses; *nevertheless / therefore*, I am going to update my antivirus software.

4. Some websites aren't reliable; *as a result / likewise*, many people are being misinformed.

5. Few people could have predicted recent advances in Internet technology; *for example / likewise*, predicting the future of the Internet is difficult.

6. Internet identity theft is something very serious; *on the other hand / as a matter of fact*, it can ruin your life.

VOCABULARY PLUS *see page 136*

6 DISCUSSION
Social networking debate

A Pair work Do you think social networking sites are a positive or negative influence? Find a partner who has the same opinion.

B Group work Find a pair who disagrees with you and your partner. Take turns explaining your reasons. Each pair gets a chance to disagree.

"The way I see it, social networking sites are a positive influence because they allow me to have friends all over the world."

"That may be true, but in my opinion, online friends aren't really true friends. In fact, . . ."

Useful expressions		
Expressing opinions	**Disagreeing**	**Giving reasons**
If you ask me, . . .	That may be true, but . . .	That's why . . .
The way I see it, . . .	I see your point, but . . .	The reason for that is . . .

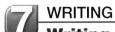

WRITING
Writing a product or service review

> Writing and posting a product or service review helps other consumers make informed decisions. Most product and service reviews contain similar features.

A Look at the information about product reviews. Then read the review below and select the things the review does. Find examples in the review with a partner.

☐ 1. names the product and explains its use   ☐ 4. suggests how it could be improved

☐ 2. explains where it can be purchased   ☐ 5. states who would find it useful and why

☐ 3. mentions positive features   ☐ 6. gives the exact price

Organize Me XPS is one of the best tools I have used for managing my busy schedule – and I have used many over the years. With this app, I'm able to organize all of my tasks and appointments in one place with just a couple of simple steps. Furthermore, a simple set-up is all it takes to share my plans with others. Having the ability to share my lists and calendars with colleagues and friends like this is extremely useful.

The only drawback some people might find is that it does not have all of the features offered by some of the more expensive productivity apps; nevertheless, it does exactly what I need it to do. In fact, the app's simplicity is its best feature. I just love the simple interface. Although the developers promise that free updates offering new features will be released soon, if you ask me, the low cost makes it a really good value as is.

If you're someone who writes notes on little pieces of paper and then loses them, get this app. It will really boost your productivity. I use it every day – for school, work, and everything else.

B Use one of these topics or your own idea to write a product or service review.

- technology you purchased
- a game or app you tried
- a restaurant you ate at
- a service you used (dry cleaner, hair salon, mechanic)

C Group work Take turns reading your reviews. Then answer the questions.

1. Whose review is the most interesting and informative? Why?
2. What additional information would you want to know as a consumer?
3. Which reviews would convince you to buy the product or use the service? Which ones would lead you to make a different choice?

1 STARTING POINT
Future shock

A Read these comments about technology. Do you agree or disagree?

WHAT'S **Your** TAKE ON TECHNOLOGY?

Joo-chan, Seoul:
"Apps are cool, aren't they? I download lots of them to my smartphone. Wouldn't it be great if phones came loaded with even more apps?"

Ana, São Paulo:
"Isn't it weird how some people use mobile devices constantly? They don't notice anything around them. It's actually dangerous, don't you think?"

Sarah, Los Angeles:
"Don't you think there are too many websites full of misinformation? Shouldn't the government fine sites that contain false information?"

Yang Ming, Taipei:
"Doesn't it seem like kids spend too much time playing violent video games? It makes kids more aggressive, doesn't it?"

B Pair work Compare your answers with a partner. Do you think the government should regulate any of these things?

2 VOCABULARY
Forms of communication

A Where do you find these forms of communication? Put them in the correct columns. Then add another expression to each category.

| banner ads | bumper stickers | crawls | infomercials | spam | text messages |
| billboards | bus wraps | fliers | pop-up ads | telemarketing | voice mail |

On television	On the Internet	On the phone	On streets or highways

B Pair work Which of the above are the most useful ways of communicating information? The least useful? Do you find any of them annoying?

"Those crawls at the bottom of TV screens aren't useful. It's impossible to read them and pay attention to a show at the same time. Don't you think they're annoying?"

VOCABULARY PLUS *see page 136*

GRAMMAR

Negative and tag questions for giving opinions

Use negative questions or tag questions to offer an opinion and invite someone to react.
Isn't it weird how some people use mobile devices constantly?
Doesn't it seem like kids spend too much time playing violent video games?
Wouldn't it be great if phones came loaded with even more apps?
Shouldn't the government fine sites that contain false information?
Apps are cool, **aren't they**?
It makes kids more aggressive, **doesn't it**?

Use the phrase *don't you think* to form negative or tag questions for opinions.
Don't you think there are too many websites full of misinformation?
It's actually dangerous, **don't you think**?

GRAMMAR PLUS *see page 119*

A Look at the Starting Point on page 58 again. Find the tag questions used by Joo-chan and Yang Ming. Why do they have different endings?

B Pair work Turn the statements into negative or tag questions. Then ask and answer the questions. Discuss your answers.

1. It's annoying how often telemarketers call.
2. They should get rid of those banner ads on the Internet.
3. It would be great if there were fewer billboards.
4. It seems like a lot of people are texting while driving.
5. It's sad when people are tricked into losing money by spam messages.
6. There are too many channels on TV these days.

DISCUSSION

It's kind of strange, isn't it?

A Pair work Do you agree or disagree with these opinions? Why?

> Millions of people are addicted to online games these days. It's kind of sad, isn't it?

> Wouldn't it be great if the Internet were turned off one day a week to give people a chance to rest?

> Don't you think a lot of people are being confused by misinformation on the Internet?

> Aren't kids today being exposed to too much information on television and on the Internet?

> Don't you find it annoying that social networking sites sell your personal information to marketers?

B Group work What other problems are caused by modern information technology? Agree on the three most pressing problems and tell the class.

"Don't you think kids today spend too much time online? Won't their grades and social development suffer because of it?"

"You might be right. But their parents should set limits for them, shouldn't they?"

5 LISTENING
Health and technology

 A Listen to a report on health problems caused by technology. Who is the main intended audience? Choose the correct answer.

- ☐ a. doctors or other health professionals
- ☐ b. frequent users of technology products
- ☐ c. designers of computers and mobile devices

B Listen again and complete the chart.

Problem	Symptoms	Advice
texter's thumb		
carpal tunnel syndrome		
gadget addiction		

6 DISCUSSION
Future technologies?

A Read about these technologies. Are any of them available now? Do you think any will be available in the future? Would you like to make use of them? Why or why not?

Technologies of Tomorrow?

You'll never be bored with the color of your clothes or furniture again. With color-changing fabric, you'll be able to select from a wide variety of colors using a remote control, changing colors whenever you want.

Wireless electricity will allow you to do away with chargers, batteries, and cords. Devices and appliances in homes and businesses will run on electricity transmitted wirelessly from a hidden power source.

A life recorder is a small wearable device that will take a video of everything you see, twenty-four hours a day, seven days a week. The sights and sounds of your entire life will be saved for years to come.

B Group work What new technologies are becoming popular? Which ones do you think are useful? What other technologies do you think will be invented in the future?

Cyber-begging

A Pair work Imagine that a stranger asked you for money to help pay off a frivolous debt. Would you help? Tell your partner. Then read the article.

Can you spare a dime for my Gucci bills?

There was a time when Karyn Bosnak couldn't pay a $59.00 bill at the grocery store. She was officially broke. She didn't have enough money to get on the subway, but she looked rich. She was a television producer, earned $900 a week, and had a closetful of designer labels like Gucci and Louis Vuitton. But she also had a $20,221.40 credit card bill and an empty bank account. Karyn decided that it was time for a change. She built a website and simply asked people to help her out by sending her a buck or two.

On the site, Karyn honestly explained her situation, Gucci shoes and all. "If 20,000 people gave me just $1, I'd be home free, and I'm sure there are 20,000 people out there who can afford to give me $1." Amazingly, it worked. Her website was visited by more than a million people. Although most donors just gave a few dollars, one generous donor sent $1,000. She was on TV and in newspapers and magazines. She was offered a book deal and a movie contract. And of course, she was able to pay off her credit card debt.

She also sold her designer clothes on eBay. In her closet, where the Gucci purses once sat, Karyn keeps all the letters that people have sent her.

She's received teddy bears, subscriptions to *Vogue*, Dunkin' Donuts coupons, backpacks, jewelry, cat food, and candles.

It's hard to understand why so many people helped a total stranger pay off her huge credit card bill. Why did they do it? Karyn explains, "I was just honest about what happened; I didn't make up some sob story about saving the world." Her donors think it's funny and original, she argues, and view it less as a charity than as an entertainment site.

Imitators have sprung up all over the Internet, some with outrageously selfish requests like a BMW or a house. Actually, Karyn was not the first person to put up a website asking strangers for money. The practice has a name: "cyber-begging." Most sites receive little traffic and even less cash.

Karyn also had thousands of enemies and critics. People sent her hate mail and scolded her on websites. Karyn says she never let this anger bother her. "They are probably jealous they didn't think of it," she explains.

Source: "Brother, can you spare a dime for my Gucci bills?" by Janelle Brown, Salon.com

B Read the article again and answer the questions. Then compare your answers with a partner.

1. Why was Karyn in financial trouble?
2. What was her main solution to her problem? What else did she do?
3. Why did so many people respond positively to her website?

C Group work Discuss these questions. Then share your answers with the class.

1. Do you think Karyn was unethical, or was she simply clever?
2. What would you have done if you were Karyn?

1 STARTING POINT
Creative professions

A Pair work How much creativity do you think these jobs require? Number them from 1 (most creative) to 4 (least creative). Explain your choices.

____ chef   ____ surgeon   ____ photographer   ____ jazz musician

"I think a chef has to be the most creative. Inventing new dishes requires a lot of creativity."

B Group work Which jobs might be right for these kinds of people? Discuss your answers.

1. someone able to think quickly
2. a person looking for adventure
3. people good with their hands
4. someone needing job security
5. a person trained in music
6. a person with a good voice

"Someone able to think quickly might be a good surgeon. You never know what might go wrong once the operation starts."

2 VOCABULARY
Creative qualities

A What qualities do creative people usually have? Complete the chart with the correct nouns or adjectives.

Noun	Adjective	Noun	Adjective	Noun	Adjective
curiosity	*curious*	innovation			passionate
decisiveness		knowledge		patience	
	determined		motivated		perceptive
	disciplined		original		resourceful

B Pair work Which of the qualities in the chart are most important to your job or studies? Discuss with a partner.

"Well, I'm studying engineering, and we get a lot of assignments, so I have to be very disciplined. It's a very competitive field."

VOCABULARY PLUS *see page 137*

GRAMMAR

Reduced relative clauses

You can shorten a relative clause by dropping the relative pronoun and the verb *be*.
Someone (**who** / **that is**) **able to think quickly** might be a good surgeon.
A person (**who** / **that is**) **looking for adventure** could be a private detective.
A person (**who** / **that is**) **trained in music** might be a good DJ.

You can also drop *who* / *that* and change the verb to the gerund.
Someone **who** / **that needs job security** might not want to be a jazz musician.
Someone **needing job security** might not want to be a jazz musician.

In many relative clauses, *who* / *that* + the verb *have* can be replaced by *with*.
A person **who** / **that has a good voice** could be a good TV journalist.
A person **with a good voice** could be a good TV journalist.

GRAMMAR PLUS *see page 120*

A Look at the Starting Point on page 62 again. Can you make the reduced relative clauses in part B into full clauses? What verb forms do the full clauses use?

B Rewrite these sentences with reduced relative clauses. Then compare with a partner.

1. Someone who hopes to be a chef should get the proper training.
   Someone hoping to be a chef should get the proper training.

2. Anyone who wants to be an actor needs both talent and luck.

3. A person who works as a comedian is always looking for new ways to make people laugh.

4. People who are clever enough to get inside the mind of a criminal would make good detectives.

5. Anyone who dreams of becoming a champion athlete has to be prepared to do a lot of hard work.

6. Someone who is interested in the latest music trends might be a good DJ.

7. A person who is responsible for a large staff has to be able to be creative with scheduling.

C Complete these sentences using reduced relative clauses and your own ideas.

1. . . . needs to take voice lessons.
   Someone dreaming of becoming a professional singer needs to take voice lessons.

2. . . . should speak English as much as possible.

3. . . . should keep up with current events.

4. . . . doesn't need to have a good speaking voice.

5. . . . should follow the latest trends in clothing.

6. . . . has to study the behavior of animals.

7. . . . usually have a great love of food and eating.

8. . . . will find the job market extremely competitive.

DISCUSSION
Creativity quiz

A How creative are you? Complete the quiz.

How Creative Are You?

	Always	Sometimes	Rarely	Never
1. Are you a risk taker?	3	2	1	0
2. Are you naturally curious?	3	2	1	0
3. Do you look for opportunities to improve things?	3	2	1	0
4. Are you sensitive to beauty?	3	2	1	0
5. Do you challenge accepted ideas?	3	2	1	0
6. Do you keep an eye out for new fashions and products?	3	2	1	0
7. Do you adapt easily to new situations?	3	2	1	0
8. Do you trust your guesses, intuitions, and insights?	3	2	1	0
9. Are you more interested in the future than in the past?	3	2	1	0
10. Do you have a creative sense of humor?	3	2	1	0

B **Pair work** Add up your score. Then check what your score means below.
Do you agree? Why or why not? Tell your partner.

	21–30	11–20	0–10
About You	Because you're open-minded, you like to keep up with the latest trends and innovations. Accepting the status quo bores you. You see mistakes as learning experiences.	You often have good ideas, but you prefer to feel them out with friends before taking action. You're up-to-date with new fashions and products, but unlikely to be the first in your group to try them.	You prefer to stick with the tried-and-true, which helps you feel safe, but you may get left behind in later years. You're content with who you are and what you know.

LISTENING
Creativity at work

◀)) **A** Listen to Samira, Alex, and Naomi talking about their occupations. What does each person do?

◀)) **B** Listen again. What do Samira (*S*), Alex (*A*), and Naomi (*N*) say they focus on in their work? Write the correct letter.

____ 1. helping indecisive clients   ____ 4. solving a wide variety of problems

____ 2. efficiency   ____ 5. new ideas to replace rejected ones

____ 3. beating the competition   ____ 6. using old concepts in new ways

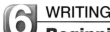

WRITING
Beginning new paragraphs

> Begin a new paragraph each time you change the focus of your ideas.

A Read this composition. The writer changes focus twice. Indicate with a *P* where the two new paragraphs should begin. Then compare answers with a partner.

Lucy Gomez is the most creative person I know. She started piano lessons when she was only four years old. At school, she was always creating interesting projects in her art class. When she was only 12 years old, she won a citywide poetry contest. Her parents were very proud of her. Lucy works as a sitcom writer for a popular TV show now. She works with a group of writers, and together they have to think of original ideas for stories. They also have to come up with funny dialogue for the actors on their show, because the actors have to play believable characters that will make the audience laugh. It is not an easy job, but Lucy does it well. She starts work late in the morning and often works until 7:00 or 8:00 at night. Lucy is very curious. She likes to travel and meet new people who have opinions that are different from hers. And she's always noting ideas, drawing quick sketches, and taking photos. She tells me that doing these things helps her turn new experiences into a source of ideas for her work. I always enjoy talking to her and am happy to know someone as knowledgeable and creative as Lucy.

B Brainstorm ideas for a composition about someone who is very creative or who is unique or different in an interesting way. Answer these questions to help you.

1. In what ways is this person special or different?
2. How does this affect his or her life?
3. Would you like to be like this person? Why or why not?

C Write a three-paragraph composition based on your ideas.

D **Pair work** Read your partner's composition and answer these questions.

1. Do the paragraphs start and end where they should?
2. Is the focus of each paragraph clear?
3. Is there any additional information you would like to know that was not included?

1 STARTING POINT
Everyday objects

A Read about these unusual uses of everyday objects. Have you ever used them in these ways?

Three Clever Ideas

1 "I have three cats, which means there's usually a lot of cat fur on my clothes. To get rid of the fur, I wrap my hand in tape, sticky side out. Then I rub the tape over my clothes, and it picks up the fur!"

2 "The zipper was stuck on my favorite jacket. Luckily, my roommate works in fashion, which is great because she knew how to fix it. She just rubbed a drop of olive oil on the zipper."

3 "Tacos can be messy to eat, which is why I wrap them in paper coffee filters. I serve them that way at parties and backyard barbecues. It works great for other messy sandwiches, too!"

B Group work Use your imagination to suggest new uses for these everyday items. Decide on the best use for each and share it with the class.

- old newspapers
- a shower curtain
- aluminum foil
- empty shoe boxes
- dental floss
- a hair dryer
- empty jars or cans
- rubber bands

"You can wrap green tomatoes in newspaper to make them ripen more quickly."

2 VOCABULARY & SPEAKING

Exploring possibilities

A Combine the verbs with the nouns to make common expressions.

Verbs			Nouns			
analyze	find	organize	a decision	a problem	a solution	possibilities
explore	make	solve	a mistake	a situation	alternatives	information

analyze a situation, solve a problem, . . .

B Pair work Discuss the questions. Then ask your partner more questions using the new vocabulary.

1. When do you make decisions quickly? When do you explore the possibilities first?
2. Who do you talk to when you need to find a solution to a big problem? Why?
3. When was the last time you analyzed a mistake you made? What did you learn from it?

VOCABULARY PLUS *see page 137*

3 GRAMMAR

Non-defining relative clauses as sentence modifiers

You can use non-defining relative clauses with *which* to make a comment about an entire sentence.
I have three cats, **which means there's usually a lot of cat fur on my clothes**.
My roommate is a slob, **which is why I want to get my own apartment**.

GRAMMAR PLUS *see page 121*

A Look at the Starting Point on page 66 again. Can you find more examples of these grammar patterns? How are the commas used?

B Match these statements with the appropriate non-defining clauses. Then compare with a partner and write two similar statements of your own.

1. I want to give away all my old books, _h_

2. I had locked my keys in my car, ____

3. I've been exploring possibilities for natural cleaners, ____

4. My son made a robot costume for himself, ____

5. Our neighbor saves her empty jars for my dad, ____

6. I downloaded a great new app that helps me organize information, ____

7. It's easy to get lost when driving in a new city, ____

8. Adam has bought some expensive software to edit videos, ____

a. which is why you saw me opening it with a coat hanger.

b. which is great since he uses them to store nails and things in his workroom.

c. which is great because I think it's solved my problem of forgetting where I store files.

d. which is why I was wiping lemon juice and salt on those copper pots.

e. which is one reason why GPS systems were developed for cars.

f. which is why he was covered in aluminum foil yesterday.

g. which is strange since there are plenty of free programs that do that well.

h. which means I have to get boxes for them.

4 SPEAKING

Key inventions

A What inventions or discoveries do you think have had the greatest impact on modern life? Make a list.

the cell phone

the television

the airplane

B Group work Compare lists with your group.

"I think the cell phone has really affected people's lives. People can talk wherever they are, which means they can always be in touch and save time."

LISTENING
Great ideas

A Look at the pictures. What do you know about these products or services? How do you think they were developed?

🔊 **B** Listen to these stories about the invention and development of the products in the photos. Complete the chart.

	Bill Bowerman	Fred Smith
How he got the idea		
The initial reaction to the idea		
What the inventor did in response		

6

DISCUSSION
Making life better

A Pair work Why do people create or invent new products? Read this list of reasons and add two more of your own.

- to help protect people's health
- to make business more efficient
- to make daily life easier
- to make life more enjoyable

- to protect the environment
- to save lives
- _____
- _____

B Group work Join another pair. Why do you think these things were created or invented? Use the reasons in part A or others of your own.

1. air conditioners
2. artificial sweeteners
3. digital cameras
4. electric knives
5. hybrid cars
6. karaoke machines
7. laptops
8. lie detectors
9. scanners

"I think air conditioners were invented to protect people's health. The summer heat can be deadly for infants and the elderly."

A unique inventor and his invention

A Read the title of the article. What do you think Daisuke Inoue invented?
Then read the article and check your answer.

The Man Who Taught the World to Sing

Daisuke Inoue was a drummer in a band near Osaka, Japan, that played versions of famous pop songs. People loved to sing along as the band played, but most of them couldn't carry a tune. Inoue's band had spent years learning how to make the untalented customer sound in tune by adjusting the music to match the customer's voice. The singers, mainly Japanese businessmen out for a night on the town, loved Inoue's unique follow-along style.

In 1971, a loyal client asked Inoue to escort him on a company trip, but Inoue could not attend. He found a solution: he recorded his band's back-up tracks, and then hooked up a car stereo and an amplifier. With this device, Inoue gave birth to the karaoke machine. By the 1980s, *karaoke*, which means "empty orchestra," was a Japanese word that required no translation across the globe.

Unfortunately, Inoue never bothered to patent the world's first karaoke machine, so he lost his chance to become one of Japan's richest men. When asked if he regretted not patenting his invention, 65-year-old Daisuke Inoue confessed, "I'm not an inventor. I am just resourceful. I simply put things that already exist together. Who would consider patenting something like that?"

Inoue's friend Robert Scott Field says, "Some people say he lost 150 million dollars. If it were me, I'd be crying in the corner, but he's a happy guy. I think he's amazed to find that he's touched so many lives." Inoue believes the little box he put together has had a huge social impact, especially in Japan. At weddings and company get-togethers, the karaoke comes out and people relax. It breaks the ice.

Although Inoue spent years in obscurity, in 1999, *Time* magazine called him one of the twentieth century's most influential people, saying he had "helped to liberate the once unvoiced."

Inoue is always getting asked silly questions, but he takes them in stride. "Women approach me all the time and ask if I can help their husbands sing better. I always say that if her husband were any good at singing, he would be making a living at it. He's bad, which means he's just like the rest of us."

Inoue didn't use a modern karaoke machine until he was 59 years old, but his favorite English songs are "Love Is a Many Splendored Thing" and Ray Charles' "I Can't Stop Loving You." "They're easy, which is good because I'm a terrible singer," said Daisuke Inoue, the man who taught the world to sing.

Source: "Mr. Song and Dance Man," by Dr. David McNeill, Sophia University, Tokyo

B **Group work** Discuss these questions. Then share your answers with the class.

1. What led Daisuke Inoue to create his invention? Do you agree he was only being resourceful, or was he actually an inventor? Explain.

2. Would you have the same attitude as Inoue if you invented something popular and received no compensation? Why or why not?

3. How do you think Inoue "helped to liberate the once unvoiced" both as a drummer in his band and as the inventor of karaoke? Do you think this is a good thing? Explain.

9 GENERALLY SPEAKING

LESSON A ► How typical are you?

1 STARTING POINT
What's typical?

A Read about the "typical" person in Italy and Japan. What information surprised you? Why?

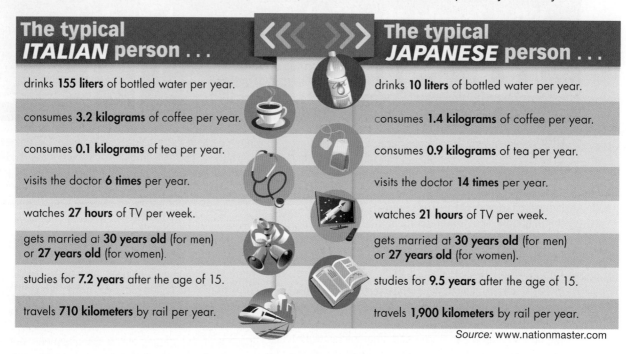

The typical **ITALIAN** person...	«« »»	The typical **JAPANESE** person...
drinks **155 liters** of bottled water per year.		drinks **10 liters** of bottled water per year.
consumes **3.2 kilograms** of coffee per year.		consumes **1.4 kilograms** of coffee per year.
consumes **0.1 kilograms** of tea per year.		consumes **0.9 kilograms** of tea per year.
visits the doctor **6 times** per year.		visits the doctor **14 times** per year.
watches **27 hours** of TV per week.		watches **21 hours** of TV per week.
gets married at **30 years old** (for men) or **27 years old** (for women).		gets married at **30 years old** (for men) or **27 years old** (for women).
studies for **7.2 years** after the age of 15.		studies for **9.5 years** after the age of 15.
travels **710 kilometers** by rail per year.		travels **1,900 kilometers** by rail per year.

Source: www.nationmaster.com

B Complete these statements. Use information from the chart.

1. Unlike the Japanese, Italians seem to drink a lot of ___*bottled water*___.
2. While the typical _____ person studies until the age of 22, the typical _____ person studies until the age of 24.
3. Both like TV, except that the typical _____ person watches more.
4. In contrast to Italians, the Japanese travel a lot more _____.
5. Both groups are fairly different, except for the age _____.

2 SPEAKING
That's just so typical!

A Pair work What are typical examples of these things in your hometown?

1. a store   2. a home   3. a job   4. a car   5. a snack food   6. a weekend activity

B Group work Join another pair and compare your answers.

"What's a typical store in your hometown?"

"We have something called 'dollar stores.' They have household goods, clothes, toys, and lots of other stuff. And everything's really inexpensive."

3 GRAMMAR

Clauses and phrases showing contrast and exception

Use *while*, *unlike*, and *in contrast to* in order to present contrasting information, especially in writing.
While the typical Italian person studies until the age of 22, the typical Japanese person studies until the age of 24.
Unlike the Japanese, Italians seem to drink a lot of bottled water.
In contrast to Italians, the Japanese travel a lot more by rail.

Use *except* (*that*), *except* (*for*), and *except for the fact* (*that*) to show an exception.
Both like TV, **except** (**that**) the typical Italian person watches more.
Italian and Japanese people are fairly different, **except for** the age they get married.
Japanese people typically consume less, **except for the fact that** they drink more tea.

GRAMMAR PLUS *see page 122*

A Look at the Starting Point on page 70 again. Notice the sentences in part B
that use phrases with *except*. Which phrase is followed by a clause?

B Here's some information about customs. How are they different in other places?
Write sentences showing contrasts and indicating exceptions.

1. When people in the U.S. go to a party, they usually arrive a few minutes late.
   Unlike people in the U.S., most people where I live arrive on time for parties.
2. Most people in Canada have cereal and milk for breakfast some days of the week.
3. Most people in the U.S. who study a foreign language in college choose Spanish.
4. In the U.K., it's common for friends to split the bill at a restaurant.
5. For people in Italy, lunch is the main meal of the day.
6. Women in Spain usually kiss people on both cheeks when they meet.

C Are you typical? Complete these sentences and compare with a partner.

1. Unlike most people where I live, *I don't own a car.*
2. In contrast to most of my friends, . . .
3. While a lot of the people where I live . . .
4. I'm similar to many of my friends, except that . . .

4 DISCUSSION

Are you typical?

Group work Choose the answer that makes each sentence true for you. Then compare
answers with your group. Are you typical in your group?

❶ I need *six or less / seven / eight or more* hours of sleep.
❷ For commuting, I rely mainly on *buses / subways / trains / taxis / a car.*
❸ I tend to eat *healthy / unhealthy snacks* between meals.
❹ I spend the most time with my friends *in person / on the phone / online.*
❺ I button my clothes from the *top down / bottom up.*
❻ A great night out should include a *movie / play / concert / sporting event.*

*"Unlike most of the people in my group, I need eight or more hours of sleep or I don't
feel rested. Most people in my group need only six hours or less."*

5 VOCABULARY
Should I just go with the flow?

A Are these adjectives, verbs, and phrases related to accepting things as they are or to making changes? Put them in the correct columns.

Adjectives	Verbs	Phrases
amenable	accept	be your own person
conservative	conform (to)	fit in
rebellious	confront	follow the crowd
(un)conventional	stand up (to/for)	make waves

Accepting things as they are	Making changes

B Group work Use the expressions in the chart in part A to describe what you think these people might be like. Give examples to explain your ideas.

1. Ed, a guy who gets along with everyone
2. Clarissa, an actor desperate for attention
3. Rob, an assistant at a law firm hoping for a promotion
4. Diana, a leader who wants to change the world

"Ed is probably amenable and does what other people want. I imagine he only confronts people if he really has to and generally follows the crowd."

VOCABULARY PLUS *see page 138*

6 LISTENING & SPEAKING
How are they different?

🔊 **A** Listen to Yoshiko, Diego, and Suzanne talking about their school experiences. Answer the questions.

1. What examples does Yoshiko give for how she is typical? In what way is she different?
2. What are three ways that Diego's life is typical? In what way doesn't he follow the crowd?
3. Does Suzanne give an example of how her life is unconventional? If so, what is it?

🔊 **B** Listen again. Do Yoshiko, Diego, and Suzanne believe they are typical or different from most people their age?

C Pair work Do you tend to go with the flow or be your own person? Discuss these questions.

1. Are your interests similar to those of your friends and family or different? Explain.
2. In what ways do the clothes you wear make you stand out or fit in?
3. How does your taste in music compare to that of other people your age?

Yoshiko in Mexico

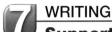

WRITING
Supporting statements

> **Supporting statements develop the topic sentence by providing key facts, reasons, or examples.**

A Read the paragraph. What's the topic sentence? Underline three supporting statements that develop the main idea in the topic sentence. Then compare your answers with a partner.

http://www.cup.org/myblog/

Unconventionally Cool: Trendspotter Josie Buchier

June 13

My friend Josie Buchier doesn't like to follow the crowd. While most of us are trying our best to fit in with everyone else, Josie likes to be her own person. For instance, she has her own unique sense of fashion, so she likes to buy all her clothes, except for her shoes, in used clothing shops. Her taste in music is also pretty unconventional. Unlike most of my friends, she can't stand pop music. She prefers to listen to Philippine and Andean folk music. She also has a very interesting job. Unlike her old nine-to-five job in a conservative department store, she now works as a trendspotter for an advertising company. This means that she spends her time looking at the latest fashion and entertainment trends among young people. Then she writes reports for her company about what's in style. This makes my unconventional friend a trendsetter that others follow, and that's pretty cool.

[4 comments]

B Finish these statements with information of your own to make topic sentences. Compare with a partner.

1. Generally speaking, most people where I live don't . . .
2. One of my best friends is . . .
3. In general, my friends tend to be . . .

C Choose one of the topic sentences and brainstorm supporting ideas. Then choose at least four supporting statements and write a paragraph.

Generally speaking, most people where I live don't mind making waves. It's their way of . . .

D Pair work Exchange paragraphs and answer these questions.

1. Do all the supporting statements relate to the topic sentence?
2. Do they develop and explain the topic sentence?
3. Do the supporting details fit together in a logical order?
4. What other facts, reasons, or examples could be added?

STARTING POINT

I never used to feel stressed.

A Read Annie's email to her friend. What problems does she have?

To: Adriana Costa
From: Annie Wilson
Subject: Missing you!

Hi Adriana,

How are things back in Cartagena? Are you glad to be home again? Sorry I haven't written lately. I have a lot of new responsibilities at work now, so I've been really stressed. My job didn't use to be so demanding!

I have to say, I miss you. You used to be such a good influence on me! These days, I oversleep. I'm even late for work sometimes! That never used to happen because I knew I had to meet you at the café in the morning. I remember how you would complain about the coffee they served. You used to call it "brown water"!

I'm spending too much money, too. Every time I go to the mall, I see something I want to buy. That's another reason I miss you! I would see some great jacket, but you wouldn't let me buy it. You would always tell me I didn't need it and drag me away!

Also, I have a noisy new roommate, Cindy. All she ever does is gab on her cell! Remember the way we would sit around talking? You always used to make me laugh. I bet that's a big reason I never used to feel stressed like I do now!

Anyway, the weekend will be here soon, so I'm sure I'll feel better then.

Write soon!

Annie

B Pair work What do you think Annie should do about her problems?

"Annie should find another friend to meet at the café in the morning."

VOCABULARY

Expressions with *keep* and *stay*

A Match the phrases to make questions. Notice the expressions with *keep* and *stay*.

1. When you're stressed, can you **keep** _e_   a. expenses down?
2. When friends move away, do you **keep / stay** ____   b. up with current events?
3. If you're sleepy while studying, what can you do to **stay** ____   c. connected?
4. What news sources do you read in order to **keep** ____   d. in touch?
5. Do you break the rules or do you **keep / stay** ____   e. things in perspective?
6. How do you save money when you need to **keep** ____   f. awake?
7. Is it important for old friends to **keep / stay** ____   g. out of trouble?

B Pair work Take turns answering the questions. Discuss your answers.

VOCABULARY PLUS *see page 138*

3 GRAMMAR

Past habitual with *used to* and *would*

Used to and *would* can both be used to describe past habitual actions or situations which are no longer true.
However, *would* cannot be used with stative verbs such as *live, be, have,* or *like*.
You always **used to make** me laugh.
My job **didn't use to be** so demanding!
Remember the way we **would sit** around talking?
I **would see** some great jacket, but you **wouldn't let** me buy it.

GRAMMAR PLUS *see page 123*

A Look at the Starting Point on page 74 again. Make a list of the things that have changed for Annie since Adriana went back to Colombia.

B Complete these sentences with *used to* or *would*. Sometimes more than one answer is possible.

The first year of high school, I wasn't a very good student. I (1) _____ *used to* _____ think school was boring. I remember my classmates (2) _____ go to the library and work on projects or study, but I (3) _____ like to play video games at a friend's house instead. We (4) _____ go right after class, and we (5) _____ spend three or four hours doing that. My parents both (6) _____ have jobs with long hours, so they never knew what time I (7) _____ get home. I thought I was smart, and that I didn't need to study to keep my grades up. But one day, I was asked to go to the principal's office. He said, "You (8) _____ be a great student. Now your grades are terrible. Explain!" That was a real wake-up call. After that, I became serious about school, and I (9) _____ study and finish my homework before playing video games. Now that my kids are in high school, I tell them about all the silly things I (10) _____ do when I was their age.

4 DISCUSSION

Personal concerns

A Pair work These people have had a change in their lives. What positive or negative impacts have these changes had?

Lucas Santos, 25, Curitiba
"Before my wife and I had our first baby, we would go out whenever we wanted. We can't do that now. I didn't use to be a worrier, but I am now."

Britney Majors, 32, Toronto
"Before my promotion, I would eat lunch in the cafeteria because that was all I could afford. Now I have money to go to nice cafés, but I just don't have the time. So, I usually eat at my desk."

Wen Ho Chen, 67, Taipei
"We used to plan on moving in with our son when we retired. But we've changed our minds. We just sold our house, and we're going to travel the world."

B Group work Think about a big change in your life. Talk about the positive and negative impacts it had.

"Last year, I was transferred to another department in my company. My new responsibilities are a lot more interesting, but I didn't use to have to work this much."

Different approaches to problem solving

A Pair work Read about these three approaches to problem solving. What method do you use? Give examples to support your answer.

What kind of problem solver are you?

Different people solve their problems in different ways. The three main approaches are assertive, meditative, and cooperative. Find out which one best describes you.

▶ **Assertive** people prefer action to talk. When they're faced with a problem, they immediately try to work out a solution.

▶ When **meditative** people have a problem, they sit and think about it, and might even do research. Sometimes, the answer comes to them if they don't act on something right away.

▶ **Cooperative** people think the easiest way to solve a problem is to ask for help. Another person's perspective can help cooperative people come up with solutions.

"I'd say I'm a meditative person. Before I bought my first car, I spent hours doing research on it by myself. It took me forever to decide!"

🔊 **B** Listen to Dominique, Carla, and Wayne talking about their personal concerns. What kind of problem solver is each person?

🔊 **C** Listen again. What are two things each person did to solve their problem?

6 ROLE PLAY

Here's an idea . . .

A Read about these people's problems. What advice would you give each person?

> My boss is so demanding. She gives me more work than I can handle.

> I can't save money because I always spend it on little things I want but don't really need.

> My last job interview went very badly. I always get tongue-tied in front of authority figures.

> I'm not enjoying things like I used to. I'm not sure why. Maybe I'm too stressed.

B Role-play each situation. Take turns giving and receiving advice.

"My boss is so demanding. She gives me more work than I can handle."

"Here's an idea. See if your co-workers feel the same way. Maybe you all can talk to the boss about it."

"I guess I could try that."

Useful expressions	
Giving advice	**Receiving advice**
Here's an idea . . .	I guess I could try that.
If I were you, I'd . . .	I just might try that.

READING

Creative problem solving

A Pair work Look at these paintings of the same landscape. How are they different? What effect does this have on what you notice first? Discuss. Then read the article.

Painting and Problem Solving: *FOUR LESSONS*

Earlier this month I escaped the office for a weeklong painting retreat in the woods of Door County, Wisconsin. While working amidst the awe-inspiring fall colors, it occurred to me that the dynamics of painting and problem solving have a lot in common. I returned home not only with newly polished painting skills but also a fresh perspective on managing problems. I learned four lessons while painting:

1 How you see things depends on your line of sight. When painting a landscape, countless choices are yours. For starters, you can choose where to place the horizon and what you eliminate from the actual setting. If the existing landscape is cluttered, for instance, you can exclude elements that detract from your focal point. Likewise, in problem solving, getting caught up in the clutter diminishes your ability to reach your desired result. Choose instead to focus on the bigger picture.

2 People can see the same landscape and represent it in totally different ways. One day I sat with two other painters in a microclimate with magnificent sugar maples. Much to my surprise, our final paintings were totally different. A similar phenomenon occurs in problem solving: Any number of people can arrive at the same situation with different ideas, skills, or resources. They can also have different designs on the end result. In this way, respecting where others are coming from is critical to problem solving.

3 When light is shined on a subject, you can explore what lies in the shadows. It can be harder to paint landscapes on cloudy days. The various forms and contrasts are less clear, and it's difficult to explore what lies in the shadows. When the sun is shining, however, the distinctions between objects are clearly visible and what lies in the shadows is revealed. The same goes for problem solving: When you shine a light on an issue, you see everything more clearly, including what opportunities or threats exist in the shadows.

4 Collaborating with people at different levels can foster appreciation for diverse ideas and perspectives. At the retreat, there were painters at every level, from first-timers to fine artists. I learned something from each one, particularly when our group came in from the woods and worked together in the studio. I opened myself up to others' unique observations and feedback, and ultimately felt more energized and creative. Additionally, I was struck by our instructor's capacity to calibrate her critiques to our individual skill levels. Similarly, in problem solving, it's important to meet others where they are, not where you might want them to be.

Odds are there is a problem on your desk today. How might even one of these four lessons help you brush up your problem-solving skills?

Source: "4 Ways to Brush Up Your Problem-Solving Skills," by Barbara T. Armstrong

B Group work Discuss these questions. Then share your answers with the class.

1. In what way is it helpful to avoid paying attention to details when solving a problem?
2. How are the second and fourth lessons in the article similar?
3. What do you think the author means by "shine a light on an issue"? How is this helpful?
4. How can the lessons from the article help you solve one of your own problems?

SELF-ASSESSMENT

How well can you do these things? Choose the best answer.

I can . . .	Very well	OK	A little
▸ Describe how information technology has changed people's lives (Ex. 1)	☐	☐	☐
▸ Describe how new technologies will change people's lives (Ex. 2)	☐	☐	☐
▸ Understand the main points of a phone conversation about personality types (Ex. 3)	☐	☐	☐
▸ Describe my personality type (Ex. 3)	☐	☐	☐
▸ Describe and compare typical behavior of parents and teenagers (Ex. 4)	☐	☐	☐

Now do the corresponding exercises. Was your assessment correct?

1 DISCUSSION
How things have changed!

A Think about how information technology has changed in the past few years. How have people's shopping habits, hobbies, and social lives been affected?

B Pair work Compare your answers with a partner.

"Video games used to be low-tech and expensive. Some games used to be available on the Internet, but few people would play them. Now, a lot of people play video games online. I think they've been greatly improved, and many are fairly cheap."

"Yeah, I think so, too. But too much time is spent playing them. My whole family is addicted – even my grandmother plays! She used to think video games were a waste of time when I played them as a kid."

2 DISCUSSION
What next?

A Pair work What do you think will happen in the next 10 years as a result of new technologies in these areas?

1. communication
2. education
3. entertainment
4. finance
5. medicine
6. sports

B Group work Compare your predictions in groups.

"Ten years from now, I think cell phones will be used by everyone. They'll even be used at work instead of office phones. What do you think?"

Team roles: The perfect "STEAM" team

 A Listen to the phone conversation between Tony and Annie. What is Tony's agency doing? Choose the correct answer.

☐ a. They're exploring the possibilities of using cell phones in advertising.

☐ b. They're analyzing the effectiveness of their advertisements.

☐ c. They're working to improve a company's image.

 B Listen again. Match the roles on the left with the personality types on the right.

Role	Personality type
1. Solver _d_	a. disciplined
2. Team manager ____	b. patient
3. Explorer ____	c. passionate
4. Analyst ____	d. creative
5. Motivator ____	e. resourceful

C Pair work Look at the roles again. Which role do you think you would be best at or would enjoy most? Why? Compare your ideas with a partner.

"I think I'd probably be best in an Explorer role. I'm pretty resourceful. What about you?"

"I'm a person with a lot of patience, but I'm not that creative. I'm more of a Team manager type."

4 SPEAKING

That's so typical!

A Complete this chart with your opinions about typical parents and teenagers.

	The typical parent	The typical teenager
What are some of their concerns?		
What is their most valued possession?		
How much time do they spend with friends?		
What do they use the Internet for?		
What do they like to do on vacation?		

B Write at least four sentences contrasting the typical parent with the typical teenager. Then compare with a partner.

"Generally, the typical teenager is concerned about friends, while the typical parent is concerned about his or her children."

1 STARTING POINT
Everyday annoyances

A Have you ever had problems similar to these? Do you agree or disagree with these comments? Why?

"The thing that I hate is when kids ride their scooters on the sidewalk."

"One thing that bothers me is when my friends don't show up on time for things."

"Something that bugs me is people who take up two seats on a crowded bus."

"The thing I can't stand is co-workers who leave their cell phones ringing on their desks."

B Group work Look at the situations in part A. Would you complain, or would you be quietly annoyed? Why?

2 LISTENING & SPEAKING
It really irks me!

A Listen to Jane and Kyle talking about irritating situations. What bothered each person?

B Listen again. Discuss the questions.

1. Whose situation do you think was more annoying, Jane's or Kyle's?
2. Who do you think handled the situation better, Jane or Kyle?
3. How would you have reacted in each situation?

3 GRAMMAR

Relative clauses and noun clauses

A relative clause can occur in the subject or the object of a sentence.
Something **that bugs me** is people **who take up two seats on a crowded bus**.
The thing **(that) I can't stand** is co-workers **who / that leave their cell phones ringing on their desks**.

Some sentences use a relative clause and a noun clause beginning with a question word such as *when*.
The thing **(that) I hate** is **when kids ride their scooters on the sidewalk**.
One thing **that bothers me** is **when my friends don't show up on time for things**.

GRAMMAR PLUS *see page 124*

A Look at the Starting Point on page 80 again. Which clauses are relative clauses? Which are noun clauses?

B Pair work Complete the sentences with your own opinions. Then discuss them with a partner.

1. One thing that irks me about my neighbors is . . .
   when they park too close to my car.
2. Something that bothers me about my friends is . . .
3. If I'm riding in a car, something that irritates me is . . .
4. The thing that aggravates me most is a friend . . .
5. The thing that annoys me about people talking on cell phones is . . .
6. . . . is one thing that bothers me at home.

4 VOCABULARY

That drives me up the wall!

A Combine the verbs with the phrases. How many combinations can you make? How are their meanings different?

Verbs	Phrases		
drive	on someone's nerves	someone mad	someone upset
get	someone crazy	someone sick	someone's blood boil
make	someone down	someone up the wall	under someone's skin

B Group work How do these things make you feel? Discuss these situations using the expressions in part A.

1. people laughing at their own jokes
2. vending machines that "steal" your money
3. finding empty ice cube trays in the freezer
4. people eating on public transportation
5. airlines not serving food on long flights

"The thing that drives me crazy is when people laugh at their own jokes, and they're not funny!"

VOCABULARY PLUS *see page 139*

5 DISCUSSION
Polite complaints

A Which of these descriptions fits you best? Give examples to support your answer.

I very rarely complain.

a silent sufferer

I only complain if I absolutely have to.

a calm, collected type

I complain because it's my right.

an activist

I complain about every little thing.

a whiner

"I guess I'm a silent sufferer. For example, I never complain in a restaurant, even if the food is awful."

"You don't? Bad food in a restaurant really annoys me. I always complain! I mean, why should I pay for terrible food? I guess I must be an activist."

B Pair work What would you do or say in these situations? Compare your answers.

1. A taxi driver is playing the radio loudly while you are trying to make a phone call.
2. Your neighbor's young son tore up all the flowers in your garden.
3. You see someone littering in a public park.

"If the taxi driver were playing the radio very loudly, I think I'd just speak louder. I probably wouldn't say anything to the driver. But I wouldn't give him a very good tip either."

6 ROLE PLAY
I hate to mention this, . . .

A Pair work Use the language in the box to create polite complaints for each situation. Then take turns acting out your complaints for the class.

1. You've been waiting in line for a long time, and someone suddenly cuts in front of you.
2. You've had a party, and one friend is still at your home long after everyone else has left. It's driving you up the wall because it's really late, and you need to get up early.
3. After you've been waiting patiently for your food for an hour, the waiter brings you the wrong order.
4. Every time you go out with your friend, she asks you to hold her belongings because she doesn't carry a bag. It's really beginning to get on your nerves.

Useful expressions

Complaining to strangers
Excuse me, but . . .
I'm sorry, but . . .

Complaining to friends/neighbors
I hate to mention this, but . . .
I'm sorry to bring this up, but . . .

B Group work Which complaints were the most effective? Which were the most polite?

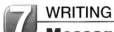

WRITING
Messages of complaint

> Writing an effective message of complaint is a powerful way to solve an ongoing problem with a product or service.

A Match the information to the points in the email.

Writing an effective message of complaint
An effective message of complaint about a purchase . . .

1. contains a clear subject line.

2. describes the product or service clearly.

3. explains the problem in detail.

4. mentions a receipt or other evidence.

5. explains exactly what you want.

6. provides contact information.

To: customerservice@phonegrp.cup.org

From: JM1990@cup.org

Subject: Damaged product —— 1

Dear Sir or Madam:

Last month, I ordered a smartphone, model number VG25S, from your website. When it arrived, I discovered that it was broken. The case was damaged, and the display screen was cracked.

At my own expense, I returned the phone to your service department over a month ago. I still have not received a replacement, nor has a customer service representative contacted me.

I have my credit card bill to prove I paid for this purchase, a one-year warranty, and a receipt from the post office. Therefore, I would like to receive a new phone as soon as possible.

Please call or email me about this matter. I look forward to your reply and hope you will handle this matter promptly.

Sincerely,

John Montgomery
101 Bee Tree Road
Encino, CA 91426
Phone: 310-555-2934

B Write an email complaining about one of these situations or one of your own.

- Your tablet came with the wrong battery charger, but you didn't notice until you brought it home. You called the store, and they refused to replace it.

- You bought airplane tickets in advance, but the airline had overbooked the flight, and you couldn't get on the plane.

C Pair work Take turns reading your emails. Did your partner follow all the steps for writing an effective message of complaint?

LESSON B ► *Let's do something about it!*

1 STARTING POINT
Why don't they do something about it?

A How many of these problems have you experienced? Compare with a partner.

"Overcrowded buses really make me mad. I wonder why they don't have more buses at rush hour."

"Umbrellas are so poorly made these days. I don't know why they always break in the wind."

"My cell phone never works around here. I can't understand why the reception is so bad."

For service in English, press 1.

"Automated phone menus drive me crazy. What I don't get is why companies don't have people answer their phones."

"The clothes in those shops are unbelievably expensive. How anyone can afford them is beyond me."

"The college course I want is really popular. My big concern is whether I'll be able to get into the class."

B Pair work Which of the problems in part A bother you the most? Explain.

"Broken umbrellas definitely bother me the most. That happened to me just the other day."
"You can say that again. I just hate it when that happens."

> **Useful expressions**
>
> **Agreeing and showing sympathy**
> I know (exactly) what you mean.
> Yeah, I hate that too.
> You can say that again.

2 LISTENING
If this is correct, say, "Yes."

A Have you ever had problems with automated phone menus? What happened?

◄)) B Listen to Gabriel using an automated phone menu. Is he successful? Choose the best summary.

- ☐ a. He completed his business successfully and will pick up his prescription this evening.
- ☐ b. He can't fill his prescription because the machine didn't recognize what he said.
- ☐ c. His pronunciation is so poor that the system didn't understand anything he said.

◄)) C Listen again. Answer the questions.

1. What's the name of the store?
2. What is his prescription number?
3. What is his phone number?
4. What time does he want to pick up his prescription?

3 GRAMMAR

Simple and complex indirect questions

Simple indirect questions use statement word order and begin with expressions such as
I wonder, I'd like to know, or *I can't understand.*

| Why don't they have more buses at rush hour? | I wonder why **they don't have** more buses at rush hour. |

Complex indirect questions also use statement word order. In addition, they begin or end with
clauses or phrases with *be.*

| Will I be able to get into the class? | **My big concern is** whether I'll be able to get into the class. |
| How can anyone afford them? | How anyone can afford them **is beyond me.** |

GRAMMAR PLUS *see page 125*

A Look at the Starting Point on page 84 again. Can you find more indirect questions?
Which ones are simple indirect questions? Which are complex?

B Rewrite these questions using the words in parentheses. Then compare
answers with a partner.

1. Will airlines ever stop losing passengers' luggage? (I wonder . . .)
   I wonder if airlines will ever stop losing passengers' luggage.
2. How do I correct a mistake on my phone bill? (I'd like to know . . .)
3. Why can't I use my cell phone in an elevator? (The thing I don't get is . . .)
4. How can I get tickets to sold-out concerts? (I want to find out . . .)
5. When will the government deal with global warming? (I'd like to know . . .)
6. Why do people complain so much? (. . . is something I can't understand.)

4 VOCABULARY & SPEAKING

I'm totally baffled!

A Look at these words that describe feelings. Put them in the correct columns.

| annoyed | confused | depressed | enraged | humiliated | insulted | mystified | stunned |
| baffled | demoralized | discouraged | frustrated | infuriated | irritated | saddened | |

Confused feelings	Angry feelings	Sad feelings
baffled	*annoyed*	

B Pair work Complete the sentences with your own information. Then discuss
your answers with a partner.

1. I'm totally baffled by . . .
2. I get so infuriated when . . .
3. I always get discouraged when . . .
4. I wouldn't be demoralized even if . . .
5. I remember feeling stunned when . . .
6. I would feel insulted if . . .

*"I'm totally baffled by people who can speak a lot of languages. How do they remember so
many different words and grammar rules?"*

VOCABULARY PLUS *see page 139*

DISCUSSION
A word to the wise

A **Pair work** Read the advice about how to avoid consumer problems. Can you add any more ideas to the list?

Buyer Beware!
SMART ADVICE FOR SMART SHOPPERS

- Buy from a reputable company.
- Make sure there's a guarantee.
- Examine your purchases before you buy.
- Do some comparison shopping.
- Find out about the return policy.
- Find out how the item should be cared for.

B **Group work** Discuss a time when you had a problem with something you bought. Would the advice in part A have helped you?

"I bought some really expensive luggage last month, and I was enraged when, after just a week, one of the wheels came off."

"Oh, you're kidding. Did you take it back to the store?"

"Yes, but they told me I couldn't return it because I'd bought it on sale. I should have asked about their return policy . . ."

Useful expressions

Sympathizing
Oh, you're kidding.
That's ridiculous.
What a pain.

ROLE PLAY
I'd like to return this.

A Read the store returns policy in part B. Is there a similar policy at the stores where you shop?

B **Pair work** Take turns role-playing a customer and a clerk at a returns counter. Use the returns policy and the situations below.

STORE RETURNS POLICY: All items must be in good condition and accompanied by a receipt. No cash refunds; store credit only. No items returned after two weeks unless under warranty. No return of items purchased on sale or with coupons.

Situation 1
- T-shirt
- have receipt
- shrank after washing
- now too small

Situation 2
- laptop
- receipt at home
- defective
- still under warranty

Situation 3
- camera
- lost receipt
- not very user-friendly
- want to exchange

"I'd like to return this T-shirt, please. I can't understand why it shrank after I washed it."

"I wonder whether you followed the washing instructions properly."

"I certainly did!"

"That's fine, then. May I see your receipt, please?"

The power of one voice

A Pair work What steps would you take if someone damaged one of your valuable possessions? Discuss with a partner. Then read the article and find out what Dave Caroll did. Did he take any of the steps you discussed?

Dave Carroll Airs a Complaint

Dave Carroll was ready to quit his 20-year career as an independent musician. Then, an airline broke his guitar and changed his life.

The airline wouldn't budge on Dave's request for $1,200 in flight vouchers to cover repairs to his $3,500 Taylor guitar. When he got "The Final No!" email after nine months of negotiations, he wrote back to say he wasn't without options.

Dave said that if he were a lawyer, he might have sued the airline, but as a songwriter, he had other tools at his disposal. He vowed to write two or three songs, make a music video for each one, and post them on YouTube.

"After months of feeling frustrated and angry about the ordeal, for the first time I felt empowered, as though a weight had been lifted from me. I changed gears from someone who *wanted* something to someone who was going to *do* something."

His goal was to reach one million views in the next year. Four days after he posted the first video, he hit a million views. The airline called him a day after the video was released to offer the same $1,200 in flight vouchers he'd asked for previously, plus an extra $1,200 in cash. Carroll refused the offer. His goal had moved beyond compensation to sharing his story and improving conditions for all travelers.

His newfound fame has revived his music career. His trilogy of songs about his experience has had approximately 15 million YouTube views. He's done media interviews and given speeches around the world. Ironically, the airline now uses his videos to train staff and pays him a license fee to do so, at his request.

He's also helped launch a website, Gripevine.com, for people to air problems and get them fixed. Companies now know that a disgruntled customer's view can go viral in a heartbeat and reach an immense audience. As Dave tells businesses, it's vital for companies to listen and learn.

Source: "Dave Carroll is still having problems with airlines," by Ellen Roseman, The Toronto Star

B Pair work Number the events in the correct order. Write *X* for the two events that are not part of Dave's story. Then take turns telling the story in your own words.

_____ a. Dave decided to use his songwriting skills to address his problem in a creative way.

_____ b. Dave rejected the airline's offer even though they'd doubled his original request.

_____ c. Dave sued the airline for the amount of money it would cost to repair his guitar.

_____ d. Dave's guitar was damaged by an airline, and they refused to compensate him.

_____ e. The airline offered Dave what he wanted after he posted his song on YouTube.

_____ f. Dave gave up on his dreams of becoming a musician after 20 years in the business.

_____ g. Dave helped start an online consumer group and relaunched his career.

C Group work Discuss these questions. Then share your answers with the class.

1. What made Dave finally feel empowered during his struggle with the airline?
2. In what ways has social media given ordinary people more power? Give examples.

1 STARTING POINT
What would you do?

A Look at the situations and people's responses. What would you do?

If you accidentally damaged a parked car in a parking lot . . .

"If the owner weren't around, I'd leave a note with my phone number."

"I wouldn't leave a note if the owner weren't around."

If you found out your co-worker got the job using false credentials . . .

"I would keep it a secret only if I liked my co-worker."

"I would keep it a secret unless my boss asked me directly about it."

If you found some money on the street . . .

"I wouldn't try to return it unless it were a large amount."

"Even if I were really broke, I'd give the money to the police."

B Pair work Now read these statistics. Do you find them surprising? Why or why not?

Of the people surveyed . . .

62% would never fail to report damaging a parked car even if nobody were present.

48% think it is unacceptable to use false credentials on a job application.

18% wouldn't keep money they found on the street.

58% would never illegally avoid paying the fare on public transportation.

25% think it's never OK to exceed the speed limit while driving.

Source: British Election Study at the University of Essex, Economic and Social Research Council

2 LISTENING
Finders keepers

🔊 Listen to Aaron and Leanne talking about finding something. Are these statements true or false, or does the person not say? Choose the correct answer.

	True	False	Doesn't say
1. Aaron's son wanted to keep the wallet and spend the money.	☐	☐	☐
2. Aaron's son received a thank-you card as a reward.	☐	☐	☐
3. The owner of the book probably didn't care much about it.	☐	☐	☐
4. Leanne will probably return the book.	☐	☐	☐

3 GRAMMAR

Present unreal conditional with *unless*, *only if*, and *even if*

Unless clauses include exceptions that would change the speaker's decision.
I **wouldn't** try to return it **unless** it **were** a large amount.
I **would** keep it a secret **unless** my boss **asked** me directly about it.

Only if clauses stress the condition for the result.
I **would** keep it a secret **only if** I **liked** my co-worker.

Even if clauses are followed by unexpected results.
Even if I **were** really broke, **I'd** give the money to the police.

GRAMMAR PLUS *see page 126*

A Look at the Starting Point on page 88 again. Look at the responses to the first situation. Are they different in meaning? If so, how?

B Choose the words that are true for you. Then complete the sentences.

1. If a cashier undercharged me, I ⟨would⟩ / wouldn't tell him if / ⟨even if⟩ . . .
   If a cashier undercharged me, I would tell him even if it were a small difference.

2. I *would / wouldn't* borrow a lot of money from a friend *only if / unless* . . .

3. I *would / wouldn't* return a gift I'd received to the store *if / unless* . . .

4. I *would / wouldn't* "temporarily borrow" an unlocked bicycle on the street *only if / even if* . . .

5. I *would / wouldn't* report my friend for skipping work *only if / unless* . . .

4 VOCABULARY & SPEAKING

It's a little unethical.

A These words describe people's ethics and attitudes. Which prefixes give them the opposite meaning? Put the words in the correct columns.

acceptable	approving	fair	legal	rational	scrupulous
agreeable	ethical	honest	logical	responsible	trustworthy

dis-	il-	ir-	un-
			unacceptable

B **Pair work** Use the vocabulary words in part A to discuss these questions.

1. Would you ever make an international call from work to save money?

2. Would you ever play a practical joke on your friends?

3. Would you ever tell a friend with a terrible new haircut that you think it's fantastic?

VOCABULARY PLUS *see page 140*

5 DISCUSSION
Ethical dilemmas

A Read these situations. What would you do?

What Would You Do ?

1 You've had plans for several weeks to visit your aunt. The day before, your friend invites you to a really great party the same night.

- Would you cancel your original plans?
- If so, would you tell the truth or "a white lie" about why you were canceling?
- Would you cancel your plans even if you knew your aunt were looking forward to seeing you?

2 You're at a convenience store, and you see someone shoplifting a can of soup.

- Would you tell the clerk?
- What if the shoplifter were a woman with a small child?
- Would it make a difference if the shoplifter looked dangerous?

3 You work full-time during the day. You're also a part-time student in an evening course, so you have a student ID card. Businesses all over town give discounts to students.

- Would you use your student ID to get the cheaper prices?
- What if you earned a high salary at your job?
- Would it make a difference if you were buying from a major chain store or from a small mom-and-pop business?

B Group work Share your answers and give reasons for each. Then agree on the best course of action for each situation.

"Unless it were a special occasion for my aunt, I might leave a little early so I could get to the party before it ended."

6 DISCUSSION
Too good to be true

A Which of these situations seem reliable? Choose those that seem legitimate.

- ☐ 1. A website offers free international phone service.
- ☐ 2. A company sends you an email asking you to confirm your credit card details online.
- ☐ 3. Someone on the street asks you to sign a petition that requires your address and phone number.
- ☐ 4. A television ad offers a set of knives worth $300 for just $75.

B Pair work Discuss these or similar situations. Share your own experiences or those of people you know.

"I once bought a kitchen appliance that I saw advertised on TV. The price was really good, and it worked well at first, but after a few weeks, it broke."

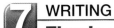

WRITING
Thesis statements

A topic sentence states the main idea of a single paragraph. A thesis statement introduces the topic of a composition. It is often located at the beginning or end of the first paragraph.

A Read the composition and choose the best thesis statement from the choices below. Then, write a *T* where you think the thesis statement should appear.

1. *I've made some bad decisions.*
2. *We learn a lot from the decisions we make.*
3. *I have good and bad memories of old friendships.*

When I'm faced with a decision that puts my ethics on the line, I think about what similar situations in the past have taught me. In my life, I've made both good and bad choices.

One of my good decisions resulted in a casual friend becoming a very close friend. A college classmate gave me a lottery ticket for my birthday. As she gave it to me, she joked that if I won, I should split the prize with her. I ended up winning $500. At the time, I was saving for a new tablet, and with the $500, I had enough money. I considered not telling my friend that I'd won. But I felt dishonest and disloyal, and I gave her half. I'll always be glad I did, and I wouldn't do it any differently today, even if I really needed all the money. Today, she is still one of my best friends.

One of my bad decisions ruined a friendship. A former classmate wanted a job with my company and asked me to recommend her. I knew she didn't have very good work habits. I told her I would do it only if she promised to work hard. She was hired, but three months later, she was fired because my boss thought she was irresponsible and her work was unacceptable. I was fairly new at the company myself, and my company is still a little unsure about trusting my judgment now. I don't have much to do with her these days.

I believe that good and bad decisions are a part of everyone's personal development. Is it possible to learn from those experiences? I think it is because even the bad ones help to prepare you for the future.

B Write a four-paragraph composition about a happy memory or a regret. Follow these guidelines.

1st paragraph: Introduce your topic in the paragraph. Begin or end the paragraph with your thesis statement.

2nd paragraph: Write about a decision you would make again.

3rd paragraph: Write about a decision you would make differently.

4th paragraph: End with a strong conclusion.

Your thesis statement . . .

- *should contain a single idea.*
- *should be neither too general nor too specific.*
- *should unify all the paragraphs.*
- *can be improved as you write.*

C Group work Take turns reading your compositions. Is the thesis statement too general? Does it need to be improved?

LESSON B ▶ *Taking stock*

1 STARTING POINT

I wish . . .

A Read these messages. Match each message with one of the values below.

a. careful spending   c. perseverance   e. career advancement

b. concern for others   d. good family relations   f. good cross-cultural relations

http://www.cup.org/connectworld/

The Connected World

Today's questions: I've had so many cool friends in my life. I wish I'd stayed in touch with all of them! Is there anything you wish you'd done differently? What do you wish you could change right now?

_____ 1. Mika22

I wish I had enough nerve to ask for a promotion. I like my job, but I've been in the same position for several years. If only my boss would consider promoting me!

_____ 2. Ivan007

I love and respect my mother and father a lot. I wish I hadn't given them such a hard time when I was growing up. I'm just happy they forgave me for all those rough times.

_____ 3. Wishful

I'm ashamed of all the money I've wasted. If only I'd saved more over the last few years. Now I want to rent my own apartment, and I can't afford to! Starting today, I'm going to stop buying things I don't need.

_____ 4. JackD

I used to travel to Mexico for my job about once a month. I probably would have been more successful if I had spoken more Spanish. I wish I'd taken a few Spanish classes.

_____ 5. SportsFan

When I was a kid, I tried lots of things – sports, languages, music – and I enjoyed them all, but I always lost interest after a while. If I had stuck with something, I could have gotten good at it.

_____ 6. Ruby65

I wish I could find the time to do volunteer work. I feel I'm not contributing enough to the community. Maybe I can find time to volunteer at the hospital in my neighborhood.

B Pair work Which person in part A are you most like? Which of the values are the most important? What are some of the values you learned when you were growing up?

"I'm similar to Ruby65. I really think it's important to show concern for other people. As I was growing up, my parents also taught me the importance of . . ."

GRAMMAR

Wishes and regrets

For wishes about the present and future, use *wish* + simple past, past continuous, or *could / would* + verb.
I **wish** I **had** enough nerve to ask for a promotion.
I **wish** I **could find** the time to do volunteer work.

For regrets about the past, use *wish* + past perfect.
I **wish** I**'d taken** a few Spanish classes.
I **wish** I **hadn't given** my parents such a hard time when I was growing up.

For regrets about the past, use *if* + past perfect and *could / would have* + past participle.
If I **had stuck** with something, I **could have gotten** good at it.

For strong wishes about the present or future, or for strong regrets about the past, use *if only*.
***If only* clauses are often used without a main clause.**
If only my boss **would consider** promoting me!

GRAMMAR PLUS *see page 127*

A Look at the Starting Point on page 92 again. Which sentences express regrets about the past? Which ones describe wishes for the present or future?

B Rewrite these statements using the words in parentheses. Compare answers with a partner. Are any of the sentences true for you?

1. I can't find the time to exercise. (I wish . . .)
   I wish I could find the time to exercise.
2. My grades weren't very good last semester. (If only . . .)
3. I don't know how to dance very well. (I wish . . .)
4. I didn't apply for that interesting job at work. (I wish . . .)
5. I'm feeling very stressed these days. (I wish . . .)
6. I never learned how to swim when I was a child. (If only . . .)
7. I gave away my old guitar last year. (If only . . .)
8. I watched too much TV and didn't read enough when I was a kid. (If only . . .)

C Complete these sentences with your own wishes or regrets and add extra information. Then compare answers with a partner.

1. If only I had enough money to . . . ! Then I wouldn't . . .
   If only I had enough money to buy a motorcycle!
   Then I wouldn't have to take the bus to class.
2. I wish I could find the time to . . . . If I could, I would . . .
3. I wish I had learned how to . . . when I was a kid. If I had, I'd . . .
4. If only I knew how to . . . . Then I could . . .
5. I wish my friends would . . . so that . . .
6. If only I had listened to my parents when they told me . . . because . . .
7. I wish they would pass a law that says . . . . If they did, . . .
8. If only I had the courage to . . . . Then I would . . .

VOCABULARY & SPEAKING
Personal values

A What words describe people's values? Complete the chart with the correct noun or adjective.

Noun	Adjective	Noun	Adjective	Noun	Adjective
compassion	*compassionate*		indifferent	selfishness	
	discreet	kindness		sensitivity	
generosity		resilience			tender
	honest		respectful		tolerant

B Pair work Which three values do you think are most important? Decide with a partner. Give your reasons.

"We thought generosity, tolerance, and honesty were most important. Generosity is an important value because if you help people, they might help you one day. Tolerance matters because . . ."

VOCABULARY PLUS *see page 140*

 LISTENING & SPEAKING
Three important values

A Listen to these on-the-street interviews. What values do these people think are important? Number the values in the order you hear them.

____ honesty   ____ privacy   ____ respect

B Listen again. Whose answer did you agree with the most? Why do you think so?

"I'd say I agreed with the first woman the most. If you're not honest, you'll only get yourself into trouble. Plus, telling the truth is the right thing to do."

 SPEAKING
Grant me a wish.

A If you could have three wishes, what would they be? Make a list.

B Pair work Compare your wishes with a partner. Then share your answers with the class.

"My first wish would be for my family to stay healthy and happy. Second, I would wish for more peace in the world. For my last wish, . . ."

Subway Superman

A **Pair work** Read the title and the first paragraph of the news article. What would you have done if you were Wesley Autrey? Discuss, and then read the article.

NEW YORK HONORS A HERO

It started as a typical day for Wesley Autrey, a 50-year-old construction worker in New York City. It was about 12:45 P.M., and he was waiting on a subway platform to take his daughters home before he went to work. He suddenly noticed a man nearby have convulsions and collapse. Mr. Autrey and two women went to help the stranger. The man, Cameron Hollopeter, managed to get to his feet, but then stumbled at the edge of the platform and fell onto the subway tracks. Mr. Autrey looked up and saw the lights of the subway train approaching through the tunnel.

What would you do? Stand horrified and watch helplessly? Most people would jump in to help, but only if there were no train in sight. Mr. Autrey acted quickly. He leapt down onto the track. He realized that he didn't have time to get Mr. Hollopeter and himself back up on the platform before the train arrived, so he lay on top of the man and pressed down as hard as he could. Although the driver tried to stop the train before it reached them, he couldn't. Five cars passed over them before the train finally stopped. The cars had passed only inches from his head. His first words were to ask the onlookers to tell his daughters he was OK.

New York loves a hero. And there was no question that Mr. Autrey's actions had been just that – heroic. He became an overnight sensation. People couldn't get enough of the story. The media named him the "Subway Superman." New York City Mayor Michael Bloomberg gave him the Bronze Medallion, the city's highest honor. (In the past, this

honor has gone to such people as General Douglas MacArthur, Martin Luther King Jr., and Muhammad Ali.) Mr. Autrey was also asked to appear on several high-profile television talk shows.

His selfless bravery was also rewarded with money and gifts. Among other things, Mr. Autrey received: $10,000 from Donald Trump, a $5,000 gift card from the Gap clothing store, a new Jeep, tickets and backstage passes to a Beyoncé concert, and a free one-year public transit pass. A "Disney ambassador" thanked him with a one-week all-expenses-paid trip to Disney World and tickets to see *The Lion King* on Broadway.

How did Autrey, a Navy veteran, react to all this? Honorably. He said, "I don't feel like I did anything spectacular; I just saw someone who needed help. I did what I felt was right."

B Read the article again. Are these statements true or false? Choose the correct answer. Correct the false statements.

	True	False
1. Autrey hadn't noticed Hollopeter before he fell onto the tracks.	☐	☐
2. There was very little space between Autrey and the bottom of the train.	☐	☐
3. Autrey jumped onto the tracks because he wanted to be a hero.	☐	☐

C **Group work** Discuss these questions.

1. Have you ever had the opportunity to help someone in trouble or in danger?
2. Why do you think so many businesses wanted to reward Mr. Autrey?

1 STARTING POINT
The benefits of studying abroad

A Read this website. Choose three benefits of studying a language abroad that you feel are the most important.

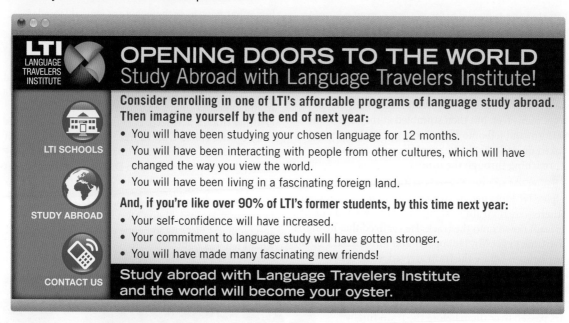

LTI LANGUAGE TRAVELERS INSTITUTE

LTI SCHOOLS

STUDY ABROAD

CONTACT US

OPENING DOORS TO THE WORLD
Study Abroad with Language Travelers Institute!

Consider enrolling in one of LTI's affordable programs of language study abroad. Then imagine yourself by the end of next year:
- You will have been studying your chosen language for 12 months.
- You will have been interacting with people from other cultures, which will have changed the way you view the world.
- You will have been living in a fascinating foreign land.

And, if you're like over 90% of LTI's former students, by this time next year:
- Your self-confidence will have increased.
- Your commitment to language study will have gotten stronger.
- You will have made many fascinating new friends!

Study abroad with Language Travelers Institute and the world will become your oyster.

B Pair work Discuss your choices. What are some other benefits of studying or living abroad?

"I think interacting with people from other cultures is the most important benefit."

2 VOCABULARY & SPEAKING
Words of encouragement

A Complete these verbs and phrases with a preposition from the box.

about	in	of	to	with

1. adjust ___*to*___
2. be excited _____
3. be scared _____
4. be familiar _____
5. become aware _____
6. get accustomed _____
7. look forward _____
8. participate _____
9. take advantage _____

B Pair work What challenges do people face when they live or study abroad? Discuss with a partner using the verbs and phrases in part A.

"Sometimes people are scared of starting a new job abroad because they aren't familiar with the routines."

VOCABULARY PLUS *see page 141*

GRAMMAR

Future perfect and future perfect continuous

Use the future perfect to emphasize that something will be completed or achieved by a particular point in the future.

By this time next year, your self-confidence **will have increased**.

Use the future perfect continuous to emphasize the duration of an activity in progress at a particular point in the future.

By the end of next year, you **will have been studying** your chosen language for 12 months.

GRAMMAR PLUS see page 128

A Look at the Starting Point on page 96 again. Can you find more examples of the future perfect and the future perfect continuous?

B These sentences about Joon's year abroad all have mistakes. Correct the mistakes using the future with *will*, the future perfect, or the future perfect continuous. Then compare answers with a partner.

1. *will have been traveling*
   By this time tomorrow, Joon ~~will travel~~ for 24 hours.

2. By the end of next week, he <u>will have been receiving</u> his student ID card and registered for classes.

3. He'll be going out more after a few weeks because he <u>will have been</u> more familiar with the city.

4. After studying English for a few months, he <u>will have felt</u> more confident about speaking to people.

5. By this time next year, his younger sister <u>will have been visiting</u> him once or twice. When she's older, she probably <u>will have wanted</u> to study abroad, too.

6. I'm sure he <u>will change</u> a lot by the time he comes back to Korea.

7. His family <u>will have been</u> surprised when he gets back because he <u>will have been changing</u> so much.

8. And just think – the next time we see him, Joon <u>will turn</u> 22 already, and he <u>will be</u> away for a year!

C Use these time expressions to write sentences using the future perfect or future perfect continuous. Then share them with a partner.

1. Before this class ends, . . .
2. By the end of the day, . . .
3. By the end of the week, . . .
4. At the end of the year, . . .
5. In two years' time, . . .
6. By the year 2030, . . .

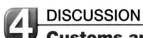
4 DISCUSSION
Customs and traditions

A Read this list of Canadian customs. Are they the same as or different from those where you live? Choose the correct answer.

	Same	Different
01 Both men and women shake hands with each other when they meet.	☐	☐
02 Business meetings are friendly, but there isn't much socializing beforehand.	☐	☐
03 Lunch is usually a fairly light meal that doesn't last long.	☐	☐
04 People are usually punctual for business appointments.	☐	☐
05 It's common to ask people you meet what kind of work they do.	☐	☐
06 Many people eat dinner early in the evening, around 6:00 P.M.	☐	☐
07 At the dinner table, the fork is generally held in the left hand and the knife in the right.	☐	☐
08 People offer to take their shoes off when entering somebody's home.	☐	☐
09 When invited to someone's home, a gift, such as flowers or dessert, is usually expected.	☐	☐
10 Most people open gifts as soon as they receive them.	☐	☐

B **Group work** How do you feel about the customs in part A? Explain your opinions.

"I think women should kiss on the cheek when they meet. Just shaking hands seems kind of cold somehow."

5 LISTENING
When in Rome . . .

A Listen to Andrew, Rachel, and Layla talking about their experiences abroad. Answer the questions.

1. What helped each of them get used to their new living situation?
2. What did each person find difficult to adjust to?

B Listen again. Did Andrew (*A*), Rachel (*R*), or Layla (*L*) do these things? Write the correct letter.

_____ 1. felt homesick

_____ 2. had fun playing a sport

_____ 3. enjoyed food with friends

_____ 4. didn't feel connected to others at first

_____ 5. ate dinner late at night

_____ 6. thought people talked about themselves too much

_____ 7. enjoyed the old buildings

_____ 8. watched comedy shows on TV

_____ 9. tried to talk about herself

WRITING
Conclusions

> The conclusion can close your composition by restating the main idea, summarizing the main points, looking to the future, making recommendations, or a combination of these methods.

A Read these two concluding paragraphs. Which methods do the writers use? Underline the parts of the conclusions that helped you decide.

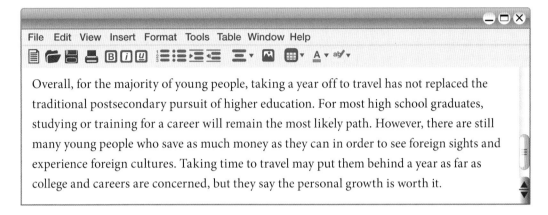

Overall, for the majority of young people, taking a year off to travel has not replaced the traditional postsecondary pursuit of higher education. For most high school graduates, studying or training for a career will remain the most likely path. However, there are still many young people who save as much money as they can in order to see foreign sights and experience foreign cultures. Taking time to travel may put them behind a year as far as college and careers are concerned, but they say the personal growth is worth it.

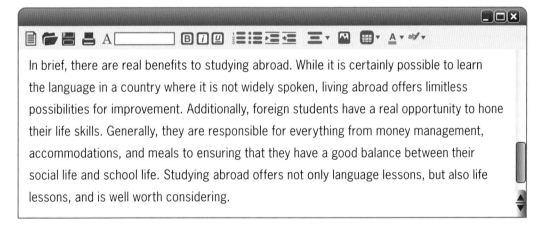

In brief, there are real benefits to studying abroad. While it is certainly possible to learn the language in a country where it is not widely spoken, living abroad offers limitless possibilities for improvement. Additionally, foreign students have a real opportunity to hone their life skills. Generally, they are responsible for everything from money management, accommodations, and meals to ensuring that they have a good balance between their social life and school life. Studying abroad offers not only language lessons, but also life lessons, and is well worth considering.

B Find these linking words or phrases in the conclusions. How are they used? Do you know any others that have similar meanings?

additionally	generally	however	in brief	overall

C Write a composition about living or traveling abroad. Choose one of these topics or one of your own. Your conclusion should use at least one of the methods described and some linking words or phrases.

- culture shock
- group travel
- independent travel
- studying abroad

D **Pair work** Exchange papers with a partner and answer these questions.

1. What methods did your partner use in his or her conclusion?
2. Are the linking words used effectively? Why or why not?
3. Can you offer any suggestions to improve your partner's conclusion?

1 STARTING POINT
Travel tips

A Read these people's experiences and the expert's advice. Can you think of any other advice?

TERRY'S Travel Tips

Get advice from Terry Tripper, the travel expert, and share your own travel tips.

Meg B. says: *A woman fell down in front of me during a sightseeing tour. I helped her up, but soon after, I couldn't find my wallet. Do you think she might have taken it?*

Terry says: It's very likely. If you hadn't been so nice, you would probably still have your wallet. It's a common scam – someone pretends to be in trouble, but actually turns out to be a thief!

Bruno H. says: *I want to share a tip my friend gave me that I used on my last vacation. If you're worried about losing your passport, like I am, don't carry it around with you. Just keep it in your hotel room.*

Terry says: That is a good tip if there is a safe in your room. If not, keep your passport with you at all times. If someone had broken into your room, you would probably still be trying to get home!

Kim N. says: *On my last trip abroad, I brought a little notebook and pen to help me communicate while shopping. If I couldn't find something, I'd draw a picture. If I hadn't had that notebook and pen, my friends wouldn't be thanking me for the awesome souvenirs I brought them!*

Terry says: That's a great idea! When phrasebooks and dictionaries don't help, a picture can be worth a thousand words. But you know there are also some great apps for that, right? Check out this <u>website</u>.

B **Pair work** What travel questions would you ask Terry? Tell your partner. Then try to offer advice to each other.

"I want to buy souvenirs from the places I'm going to visit, but I also like to travel light. Should I store them at the airport or somewhere else?"

"The best thing would be to mail them home. If you don't mind waiting, use surface mail instead of airmail. It's cheaper."

2 LISTENING
Things went wrong.

◀)) A Listen to Cindy and Scott talking about their travel problems. What happened to each person?

◀)) B Listen again. Choose the statements you think are probably true. Compare your answers with a partner. Give reasons.

☐ 1. Cindy has a unique, easy-to-see name tag on her luggage.

☐ 2. Cindy travels frequently.

☐ 3. Scott likes peace and quiet when he travels.

☐ 4. Scott slept soundly all the way to Panama City.

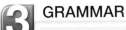

③ GRAMMAR

Mixed conditionals

Use *had / hadn't* + past participle and *would / wouldn't* to talk about hypothetical events in the past that have effects on the present.
If you **hadn't been** so nice, you **would** probably still **have** your wallet!
If someone **had broken into** your room, you **would** probably still **be trying** to get home!

GRAMMAR PLUS *see page 129*

A Look at the Starting Point on page 100 again. Find another mixed conditional sentence. Does this sentence describe actual or hypothetical events?

B Complete these sentences with the correct form of the verbs in parentheses.

1. If I _____*had been*_____ (be) more adventurous when I was younger,
   I _____*wouldn't have*_____ (not have) any regrets about the things I missed.

2. The airline lost my luggage. If I _____ (bring) a change of clothes
   in my carry-on bag, I _____ (not shop) for new clothes now.

3. This flight is so long! If I _____ (not buy) an economy ticket,
   I _____ (be) more comfortable now.

4. If you _____ (learn) to speak some Mandarin before moving to
   Taipei, you _____ (be able to) ask someone for directions now.

5. If Martha _____ (not become) a flight attendant, she probably
   _____ (not travel) as much as she does.

④ DISCUSSION

Your own trip

A Pair work Have you ever had problems on vacation? Tell your partner.
Use the topics below or your own ideas.

- health   • accommodations   • food   • safety
- language   • getting around   • costs   • weather

"I went to the beach last week, but the weather was awful."
"Why? Was it rainy?"
"No, it was too sunny. If it hadn't been so sunny, I wouldn't have this terrible sunburn now."

B Group work Share your bad travel experiences. Get advice about what you could have done differently.

5 VOCABULARY
One word or two?

A Combine the items from the boxes to make compound adjectives.

culturally	assured	hearted	motivated
non	aware	judgmental	reliant
open	conforming	minded	sensitive
self			

culturally aware, nonjudgmental, open-minded, . . .

B Pair work Are the characteristics in part A important when you travel? Give an example for each one.

"If you're culturally aware, you'll find it easier to accept cultural differences."

VOCABULARY PLUS see page 141

6 ROLE PLAY
Planning a trip

A Group work Imagine you are planning a vacation. Discuss these questions. Write notes about what your group decides for each question.

1. Where would you like to go?
2. How long would you like your stay to last?
3. Would you like to go with a tour group or on your own?
4. What type of accommodations do you prefer?
5. What kinds of activities would you like to do during the day?
6. What sorts of evening activities would you prefer?
7. What would each person's budget be?
8. What types of transportation would you plan on using?

B Class activity Choose someone in your group to act as a travel agent and present your vacation to the class. The class votes on the best itinerary.

"We have planned a truly exotic vacation for you in the remote Galápagos Islands! You'll stay for seven unforgettable days in a five-star resort . . ."

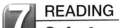

A What are the best ways to experience a new place when you travel? Make a list. Then read the article to compare your list with the author's.

Get Yourself LOST

Travelers to a new city are often encouraged to take a bus tour. The thinking is that they can later return to the places that **captivated** them, but that's nonsense! What you see from the inside of a fast-moving bus is sanitized and unreal, utterly removed from the authentic sights, sounds, and smells outside.

The best way to experience any destination is by foot, without an itinerary, wandering where your spirit leads you. Even in the largest cities, the **savvy** traveler **plunges** into the very center of town and walks down the nearest street, experiencing the actual life of the people while looking into the grocery stores and courtyards. You eventually get to many of the same sites that are on the bus route – the museums, the monuments, the city hall – but you will have witnessed so much more because you will have felt the contemporary life of the city you're visiting.

"But what if I get lost?" people ask. No one ever gets permanently lost in a major city. Eventually, a trolley or bus passes with the words "Central Station" on its front and you can easily return to the center of town. Besides, the most wonderful things can happen if you do get lost, such as stopping at a sidewalk café to sit and relax and then asking directions from the locals at the next table. Hopefully, your trip may be **enhanced** by this encounter. Here are a few ways to make the most of your travels:

❯ KNOW BEFORE YOU GO. Before you depart, spend time learning about the history and culture of your destination so you will better understand the place you're visiting.

❯ MOVE AROUND LIKE A LOCAL. Use the local subways, trams, and buses. You'll not only save money, you'll learn how people live there, and you'll gain a realistic perspective of the city.

❯ CHECK THE BULLETIN BOARDS. Bulletin boards list free lectures, concerts, workshops, and social gatherings, giving you a chance to join or meet the area's most **dynamic** residents.

❯ TAKE A WALKING TOUR. If you must book a guided tour, select the nonstandard, inexpensive kinds conducted on foot.

So, the next time you feel lured by a sightseeing bus tour, save your money and instead, wander around on your own. I promise you a time you'll remember fondly.

Source: "Get Yourself Lost," by Arthur Frommer

B Find the boldfaced words in the article. Then choose the correct words to complete the sentences.

1. If something **captivates** you, you're *upset / captured / delighted* by it.
2. A **savvy** traveler is *refined / experienced / adventurous*.
3. When you **plunge** into an activity, you probably *walk away from it / throw yourself into it / stumble into it*.
4. If you **enhance** your reading skills, you *upgrade / restore / prolong* them.
5. **Dynamic** people are more *cautious / unstable / interesting* than others.

C Pair work How do your travel habits compare with those in the article? Which ideas do you think you'll try the next time you visit a new city? Why?

COMMUNICATION REVIEW

UNITS 10–12

How well can you do these things? Choose the best answer.

I can . . .	Very well	OK	A little
▶ Describe annoying behavior (Ex. 1)	☐	☐	☐
▶ Make and respond to customer complaints (Ex. 1)	☐	☐	☐
▶ Discuss hypothetical situations in my present and future life (Ex. 2)	☐	☐	☐
▶ Understand the main points of a training workshop about customer service (Ex. 3)	☐	☐	☐
▶ Express and explain my opinions in a discussion about living and working in a different culture (Ex. 4)	☐	☐	☐
▶ Make hypotheses about past and present events in my life (Ex. 5)	☐	☐	☐

Now do the corresponding exercises. Was your assessment correct?

ROLE PLAY
Annoying customers

A What do you think annoys these people about their passengers or customers?

1. bus drivers
2. flight attendants
3. tech support workers
4. waiters/waitresses

"Something that probably makes bus drivers crazy is when people complain that the buses are running late. It usually isn't the drivers' fault."

B Pair work Take turns playing the role of a customer complaining and an employee responding to the complaints.

DISCUSSION
I'd like to try . . .

A Look at these questions and write answers that are true for you.

1. What is something you'd like to try, even if it were a little risky?
2. What is something you would do only if it were a matter of life or death?
3. Where is someplace you wouldn't want to go unless someone went with you?

B Pair work Discuss your answers with a partner.

"I'd like to try scuba diving at night, even if it were a little risky. I think diving in the ocean at night must be incredible."

3 LISTENING
Training

🔊 **A** Listen to a training workshop. What job are the trainees going to do?

🔊 **B** Listen again. Are these statements true or false? Choose the correct answer.

	True	False
1. Sammy would try to get the customer on a flight the same day.	☐	☐
2. Andrea says the customer should have left more time between flights.	☐	☐
3. Ricardo says the customer should be ashamed for being late.	☐	☐
4. Hannah would direct the customer to a place where she could get refreshed.	☐	☐

4 DISCUSSION
Culture shock

A Pair work How important are these personality traits for someone who is living and working in a new culture? Number them from 1 to 6 (1 = most important, 6 = least important).

It's important to be . . .

☐ culturally aware   ☐ nonjudgmental

☐ open-minded   ☐ self-assured

☐ self-aware   ☐ self-reliant

B Group work Join another pair. Explain your rankings to the group and discuss any differences of opinion.

5 DISCUSSION
What if . . . ?

A Pair work Discuss the questions.

How would your life be different today if . . .

1. you'd been born in another country?
2. you'd grown up in a much smaller or larger family?
3. you hadn't learned any English?
4. you hadn't met your best friend?

B Group work What event or circumstance has had the biggest effect on you? How would your life be different if that event hadn't happened?

"I think growing up in an extended family had the biggest effect on me. If my grandmother hadn't been living with us, I wouldn't have such an awareness of my culture and my ancestors."

GRAMMAR PLUS

1A Verbs followed by gerunds

These verbs are followed by a gerund.

deny   discuss   finish   mention   practice   quit   resist   suggest

These verbs are followed by an infinitive.

arrange   claim   decide   demand   deserve   expect   pretend   refuse   volunteer

Some common expressions are always followed by gerunds.
She **had fun / a good time** arranging the party.
He **has trouble / a tough time** getting his assignments in on time.
He**'s busy** cooking dinner right now.
She never **worries about** cleaning up after herself.

Some verbs take either a gerund or an infinitive, but the meaning of the sentence will be different.
I **stopped to drink** some coffee. *(I ended one activity and began another.)*
I **stopped drinking** coffee. *(I don't do that activity anymore.)*
I **stopped running** when I got tired. *(I temporarily ended the activity.)*

1 Complete these sentences with the gerund or infinitive form of the verb in parentheses.

1. I practiced ___*speaking*___ (speak) English with an American friend last night.

2. He volunteered _____ (help) at the hospital fund-raiser.

3. They discussed _____ (go) somewhere exotic on their vacation this year.

4. She's stopped _____ (talk) to him because they had a big argument.

5. My great-grandmother has trouble _____ (get) to our family reunions.

6. Laura always denies _____ (be) wild and crazy, but she really is.

2 Choose the best answer to complete the sentences.

My friend Shanda is pretty cool and very outgoing. She's usually busy (1) *to do /* (doing) a million things at once. Last week, I suggested (2) *to go / going* out for dinner and (3) *to see / seeing* a movie. We arranged (4) *to meet / meeting* at 7:00. Well, I know she doesn't worry about (5) *to be / being* on time, but she didn't show up until 7:30. At first, she said it took her a long time to finish (6) *to get / getting* ready. Then, after the movie, she couldn't resist (7) *to tell / telling* me what really happened. She was having such a good time (8) *to play / playing* video games with her brother that she forgot about our plans. It's a good thing I'm the laid-back type!

1B Noun clauses after *be*

The downside of, the upside of, the hard part about, the good thing about, the only thing about, the trick to, the secret to, and *one difficulty with* are used in complex phrases that introduce noun clauses after *be.*

The downside of sharing a bedroom is (that) it's hard to have any privacy.
The hard part about being a twin is (that) people are always calling you by the wrong name.
The trick to living in a crowded house is (that) you have to find a private space of your own.
One difficulty with being the youngest is (that) everyone is always telling you what to do.

The phrases ending with a preposition can be followed by a gerund phrase, *not* + a gerund phrase, or a noun phrase.
The secret to **getting along with your siblings** is (that) you have to respect their privacy.
The good thing about **not being in a big family** is (that) you always get to choose what's on TV.
The upside of **a large family** is (that) you always have someone to spend time with.
The only thing about **working moms** is (that) they have less time to spend with you.

1 Complete the sentences with *about, of, with,* or *to.*

1. The best thing _____*about*_____ my grandmother living with us is that she's a great cook.

2. The upside _____ being a two-income family is we can afford a few small luxuries.

3. One difficulty _____ living with my in-laws is that they want everything their way.

4. The trick _____ living in a large family is you have to learn to respect each other.

5. The hard part _____ strict parents is you always have to remember the rules.

6. The problem _____ not going to our family reunion is I won't see my cousins.

2 Rewrite the sentences. Change the noun phrases in boldface to gerund phrases.

1. The trouble with **a big family** is it's expensive to feed everyone.
   The trouble with having a big family is it's expensive to feed everyone.

2. The trick to **a two-income family** is you have to schedule family time together.

3. The hard part about **a big house** is there's so much work to do.

4. The upside of **a big house** is no one has to share a room.

5. The only bad thing about **little brothers** is I always have to babysit them.

6. One good thing about **little sisters** is they really look up to you.

7. One problem with **an extended family** is we had to get a bigger car.

8. The greatest thing about **a small house** is the bills are a lot lower.

Some past modals and phrasal modals of obligation are stronger than others.

Strong obligation: To show that there was no choice about doing the action, use *had to*.
(Note that *must* is not used in the past.)
My parents **had to** go to school on Saturdays.

Expectation: There was a general expectation that an action was required or prohibited.
She **was supposed to** talk to her professor after class. *(But she probably didn't.)*
He **wasn't supposed to** drive the car to school. *(But he probably did.)*

Advisability: There was a good idea or a correct action in a particular situation, but it was or was not done.
He **should have** taken better notes in class. *(But he didn't.)*
She **shouldn't have** bought such an expensive jacket. *(But she did.)*

Necessity: The action was considered to be necessary or unnecessary. However, unlike *had to*, there is a choice about doing or not doing the action.
I **needed to** make an appointment with the counselor.
I **didn't need to** buy the textbook, but I thought it looked interesting.

No obligation: There is complete choice about doing the action.
I **didn't have to** take piano lessons, but I wanted to.

1 Choose the correct answer to complete the sentence.

1. Jan *should have* / *shouldn't have* ignored the problem because it only got worse.

2. I *was supposed to* / *didn't have to* go on vacation, but I didn't save enough money.

3. Yoko *needed to* / *wasn't supposed to* ignore her parents' advice, but she did.

4. He fixed the leak himself, so he *didn't need to call* / *should have called* a plumber.

5. When I got older, I *had to* / *wasn't supposed to* learn to solve my own problems.

6. I *needed to* / *didn't have to* book my flight so early, but I wanted a good seat.

2 Complete the sentences with *(not) had to*, *was (not) supposed to*, *should (not) have*, or *(not) needed to* and the correct form of the verb in parentheses. Sometimes more than one answer is possible.

1. A: I heard Rob's cell phone rang in the middle of the test. What happened?
   B: He __*had to leave*__ (leave) the room immediately and was given a failing grade.

2. A: You're home early, Jenny. I thought your English exam lasted until 4:00.
   B: I finished early, and the teacher said I _____ (stay) if I didn't want to.

3. A: Have you seen Steven this morning? He's late for the test.
   B: No, I haven't. He _____ (meet) me for breakfast, but he didn't show up.

4. A: The teacher recommends using a pencil on tests so you can erase wrong answers.
   B: Yes, and I _____ (follow) his advice. I made a real mess with my pen.

2B Modals with multiple uses

Degrees of certainty range from very certain to uncertain.

Very certain: To show that you think something was probable in the past, use *must have*, *must not have*, *can't have*, **or** *couldn't have*.
Jake had a stomachache last night after dinner. He **must have** eaten too much.
Sofia was at a movie with me last night. You **couldn't have** seen her at the mall!

Uncertain: To show that you think something was possible in the past, use *could have*, *may have*, *might have*, *may not have*, **or** *might not have*.
Jun Ho is usually here by now. He **could / may / might have** missed the bus this morning.
Tanya was supposed to meet me before school. She **may / might not have** gotten the message.

To give opinions or advice, there are a greater number of modals available for talking about the present or future than there are for the past.

Present or future: Use *must (not)*, *have to*, *have got to*, *had better (not)*, **or** *should (not)*.
Parents **have got to** monitor the shows their children watch.
The kids **had better not** spend so much time indoors playing computer games.

Past: Use *should (not) have*.
I **should have** listened to the advice my parents gave me about having a healthy lifestyle.
We **should not have** ignored the scientists' warnings about global warming.

Choose the correct answer to complete the sentence.

1. A: Kimberly didn't come to the party last night. I wonder why.
   B: I'm not sure. She *could have* / *should have* been sick, I guess.

2. A: Where's my umbrella? It was right here by the door.
   B: Oh, I'm sorry, Paul. My sister *couldn't have* / *must have* taken it.

3. A: I got a terrible cramp in my leg while I was jogging yesterday.
   B: Hmm. You *must not have* / *may have* done your stretches properly first.

4. A: I had to ask Natalie twice to turn down the TV.
   B: She *might not have* / *must have* heard you the first time.

5. A: They said the meeting was at 7:30, but it had already started when I got there.
   B: They told me 7:00. You *can't have* / *must have* been told the wrong time.

6. A: Marnie wasn't at work yesterday. Was she sick?
   B: Well, she *couldn't have* / *must have* been too sick. I saw her at the park.

7. A: I only used your camera to take a few pictures. I don't see why you're so upset.
   B: Well, you *couldn't have* / *shouldn't have* been using it without my permission.

8. A: Sorry I'm late. We were playing baseball, and I didn't notice the time.
   B: You *may not have* / *couldn't have* been doing that. It's been dark for an hour!

3A Defining and non-defining relative clauses

> *That* can be used for people or things in defining relative clauses. However, it cannot be used as a replacement for *where* or *when* with the meaning "in which," "at which," or "during which."
> Many of the people **that live in Paris** leave the city in August to vacation in other places.
> A statue of ducks **that can be found in Boston** is a popular tourist attraction for children.
> Pamplona is that city in Spain **where the bulls run through the streets during a summer festival**.
> Summer is the season **when New York is crowded with tourists from all over the world**.
>
> *That* cannot be used in non-defining relative clauses. *Who*, *which*, or *where* are used instead.
> Cairo, **which has fascinated Europeans for ages**, draws countless tourists each year.
> Our tour guide, **who knew a great deal about souvenirs in Otavalo**, helped us buy some beautiful presents for our friends.

1 Complete the defining relative clauses with *that*, *who*, *when*, or *where*. Sometimes more than one answer is possible.

1. People ___*who / that*___ live in cities have more stress than people _____ live in small towns.

2. Amy likes to stay in hotels _____ there are lots of theaters and restaurants nearby.

3. Some city people have cottages by lakes _____ they can swim and relax during the summer season.

4. My family and I always visit Brazil in the month _____ the Carnaval festival begins.

5. Many office workers like to have lunch in a park _____ they can sit in the sun and enjoy the nature _____ is all around them.

6. The city is better for students _____ want to work in the summer because it's the place _____ the job market offers the most opportunities.

7. People _____ live in towns _____ there is no public transportation system often own cars.

8. If you're going to Asia in April, Tokyo is a city _____ I recommend visiting because spring is the season _____ the cherry trees are in bloom.

2 Match the information about these cities. Then make sentences with non-defining relative clauses.

1. New Yorkers / huge baseball fans __*c*__
2. Saint Petersburg / the Hermitage is located ____
3. Athens / 2004 Summer Olympics were held ____
4. Sydney / famous for its Opera House ____
5. Venice / built on 118 small islands ____
6. Hawaii / has warm weather all year ____

a. was also the location of the first games.
b. is a popular winter destination.
c. have two pro teams in their city.
d. is crossed by many canals.
e. was Russia's capital for many years.
f. also has a well-known bridge.

New Yorkers, who are huge baseball fans, have two pro teams in their city.

3B Order of modifiers

Shape (*round*, *thin*), color (*red*, *blue*), and material (*silk*, *plastic*) are also used to describe nouns. They appear in the following order:

Quality	Size	Shape	Age	Color	Type	Material	Noun
quaint	little	winding					streets
picturesque			old	brightly colored	resort		hotels
	small				Thai	wooden	fishing boats

1 Put the words in the correct order.

1. He bought a *red / house / brick / little* in the center of town.
   He bought a little red brick house in the center of town.

2. They're renting a *cottage / pink / traditional / square* beside the river.

3. He hated living in a *border / town / remote / little* with its *wooden / houses / run-down*.

4. The town had many *old / buildings / cement* with *steel / dirty / black / roofs*.

3B Connecting contrasting ideas

There are three ways to connect contrasting ideas.

To begin an adverb clause, use *although* or *even though*.
I'd like to live in a small town someday **even though** I love all the opportunities in big cities.
Although I love all the opportunities in big cities, I'd like to live in a small town someday.

To begin an independent clause, use the transition words *however*, *nevertheless*, or *on the other hand*. Note the punctuation with transition words.
I love big cities. **However / On the other hand**, I'd like to live in a small town someday.
I love big cities; **nevertheless / however**, I'd like to live in a small town someday.

To begin a noun phrase, use the prepositions *despite* or *in spite of*.
Despite all the opportunities in big cities, I'd like to live in a small town someday.
I'd like to live in a small town someday **in spite of** all the opportunities in big cities.

2 Complete each sentence with a word or phrase from the box. Sometimes more than one answer is possible.

although	however	in spite of	on the other hand	nevertheless

1. This is a great city; _*nevertheless / however*_, it's too crowded.

2. _____ living downtown is expensive, there's a lot to do.

3. The summer is beautiful here. _____, it's terrible in the winter.

4. _____ the high crime rate, I'm not afraid to walk home alone after dark.

4A Reduced time clauses

In a reduced time clause, the subject of the clause is omitted and the verb is changed to an *-ing* form. A time clause with *before*, *after*, or *while* can be reduced only if the subject in the sentence's other clause is the same.
Before **I go to sleep**, I like to read.
Before **going to sleep**, I like to read.
I like to read before **going to sleep**.
Before **the baby goes to sleep, his mother reads** to him.

Once, every time, till, as, the first / next / last time, and many other time expressions can be used in time clauses. Time clauses beginning with these expressions cannot be reduced.
As soon as / Once I drink that first cup of coffee, I'm ready for the day.
Whenever / Every time I stay out late, I have trouble getting up the next morning.
I always stay at the office **until / till** I've finished all my work.
I like to watch TV **as** I'm eating dinner.
The last time I drank too much coffee, I was jittery all day.

1 Which of these time clauses can be reduced (*R*)? Which ones cannot be reduced (*N*)? Write the correct letter.

__N__ 1. Ever since I can remember, I've been a night owl.

_____ 2. Once I fall asleep, I almost never wake up until morning.

_____ 3. My mother races off to work right after I leave for school.

_____ 4. Every time Jerry comes to visit, he keeps me up past my bedtime.

_____ 5. As soon as I get up in the morning, I drink a large glass of water.

_____ 6. I always listen to music while I run.

_____ 7. I often doze off as I'm watching TV at night.

_____ 8. Whenever I drink coffee after 3:00, I have trouble falling asleep.

_____ 9. I always have breakfast at a local café before I start classes for the day.

_____ 10. The last time I stayed at a hotel, the bed was really uncomfortable.

2 Rewrite the sentences using reduced time clauses.

1. I usually watch the news while I have breakfast.
   I usually watch the news while having breakfast.

2. My sister won't drink orange juice after she brushes her teeth.

3. She does a lot of housework before she leaves for work in the morning.

4. Power nappers work better after they sleep for a short time during the day.

5. You probably shouldn't eat anything heavy before you exercise.

6. If I listen to soft music while I study, I can concentrate better.

7. After I'm in an argument, I need to be by myself for an hour or two.

8. Before I chill out at night, I make sure everything is ready for the morning.

4B Clauses stating reasons and conditions

The following are all additional commonly used clauses that state reasons and conditions.

Now that introduces a change in general circumstances that explains the main clause. *Now that* means "because now."
Now that I have a job that starts early, I have to leave the house by 6:30.

Whether or not introduces a condition that might or might not occur and which will not influence the main clause. Note its two possible positions.
She goes jogging every morning **whether or not** it's bad weather.
She goes jogging every morning **whether** it's bad weather **or not**.

Provided / Providing (*that*) introduces a condition that must be met for the main clause to be true.
Provided that I get all my schoolwork done, my weekend will be free.
Providing that I get a promotion, I'll stay with my company a few more years.

1 Match each sentence on the left with the best meaning on the right.

1. She always has breakfast whether she's in a hurry or not. __c__

2. Now that she works the afternoon shift, she always has time for breakfast. ____

3. Unless her mother makes it, she doesn't bother with breakfast. ____

4. She only eats breakfast if she's hungry. ____

5. Provided that she has enough time, she has breakfast. ____

6. As long as she has breakfast, she can concentrate in class. ____

a. She has plenty of time to eat something in the morning.

b. She skips her morning meal when she doesn't feel like eating anything.

c. She eats something every morning.

d. When she is in a hurry, she doesn't eat breakfast.

e. She never makes her own morning meal.

f. If she doesn't eat, she can't think clearly.

2 Choose the correct answer to complete the sentence.

1. He won't be late for work (as long as) / unless the bus is on time.

2. *Considering that / Just in case* I took a nap, I shouldn't feel this drowsy.

3. I'll wake up on time tomorrow, *provided that / unless* I set my alarm clock.

4. He jogs after work *now that / unless* he's too tired at the end of the day.

5. My brother usually goes to bed early *now that / whether or not* he's sleepy.

6. *Now that / Even if* I'm going to bed later, I'm getting up later.

7. I'm afraid to nap at lunch *even if / just in case* I start snoring at my desk.

8. *Even if / Provided that* I'm totally exhausted, I can't sleep on airplanes.

5A Infinitive and gerund phrases

In a sentence with *It's* + adjective + infinitive, it is possible to follow the adjective with *for* and an object. The object can be a pronoun or a noun.
It's difficult for her to talk about her feelings openly.
It's customary for North Americans to make frequent eye contact.

For sentences in the negative, use *not* + infinitive or *not* + gerund.
It's considered rude **not to thank** people who give you gifts.
Not thanking people who give you gifts is considered rude.

Adjectives of feeling (*glad*, *happy*, *pleased*) cannot be used with the *It's* + adjective + infinitive structure. Instead, the sentence needs to say who has (or doesn't have) these feelings.
Most parents are happy to see their children go to college.
People are always delighted to get compliments.

1 Rewrite the sentences using infinitive or gerund phrases.

   1. It's important to make a good first impression.
      Making a good first impression is important.

   2. Arriving late for an appointment is inappropriate in most countries.

   3. It's fairly typical for college students to get to a party late.

   4. It's considered rude not to be punctual for a dinner party.

   5. Keeping the conversation going is easy for Elyse.

   6. Showing the bottom of your feet is offensive in some places.

   7. It's good form to bring a small gift to a dinner party.

   8. Talking about politics is sometimes risky.

   9. It's customary for some parents to brag about their children.

  10. Thanking the hostess the day after a party is a nice idea.

2 Write sentences with infinitive phrases using the words below.

   1. Tom / always happy / lend money to his friends
      Tom is always happy to lend money to his friends.

   2. Wendy / unusual / arrive late to class
      It's unusual for Wendy to arrive late to class.

   3. Donald / relaxing / not have homework over the weekend

   4. Min / always glad / help a friend in need

   5. many tourists / surprised / learn about some American customs

   6. students / inappropriate / interrupt a teacher

   7. new employees / often afraid / ask their bosses for help

   8. dinner guests / customary / thank their hosts

   9. businesspeople / important / be punctual for appointments

5B Reported speech

The modals *can, may, must, have to,* and *don't have to* change in reported speech. *Might* and *should* do not change. Also notice how the pronouns change in reported speech.

Statements	Reported statements
"You **can** go to the party with **me**."	She said I **could** go to the party with **her**.
"I **may** go to a movie tonight."	He said he **might** go to a movie tonight.
"We **must** tell him the truth."	They said they **had to** tell him the truth.
"He **has to** go to the bank."	He said he **had to** go to the bank.
"You **don't have to** pay me back."	She said I **didn't have to** pay **her** back.
"We **might** get married."	She said they **might** get married.
"I **should** replace **my** old laptop.	He said he **should** replace **his** old laptop.

Say and *tell* are used differently in reported speech. *Tell* must be followed by a noun or object pronoun. *Say* is not followed by a noun/pronoun object.

Statements	Reported statements
"Don't park the car there."	She **told me** not to park the car there.
	She **said** not to park the car there.

When a very recent statement is being reported, no tense change is necessary.
A: I didn't hear that. What did she say?
B: She said she **wants** to go out for dinner.

Review the rules for reported speech on page 41. Change these conversations to reported speech.

1.   Ryan: I'm thinking of applying for a promotion at work.
     Emma: What kind of promotion is it?
     Ryan: Our department needs a new manager.
     Emma: You should definitely apply!
     Ryan: I'm a little nervous because there's a big interview.
     Emma: You just have to practice. I can help you.
     Ryan told Emma he was thinking of applying for a promotion at work.

2.   Karl: Do we have to sign up for our after-school club?
     Tanya: You can sign up until noon.
     Ava: Don't wait too long. The good clubs are filling up fast.
     Karl: I'll do it after I eat my lunch.

3.   Larry: I'm going to the Galápagos Islands in April.
     Jason: That's wonderful! You must send me some photos.
     Larry: I'll send you some. I promise! But why don't you go with me?
     Jason: I can't go. I may be starting a new job in April.

6A Present perfect vs. simple past

Use the present perfect to report a repeated past event that could continue into the present.
Thieves **have robbed** three banks this year.
The seal **has painted** four pictures so far.

Use the present perfect to report an event that has an effect on the present, or is still relevant.
She**'s been** more careful since she lost her car keys.
The store **has had** a security camera for a month now.

1 Complete these sentences with the simple past or the present perfect form of the verbs in parentheses.

1. The police ____caught____ (catch) the robber when he _____ (sell) the stolen art.

2. Unbelievably, the same woman _____ (win) the lottery twice since May.

3. So far, the children _____ (raise) more than $500 for charity.

4. Since the city _____ (pass) its new laws last year, crime _____ (fall).

5. The kidnappers _____ (not call) and _____ (not demand) any ransom yet.

6. No storms _____ (strike) since the summer _____ (begin).

6A Present perfect vs. present perfect continuous

Some verbs, such as *live, work, study, give/take (lessons)*, and *teach*, express the idea of an ongoing action. They can usually be used in either the present perfect or the present perfect continuous.
He **has lived** in London for eight years.
I **have taken** violin lessons since I was three.

He **has been living** in London for eight years.
I **have been taking** violin lessons since I was three.

2 Review the rules for the present perfect and the present perfect continuous on page 45. Then choose the correct form of the verb to complete the article. Sometimes more than one answer is possible.

It's a sad day for many who (1)(*have lived*) / (*have been living*) in this town since they were children. The town council (2) *has decided / has been deciding* to take down the old fishing pier.

Fisherman Bob Kates said, "I (3) *have worked / have been working* here since I was young. Generations of kids (4) *have taken / have been taking* swimming lessons here. I myself (5) *have jumped / have been jumping* off this pier many times, especially on hot summer days. However, today the temperature (6) *has reached / has been reaching* 36 degrees Celsius, but nobody can jump off the pier as the town (7) *has already put up / has already been putting up* barriers. It's true that the pier (8) *has been / has been being* in pretty bad condition for a while now, so I guess it's a safety issue."

It's not all bad news for Mr. Kates. The town (9) *has studied / has been studying* proposals for replacing the pier for a year now, and in fact, planning for a new and improved pier (10) *has already begun / has already been beginning*.

6B Adverbs with the simple past and past perfect

> *When* and the simple past and past perfect can be used to express different time relationships.
> **When** I arrived in Bangkok, my connecting flight **had already departed**.
> **When** I arrived in Bangkok, my friend **met** me at the airport.
>
> When *before* makes the sequence of events clear, the simple past or past perfect can be used.
> It **began** to rain **before** she boarded the plane.
> It **had begun** to rain **before** she boarded the plane.
>
> *Yet* and *already* are used with both the present perfect and past perfect to show that an event took place earlier.
> It **had already started** raining when I arrived in Bangkok.
> It **hadn't started** raining **yet** when I arrived in Bangkok.

Choose the correct form of the verb to complete the story.

The taxi arrived to take Erica to the airport for her flight to London. Until that day she (1) *was never /* (*had never been*) on an international flight. The travel agent (2) *told / had told* her to get to the airport early, so she (3) *arrived / had arrived* four hours before her flight was due to leave. When she (4) *got / had gotten* there, she (5) *realized / had realized* she had plenty of time to spare, so she (6) *decided / had decided* to have some coffee and a snack and look at the newspaper before she (7) *checked in / had checked in*. She (8) *already bought / had already bought* some chocolate bars to eat on the plane, so she decided to have one of those. She sat at the counter and ordered a coffee.

When her coffee (9) *came / had come*, she pulled her favorite section out of the newspaper, carefully refolded it, and put it on the counter beside her. When she (10) *reached / had reached* for her chocolate bar, she saw that someone (11) *already took / had already taken* it out of the package and (12) *broke / had broken* it into eight tidy squares. She looked beside her and saw a distinguished-looking businessman. Before that, she (13) *didn't really notice / hadn't really noticed* him. She watched as he picked up a piece of the chocolate and calmly popped it into his mouth. She (14) *never saw / had never seen* such rude behavior in her life, so still staring at him, she (15) *picked up / had picked up* a piece and ate it. By now, he was staring back. He picked up another piece and ate it. So did Erica. Finally, there was only one piece left. Erica (16) *took / had taken* it.

The man stood up. He said, "Look. If you're that hungry, buy yourself a donut!" He (17) *slammed / had slammed* a dollar bill down on the counter and stormed out. In her entire life, she (18) *was never / had never been* so shocked. Muttering to herself, Erica began to gather up her things. Suddenly, she stopped, standing as still as a statue. There, under her newspaper, (19) *was / had been* her chocolate bar, exactly where she (20) *put / had put* it before the whole fiasco began.

> If the agent (the person or thing doing the action) is unknown or obvious from the context, it's better to use a passive form. However, if the person or thing doing the action needs to be emphasized, it's better to use an active form.
> The spyware **is being used** to collect information about college students. *(Agent is unknown.)*
> Social networking sites **have been used** in criminal investigations. *(Agent is clear from context.)*
> A criminal organization **has created** this virus, not an amateur hacker. *(Agent is emphasized.)*
>
> **The passive is very rarely used with the present perfect continuous. Use the passive of the present perfect instead.**
> People **have been posting** more videos to the Internet this year than ever before.
> More videos **have been posted** to the Internet this year than ever before.

1 For each pair of sentences, is it better to use the passive or active form? Choose *a* or *b*.

1. ☑ a. More U.S. employers will likely allow access to social networking sites.
   ☐ b. Access to social networking sites will likely be allowed.

2. ☐ a. Soon, inventors will invent smartphones that don't require a battery.
   ☐ b. Smartphones that don't require a battery will be invented soon.

3. ☐ a. Most cell phone companies are now offering unlimited-use plans.
   ☐ b. Unlimited-use plans are being offered now.

4. ☐ a. Teachers might be teaching more high school students with educational computer games.
   ☐ b. More high school students might be taught with educational computer games.

2 Complete the sentences with the correct active or passive form of the verb in parentheses.

1. Recently, social networking sites *have become* (become) popular with all age groups.

2. Every week, free software _____ (download) on computers everywhere.

3. In the years to come, podcasts _____ (use) more often in educational programs.

4. Lately, children _____ (ask) for cell phones at a younger and younger age.

5. More sophisticated viruses _____ (create) all the time.

6. For years, hackers _____ (try) to use spyware to commit identity theft.

7. In years to come, more and more data _____ (store) in the cloud.

8. I recently discovered that my neighbors _____ (use) my Wi-Fi many times.

9. In the next decade, more job interviews _____ (hold) online.

10. Since I last visited this blog, several older posts _____ (remove).

7B Negative and tag questions for giving opinions

Use past negative and tag questions to offer an opinion about a past event and invite someone to react.

Wasn't it weird how the manager's microphone kept turning on and off during his speech?
Didn't it seem like the manager's speech would never end?
Shouldn't the company have provided us with coffee before the speech?
The manager's speech was really boring, **wasn't it**?
The manager has given some pretty boring speeches, **hasn't he**?
The manager's speech had just put about everyone to sleep when the fire alarm rang, **hadn't it**?

In informal spoken English, *they* can be used as the pronoun in tag questions when the subject is *somebody, someone, everybody, everyone, nobody,* or *no one.*
Everyone we know had a cell phone in school, didn't **they**?   Yes, they did.
Somebody has hacked into your computer, haven't **they**?   Yes, they have. / No, they haven't.

Use an affirmative tag question when the subject is a negative, such as *nobody* or *nothing.*
Nobody left any voice mail messages, **did they**?   Yes, they did. / No, they didn't.

1 Turn the statements into negative questions.

1. It would have been great if telemarketers had never gotten my number.
   Wouldn't it have been great if telemarketers had never gotten my number?

2. It was awful how much paper we wasted on fliers that nobody read.

3. Jill should have kept her text messages much shorter.

4. It was weird how those pop-up ads made my computer freeze.

5. It seemed like we spent all day looking for an Internet café.

6. It would have been great if we could have paid less for our computer.

7. We should have spent less time playing video games as kids.

8. It was sad how Mark got really addicted to social networking sites.

2 Complete the sentences with tag questions.

1. There were several voice mail messages for me, _weren't there_?

2. There haven't been any new rules about using social media at work, _____?

3. Someone told him there was a problem with his phone, _____?

4. You gave your computer password to someone, _____?

5. There was nothing he could do with his obsolete computer, _____?

6. Nobody we know ever actually clicked on those banner ads, _____?

7. She had already complained about the telemarketers, _____?

8. You used to have a robot vacuum that constantly cleaned the house, _____?

8A Reduced relative clauses

Non-defining relative clauses with *be* can be reduced in the same way as defining relative clauses. Notice the use of commas.

Einstein, **who is thought to be one of the greatest minds of the twentieth century,** struggled in school.
Einstein, **thought to be one of the greatest minds of the twentieth century,** struggled in school.
Curtis James Jackson III, **who is better known as the singer 50 Cent,** used to be a boxer.
Curtis James Jackson III, **better known as the singer 50 Cent,** used to be a boxer.

1 Rewrite these sentences using reduced relative clauses.

1. The photographer who lives upstairs has won many awards for his creativity.
   The photographer living upstairs has won many awards for his creativity.

2. Professional cooking, which is considered a tough business, requires both patience and skill.

3. Movie stars who are constantly hounded by the press deserve more privacy.

4. Roger Federer, who is ranked among the world's best tennis players, is considered very disciplined.

5. The Summer Olympics, which are held every four years, are broadcast around the world.

6. Children who are talented at music should take private lessons if possible.

2 Combine the sentences. Rewrite them as one sentence containing a reduced non-defining relative clause.

1. Lady Gaga is generally believed to be very confident and professional. She claims she is actually shy.
   Lady Gaga, generally believed to be very confident and professional, claims she is actually shy.

2. Yohji Yamamoto is famous for his modern fashion designs. He often uses the color black.

3. Jessica Alba has been interested in acting since the age of five. She first appeared in a film at age 13.

4. The movie *Twilight* was adapted from a novel by Stephenie Meyer. It stars Robert Pattinson.

5. Mark Zuckerberg is celebrated for creating Facebook. He attended Harvard University.

6. Justin Bieber is originally from Canada. He began his professional singing career in the U.S.

7. Tim Berners-Lee is credited with inventing the Web. He published the first website in 1991.

8. Jamie Oliver is known for his food-focused TV shows. He advocates healthier food in schools.

8B Non-defining relative clauses as sentence modifiers

Non-defining relative clauses can be used as sentence modifiers and can contain almost any verb. Some of the most common ones are *surprise*, *depress*, *encourage*, *suggest (that)*, *contribute to*, and *result in.* Note that the verbs that describe emotion must be followed by an object.

My husband tried to repair a leak with aluminum foil, **which has resulted in a ruined silk carpet**.

My teacher praised my English today, **which encourages me to study harder**.

Peter has been happier since he took up golf, **which suggests that hobbies are good for a person both mentally and physically**.

I learned how to clean jewelry with toothpaste, **which depressed me because it meant I had wasted a fortune on expensive cleaners**.

I've started making my own clothes, **which has contributed to financial savings and a full closet**!

1 Match these statements with the appropriate non-defining clauses.

1. I use dental floss to string beads for jewelry, __*c*__

2. My sister always loved school, ____

3. Robert moved to a small town, ____

4. I just had a big fight with Ana, ____

5. Paul is really good at solving problems, ____

6. Amy jogs every morning, ____

7. I've had a private tutor for the past few months, ____

8. The class I wanted to take is already full, ____

a. which surprised us since he loves cities.

b. which has contributed to weight loss and more energy.

c. which is why I have so much of it.

d. which is why people always go to him for help.

e. which has resulted in better grades for me.

f. which encouraged her to go into teaching.

g. which means I'll have to explore alternatives in the course schedule.

h. which depressed me because she's my best friend.

2 Complete the sentences with a phrase from the box.

which resulted in	which suggested	which depressed
which encouraged	which means	which surprised

1. I'm working late tonight, _____*which means*_____ I'll take a later train home.

2. My friend was in a local play, _____ me to try acting.

3. Our team lost the championship, _____ me and my friends.

4. Prices went down last year, _____ savings for many people.

5. Ted sent me a nice birthday card, _____ me since he usually doesn't do anything special for people's birthdays.

6. Dinner tasted terrible, _____ that I didn't follow the recipe correctly.

9A Clauses and phrases showing contrast and exception

The following are additional common phrases that show contrast and exception.

Use *whereas*, especially in formal writing, to present contrasting information.
Whereas the bottled water market is huge in Italy, it is very small in Japan.

Use *except (for)* or *with the exception of* to show an exception within a group.
Everyone in my family, **except for** my mother, plays a musical instrument.
Everyone in my family, **with the exception of** my mother, plays a musical instrument.

1 Circle the correct answer to complete the sentence.

1. (While)/ Unlike Leo prefers a big breakfast, I just have coffee.

2. No one in the class, *except that / with the exception of* Eva, can speak German.

3. *In contrast to / While* city people, those who live on farms must have a car.

4. *Unlike / Except for* Thai women, Spanish women greet each other with a kiss.

5. I'm a typical Canadian, *whereas / except for the fact that* I don't like hockey.

6. Most Americans have dinner by 7:00, *whereas / unlike* in Spain people eat later.

7. Everyone on our street, *except that / except for* my family, has a pet.

8. *Unlike / While* me, all my friends are addicted to reality shows on TV.

2 Read about Alonzo and Jun. Complete the sentences with an expression to show contrast or exception. More than one answer is possible.

Alonzo (26 years old) . . .	Jun (21 years old) . . .
finished college four years ago.	is in his third year of college.
considers himself to be pretty typical.	doesn't think he's really typical.
plays and watches all kinds of sports.	doesn't play any sports.
isn't crazy about baseball.	doesn't watch any sport but baseball.
has a high salary and eats out often.	doesn't work and always cooks at home.
wears a suit on weekdays.	always dresses very casually.

1. Jun is still in college, *whereas / while* Alonzo has already graduated.

2. Alonzo considers himself to be pretty typical, _____ Jun doesn't.

3. _____ Jun, Alonzo is a big sports fan.

4. Alonzo is a fan of most sports _____ baseball.

5. Alonzo has dinner in restaurants, _____ Jun usually can't afford to eat out.

6. _____ Alonzo, Jun hardly ever dresses up.

7. Alonzo has a good job, _____ Jun isn't working now.

8. Jun and Alonzo are very different, _____ they are both in their 20s.

9B Past habitual with *used to* and *would*

To ask questions about a habitual action or situation in the past, use *Did . . . use to . . . ?*
(NOT *Would . . . ?*).
Did you use to listen to rock music when you were younger?
Did you use to share a bedroom with your little brother?

Use the negative question *Didn't . . . use to . . . ?* to confirm a guess about habitual actions
or a situation in the past.
Didn't you use to work at a grocery store after school?
Didn't he use to play on the school soccer team?

1 Write the questions to these responses. Use *Did . . . use to* or *Didn't . . . use to*.

1. A: *Did / Didn't you use to live in San Francisco?*
   B: Yes, I did. I lived in San Francisco for about two years.

2. A: _____
   B: A lot? No, as a matter of fact, I've never drunk coffee.

3. A: _____
   B: No, he never did. Actually, Pete's allergic to cats.

4. A: _____
   B: In the school band? Yes, I did. I played the flute.

5. A: _____
   B: Yes, I always rode my bike in elementary school, but I'd take the bus on rainy days.

6. A: _____
   B: Yeah, my hair was really long, but I had to cut it when I joined the swim team.

2 Choose the correct answer to complete each sentence. Sometimes both are possible.

1. Lesley *would* / *used to* live in Brazil before she moved to Turkey.

2. We *would* / *used to* have fun during summer vacations.

3. They *would* / *used to* have a house by the ocean, but they've sold it.

4. Serena *would* / *used to* go mountain biking every weekend.

5. *Would her parents* / *Did her parents use to* own a Mexican restaurant ten years ago?

6. My mother *would* / *used to* volunteer at the hospital every winter.

7. Alex *would* / *used to* like to build models of cars and ships.

8. *Would you* / *Did you use to* be good at fixing cars when you were younger?

10A Relative clauses and noun clauses

In some relative clauses, the relative pronoun (*who*, *that*, or *which*) can be omitted.

In an object relative clause, a relative pronoun (*who*, *that*, or *which*) is optional. Relative pronouns are only required when they function as the subject of a relative clause.
My friend told our classmates a secret. I had told him that secret.
My friend told our classmates a secret (**that**) I had told him.

In a subject relative clause, a relative pronoun (*who*, *that*, or *which*) is necessary because it functions as the subject of the relative clause.
I have a roommate. She never cleans the kitchen.
I have a roommate **who** never cleans the kitchen.

1 Choose the sentences where the relative pronoun (*who*, *that*, or *which*) is optional.

- ☑ 1. The restaurant that we had dinner at last night overcharged us.
- ☐ 2. One thing that makes me sick is really selfish people.
- ☐ 3. People who chew gum loudly really get on my nerves.
- ☐ 4. Someone's cell phone kept ringing all through the movie that I saw last night.
- ☐ 5. I had a big argument with a store clerk who refused to give me a refund.
- ☐ 6. My teacher gets mad at every little noise that our class makes.
- ☐ 7. The town fined a neighbor who burned garbage in her backyard.
- ☐ 8. The people in the line which he tried to cut into complained to the theater manager.

2 Complete the sentences with *who* or *that*. If the pronoun can be omitted, write *X*. Sometimes more than one answer is possible.

1. One thing _____*that*_____ gets me down is people ___*who / that*___ lie to me.

2. I like people _____ stand up for something _____ they believe in.

3. Something _____ makes me sad is people _____ have no place to live.

4. Something _____ I can't do is keep up with technology.

5. I was a kid _____ had parents _____ made a lot of rules.

6. The thing _____ aggravates me most is people _____ are cruel to animals.

10B Simple and complex indirect questions

If the beginning clause of an indirect question is in statement word order, the sentence is a statement and ends with a period.
I'm curious about why he didn't complain to the landlord.
I'm not sure who is responsible for repairing the roads.
The big question is if / whether we can get the city officials to listen to our concerns.

If the beginning clause of an indirect question is in question word order, the sentence is a question and ends with a question mark.
Do you have any idea if / whether I need a visa to visit China?
Could you tell me where I can go to pay my parking ticket?
Don't you wonder how a place with such poor service stays in business?

1 Rewrite these sentences using the words in parentheses.

1. Why can't the city add more streetlights? (I don't understand . . .)
   I don't understand why the city can't add more streetlights.

2. Is the city going to improve the rush hour bus service? (Do you know . . .)

3. Why are prices going up so fast? (. . . is something that baffles me.)

4. How can I finish the work before the deadline? (I have no idea . . .)

5. Have you saved enough money for school? (Would you mind telling me . . .)

6. Why aren't there any bike paths in the city? (. . . is beyond me.)

7. How am I going to find time to enjoy myself? (My main problem is . . .)

8. When are they going to build a new hospital? (Do you have any idea . . .)

9. Who decided to close the swimming pool in the park? (Don't you wonder . . .)

10. Is tuition going up again next year? (I have to find out . . .)

2 Rewrite these sentences as direct questions.

1. I haven't got a clue what we're supposed to do for homework tonight.
   What are we supposed to do for homework tonight?

2. How people can leave their children home alone is mystifying to me.

3. What I don't get is how I can keep up with all this new technology.

4. Why there isn't a pedestrian zone downtown is my number-one question.

5. I'd like to know who should be responsible for keeping our city clean.

6. Tell me what I have to do to get my driver's license.

7. When the next meeting will be is something I haven't found out yet.

8. I wonder if I should complain about my neighbor's loud parties.

11A Present unreal conditional with *unless*, *only if*, and *even if*

To ask a follow-up question after a yes/no question, a shortened conditional can be used, especially in spoken or informal English. The positive shortened conditional is *if so*, and the negative shortened conditional is *if not.*
Would you consider lying to a good friend to avoid hurting your friend's feelings? **If so**, what kinds of things would you lie about?
Are you sure your friends are loyal and trusting? **If not**, you shouldn't tell them your secrets.

1 Match the yes/no questions on the left with the follow-up questions on the right.

1. Would you say anything if a colleague called you by the wrong name? __c__

2. If the man next to you on the bus fell asleep on your shoulder, would you wake him up? ____

3. Would you remain silent if you disagreed with your boss in a meeting? ____

4. Would you report it if you saw a friend steal a small item from a store? ____

5. If people you secretly disliked invited you to a party at their home, would you go? ____

6. If a cat always came to your house for food, would you keep it? ____

a. If not, what would you say?

b. If not, would you confront your friend?

c. If so, what would you say?

d. If not, would you try to find its owner?

e. If so, how would you wake him up?

f. If not, what excuse would you give?

2 Review the rules for the present unreal conditional with *unless*, *only if*, and *even if* on page 89. Choose the correct answer to complete each sentence.

1. I wouldn't lie to a friend (*unless*)/ *only if* it was in his or her best interests.

2. If you found money on the street, would you turn it in to the police? *If so / If not*, what would you do with it?

3. Would you report a shoplifter *only if / even if* the person looked poor? *If so / If not*, would you tell the store manager, or would you call the police?

4. He wouldn't lose his temper *only if / even if* he were really angry.

5. Would you confront a friend who gossiped about you behind your back? *If so / If not*, what would you say?

6. I wouldn't read anyone else's mail *even if / only if* I were really curious.

7. Would you make a promise if you already knew you couldn't keep it? *If so / If not*, what would you do later when you didn't keep the promise?

8. I would criticize my friends *unless / only if* I knew a way to help them improve.

11B Wishes and regrets

Wishes and regrets often use comparative words, such as *(not) enough*, *more*, *less*, and *better*, and intensifiers, such as *really* and *very*.

I did**n't** save **enough** money last summer.
I wish I had saved **more** money last summer.

I spent **too much** money on video games last year.
If only I had spent **less** money on video games last year.

I bought **too many** clothes this weekend.
I wish I had bought **fewer** clothes this weekend.

I **don't** understand math very **well**.
I wish I understood math **better**.

I got **really** angry at my friend last night.
If only I had**n't** gotten **so** angry at my friend last night.

1 Complete the wishes and regrets with a word from the box.

> better   fewer   harder   less   more   so

1. I don't have enough time to do volunteer work.
   I wish I had _____*more*_____ time to do volunteer work.

2. I don't know how to swim very well.
   I wish I knew how to swim _____.

3. I drank too much coffee before bed last night.
   If only I had drunk _____ coffee before bed last night.

4. The teacher thought the questions on the exam were much too easy.
   The teacher wished the questions on the exam had been _____.

5. Our class has too many assignments this week.
   I wish our class had _____ assignments this week.

6. I felt really sleepy in class and couldn't pay any attention.
   I wish I hadn't felt _____ sleepy in class and had paid attention.

2 Rewrite these sentences using the words in parentheses.

1. I wasn't very obedient in elementary school. (I wish . . .)
   I wish I had been more obedient in elementary school.

2. I refused to take piano lessons when I was young. (If only . . .)

3. I fell asleep at the computer last night, and now my essay is late. (I wish . . . Then . . .)

4. I exercised too much yesterday, so now I feel really tired. (If only . . . Then . . .)

5. Bob is shy and doesn't make friends easily. (Bob wishes . . .)

6. I'm not a very good cook. (If only . . .)

12A Future perfect and future perfect continuous

When using the future perfect or future perfect continuous, the particular point in the future is often referred to in another part of the sentence.

By this time next year, your commitment to language study is going to have gotten stronger.
On August 1, I will have been living overseas for six months.
After a few months, you're going to have made real progress with English.
Before next spring, he will have finished most of his course work.
By the time you arrive in New York, Marisa will have already received the package you sent.
When the van arrives, I will have been packing for two days, and I probably won't have finished.
Before I leave for Paris, I will already have sold my house and put my things in storage.
After I finish this, I will have completed everything on my "to do" list.

1 Underline the words in each sentence that refer to a point in the future.

1. By the spring, Nate will have visited over a dozen different countries.

2. When the end of the week arrives, I will have written four exams.

3. Before long, I'll have been working on this puzzle for an hour. It's impossible!

4. I can't believe he's still sleeping! At 11:00, he'll have been sleeping for 12 hours.

5. When she leaves the house, she'll have had six cups of coffee.

6. If it continues, on Tuesday it will have been raining for three weeks.

7. After I stop working, I will have painted three of the rooms in my house.

8. By the time the plane lands, we will have been in the air for seven hours.

2 Complete the sentences with the future perfect or the future perfect continuous form of the verb in parentheses.

1. By the end of class, I ___*will have learned*___ (learn) about the future perfect tense.

2. By the year 2030, I _____ (work) for several years.

3. Before she's 30, Sue _____ (make) her first million dollars.

4. At the end of his trip, Seth _____ (visit) four different countries.

5. After I finish this book, I _____ (read) all the titles you recommended.

6. By 11:00, how long _____ Dan _____ (watch) TV?

7. When I finish college, I _____ (be) in school for 16 years.

8. Pretty soon, I _____ (wait) for her for an hour. I'm getting annoyed!

9. We're late. By the time we get there, they _____ (finish) dinner.

10. On Friday of this week, Kara _____ (travel) for two months.

12B Mixed conditionals

Conditionals can appear in many forms. They can describe how situations in the past affect situations in the past, the present, or the future.

Use a past form in both the *if* clause and the result clause to talk about true events in the past.
When I was younger, if I **didn't behave** well, my parents **were** disappointed.
If we **got** lost during our trip last year, we just **asked** someone for directions.

Use the past perfect in the *if* clause and *would / wouldn't have* + the past participle of the verb in the result clause to talk about hypothetical situations in the past that had effects on the more recent past.
If I **had been born** with a good voice, I **would have started** my own band a long time ago.

Use the past perfect in the *if* clause and *would / wouldn't* + verb in the result clause to describe hypothetical situations in the past that have effects on the present.
If I **had studied** harder when I was in school, I **would have** a better job today.

Use the past perfect in the *if* clause and *would / wouldn't* + verb in the result clause to talk about hypothetical situations in the past that have effects on the future.
If she **had booked** her flight before now, she **would be** in Paris next week.
If I **hadn't taken** a year off from school, I **would be graduating** this June.

Complete these sentences with the correct form of the verbs in parentheses. Sometimes more than one answer is possible.

1. As a kid, I always ____*enjoyed*____ (enjoy) school if I _____ (like) the teacher.

2. If I _____ (study) harder last year, I _____ (not have to) repeat the course this year.

3. If he _____ (not speak) Greek, his trip to Athens last year _____ (be) so enjoyable.

4. When I was young, if I _____ (see) a scary movie, I _____ (have) bad dreams.

5. When I was a kid, if my father _____ (go away) on a business trip, he always _____ (call) at 8:00 to say "Good night" to us.

6. If I _____ (spend) less money when I was younger, I _____ (have) a nice little nest egg in a few years.

7. If I _____ (not have) a fight with my friend yesterday, I _____ (go) to the party tonight.

8. If she _____ (show) more interest since she was hired, she _____ (get) the next promotion.

9. If I _____ (not lose) my passport, I _____ (fly) to Lisbon tonight.

10. If she _____ (not start) figure skating when she was four, she _____ (not be) in the last Olympics.

VOCABULARY PLUS

1A Personality collocations

Choose the correct words to complete the sentences.

1. I'm thinking about different careers. Since most people think I'm (calm and cool) / wild and crazy / friendly and outgoing, I'd probably be a good air traffic controller. Also, I love planes! –**Jen**

2. I enjoy shopping and have always wanted to work in retail. My family thinks I'm friendly and outgoing / shy and reserved / neat and tidy and advises me to become a sales manager. –**Eva**

3. I'll do anything to make people laugh. My friends think I'm wild and crazy / laid-back and relaxed / kind and generous. They think I might have a future as a comedian. –**Matt**

4. I've traveled to many countries on my own. Since I'm laid-back and relaxed / neat and tidy / strong and independent and enjoy photography, I want to become a photojournalist. It would be exciting to travel around the world to cover major news events. –**Paolo**

5. I tend to be friendly and outgoing / shy and reserved / honest and sincere, so I prefer to work alone. I plan to become a software developer. –**Jim**

1B Compound family terms

Combine the prefixes and the suffix with some of the words for family members to complete the conversation. Some prefixes will be used more than once.

great-	grand-	great-grand-	-in-law

aunt	brother	father	mother	nephew	niece	uncle

Sara: Hi, Alex! The whole family is here at the wedding! Do you see my (1) _great-grandmother_ over there?

Alex: Is she your mom's grandmother or your dad's grandmother?

Sara: My mom's. And look, there's Raul. He's married to Hugo's older sister. He's Hugo's (2) _____, but they get along better than most brothers.

Alex: Who's your favorite relative?

Sara: Oh, my (3) _____ Vera, my grandmother's sister. Although Vera has five (4) _____ besides me, I'm probably the closest. She lived next door when I was growing up and taught me to play the guitar.

Alex: That's cool . . .

Sara: Hey, do you see my (5) _____ Pat making my dad laugh? Pat is my father's uncle. It's always fun to hear his stories!

Alex: So, who is the other person with them?

Sara: Oh, that's my (6) _____, you know, my dad's grandfather. Let's go and say hello.

2A Collocations with *problem*

Choose the correct words to complete the sentences.

Problem-Solving Tips

1. The best way to *run into* / *deal with* a problem is to figure out what it is.

2. After you *identify* / *ignore* a problem, analyze it and think of possible solutions.

3. It's a mistake to believe that if you *ignore* / *cause* a problem long enough, it will go away.

4. Don't *aggravate* / *run into* problems by worrying too much about them and coming up with poor solutions.

5. Sometimes discussing a problem with others will help you *cause* / *solve* it.

6. Don't blame your problems on other people. It's best just to *deal with* / *avoid* problems as soon as possible.

2B Verbs of belief

Replace the underlined words with the correct form of the word or phrase from the box that means the same thing.

1. **be positive   doubt   suppose**

    The archaeologist dug up pieces of pottery in the castle ruins. After studying the pottery markings, he <u>was sure</u> that it was from the 16th century.   ___*was positive*___

2. **assume   be certain   have a hunch**

    Based on clues at the crime scene, the detective <u>suspected</u> that the husband must have known something about his wife's disappearance. _____

3. **guess   know for a fact   suppose**

    The accountant carefully reviewed his client's records and <u>was certain</u> that all of his earnings and expenses were reported correctly. _____

4. **be sure   doubt   suspect**

    After examining the brushstrokes of the painting, the art expert <u>figured</u> that it must be a forgery. _____

5. **be certain   have a hunch   suppose**

    The lab technician studied the tooth under a microscope. She <u>was sure</u> it belonged to a humpback whale. _____

6. **be positive   doubt   guess**

    When the reporter investigated the story, he <u>had a hunch</u> that the politician was lying about the bank loan. _____

3A Features of cities

Use five more words or phrases from the box to complete the conversation.

climate	crime rate	hotels	neighborhood	transportation system
cuisine	green spaces	job market	nightlife	

Su-ho: Where do you want to live after you finish college?

Ines: Well, I have to support myself and pay my rent and other expenses. That means I'll need to live in a city with a strong (1) ___*job market*___.

Su-ho: Yeah. And you enjoy the outdoors, so you probably want parks and other (2) _____.

Ines: Yes, you're right. I want places to run and bike. I love being in the sun, so a place with a good (3) _____ is also important.

Su-ho: That's true. You always complain about the cold winters here. Oh, and I know you also love trying new restaurants.

Ines: You know me so well! I'll definitely want to explore restaurants with many different kinds of (4) _____.

Su-ho: What else do you want a city to offer?

Ines: Well, I love going to jazz clubs and concerts, so a city with an active (5) _____ would be perfect. How about you? What's important to you?

Su-ho: I'd like to live in a friendly (6) _____ where I can meet people. That will make it easier to live in a new city.

3B Compound terms for towns

Cross out the phrases that do <u>not</u> fit the meaning of the sentences.

1. Thousands of visitors come to this *resort town* / ~~*rural town*~~ / *tourist town* each year to enjoy its beaches, hotels, and restaurants.

2. This *industrial town* / *coastal town* / *mountain town* does not have many factories or businesses, but it has amazing views and clean air.

3. This *mountain town* / *coastal town* / *port town* is located in a valley near a river, with convenient access for boats and ships.

4. This *suburban town* / *industrial town* / *rural town* has many gardens that are famous for gorgeous flowers and fruit trees.

5. Not many people live in this *resort town* / *mountain town* / *suburban town*, but many people vacation here because it offers activities such as skiing and hiking.

6. Most of the people in this *border town* / *college town* / *suburban town* are elderly, so there isn't much of a nightlife.

4A Phrasal verbs related to energy and sleep

Choose the correct words to complete the sentences.

1. I'm feeling tired, and I have to write a paper tonight. I think I'll take a quick walk in the fresh air to *burn out / sleep over / (perk up)*.

2. Lea taught four English classes today, and tonight, she had to run a faculty meeting. She really needs to *race off / chill out / burn out* for a while.

3. Ben will have to leave for the airport at 5:00 in the morning. He should probably *turn in / perk up / calm down* early tonight.

4. Dina lives in a town that's over an hour away from her office. When she has to work late, she often *races off / calms down / sleeps over* at a friend's place near the office.

5. Ellen invited us over for a dinner party last night. I had a great time, but I had to *race off / doze off / calm down* to catch the last train home.

6. I enjoy reading mystery novels on the bus, but if I'm tired, I sometimes *sleep over / burn out / doze off* after reading just a few pages.

4B Expressions related to sleep

Cross out the phrases that do not fit the meaning of the sentences.

Val: I'm exhausted this morning. I (1) *had a sleepless night / slept like a log / tossed and turned* last night. I even had some warm milk at 2:00 and still couldn't get to sleep.

Eva: Have you ever thought of going to bed earlier? If you put on some soft music and relaxed, you'd probably (2) *be wide awake / nod off / feel drowsy* in 10 or 15 minutes.

Val: Yes, I've tried that, but it doesn't help. Maybe I should cut back on coffee. The caffeine may be the reason why I'm (3) *fast asleep / wide awake / tossing and turning* in the middle of the night.

Eva: I take a hot bath every night and am usually (4) *sleeping like a log / sound asleep / taking a power nap* by 10:30. Speaking of sleep, I hope I can stay awake tonight. It's 8:00, and I still have a lot of homework to finish.

Val: How about taking a quick power nap before doing your homework? That way, you won't (5) *drift off / be wide awake / feel drowsy* at your desk this evening.

Choose the correct words to complete the conversation.

Liu: I'm going to an academic conference in Los Angeles next week. It'll be my first time in the U.S., and I want to behave in an (1) (appropriate) / offensive / unusual way. Can I address people by their first names?

Jing: When you first meet people in the U.S., it's (2) polite / offensive / rude to address them by using their title and last name. Once you start talking, if the other person uses your first name, then you can do that as well.

Liu: OK, I'll try to remember that. Something else I want to know – do people kiss on the cheek when they first meet? Or is it better to shake hands?

Jing: In a professional setting, it's (3) rude / strange / normal to shake hands. Americans don't usually kiss strangers on the cheek.

Liu: I'm also wondering how to start conversations with people I meet for the first time.

Jing: Well, I think it's (4) inappropriate / typical / bad form to start by mentioning something interesting that a speaker said in a recent session. You might also ask someone's opinion about a conference topic.

Liu: OK. Now, sometimes when I get excited about an idea, I interrupt the other person with a lot of questions. Is that all right?

Jing: That's OK with friends, but when you meet new people, it's considered (5) polite / a compliment / bad form. You should let the other person finish talking.

5B Expressions for reported speech

Use phrases from each box to complete the conversations.

1.
advised me to	claimed that	promised to	wanted to know

A: My sister borrowed my car. She ____claimed that____ her car was being repaired.

B: She _____ if I knew a good mechanic. It sounded like a big repair job!

2.
claimed that	encouraged me to	explained that	wondered

A: My parents _____ take a trip to Brazil this summer.

B: That's fantastic! I _____ where you were planning to travel this year.

3.
advised me to	claimed that	wanted to know	warned me not to

A: My dad doesn't like my boyfriend because he plays in a band. He _____ find someone who's more serious about a career.

B: My father thinks the same way. He _____ date artists or writers!

4.
advised me to	encouraged me to	explained that	promised to

A: Ted was late again! He _____ he'd been studying and lost track of time.

B: Knowing Ted, I'll bet he _____ never be late again!

6A News events

Use four more events from the box to complete the headlines for the news stories.

Epidemic   Hijacking   Natural Disasters   Recession
Famine   Kidnapping   Political Crisis   Robbery

1. _Natural Disasters_ **Affect Economy**
   Last month's earthquake and storms caused significant damage to roads, bridges, and homes. The cost of repairs is putting a huge strain on the national economy.

2. _____ **of a Plane in Miami**
   Two men got on a plane at Miami National airport, threatened the pilots, and ordered them to fly to an unknown destination.

3. **Economy Falls into** _____
   Economists report that the unemployment rate has risen and consumer spending is slowing because people are saving money instead of purchasing goods.

4. _____ **Averted**
   The mayor is now under investigation and agreed to step down to avoid a government scandal. A special election will be held next month to fill his position.

5. **Experts Offer Tips to Prevent** _____
   Each year, thousands of people go missing. To prevent being taken against your will, security experts suggest that you change the routes you drive or walk every day and let your family or close friends know where you are going.

6B Storytelling expressions

Use phrases from each box to complete the story.

And in the end,   The next thing we knew,
I'll never forget the time   The thing you have to know is

(1) _I'll never forget the time_ it snowed in July. I was on vacation in the mountains with some friends, staying in a resort hotel. We went hiking and swimming every day. The weather was perfect – sunny and warm. One day, the temperature suddenly dropped, and the wind picked up. (2) _____ it was snowing big, fat flakes. It snowed for hours! (3) _____ that we were absolutely not ready for snow! We were wearing T-shirts, cotton pants, and sandals. Who knew we'd need snow boots in July?

It all started when   So finally,
I forgot to mention that   That reminds me of the time when

During the storm, we stayed inside, ordered sandwiches, and played board games. Oh, (4) _____ we lost electricity for a few hours, and we couldn't watch TV or play video games. (5) _____ the snow stopped, and the sun came out again. We borrowed some skis and boots from the hotel and went skiing on a summer day!

Use four words from the box to correct the underlined mistakes in the sentences.

| apps | the cloud | download | post | spyware | Wi-Fi |

1. My aunt recently started to <u>text</u> her recipes online to share with others. _____

2. Kyle said that <u>a blog</u> was secretly recording my online activity. _____

3. Angela downloaded some <u>podcasts</u> to play games on her smartphone. _____

4. My apartment building has installed <u>a virus</u>, so I can use my laptop anywhere in the building to get on the Internet. _____

7A   Expressions for connecting ideas formally

Choose the correct words to complete the text.

Does technology keep you up at night?

Technology has had a positive impact on our lives, for the most part. (1) *Similarly /* (As a matter of fact)*/ Additionally*, it's hard to imagine how we could live without our computers, smartphones, and apps. These things have made our lives so easy! (2) *Therefore / Nevertheless / As a result*, some technology issues keep me up at night. (3) *Likewise / On the other hand / For example*, what can we do about spyware? As soon as we download software to get rid of it, someone creates a new way to spy on our computers. (4) *For instance / In fact / Furthermore*, there's spyware's nasty cousin, the virus, which can ruin anyone's day. It's a constant battle to overcome these issues, but we can take some common sense steps. Always remember to back up your documents. (5) *In fact / Additionally / As a result*, update your software whenever you get alerts from the manufacturers. Doing these things can help keep technology a positive part of daily life.

7B   Words for forms of communication

Cross out the words that do <u>not</u> fit the meaning of the sentences.

A: We're planning an ad campaign to launch a new athletic shoe. In addition to some television ads that look like cool music videos, we'll use (1) *billboards / ~~voice mail~~ / bumper stickers.*

B: Are you also considering (2) *banner ads / pop-up ads / spam* to reach wider audiences?

A: Yes, they're on our list of possibilities. We're also wondering if we should hire a professional basketball player to appear on (3) *a crawl / a bus wrap / an infomercial.*

B: That's a great idea. Now, you may want to know that our research showed that younger audiences think print ads are old-fashioned. They want everything to be digital, so don't use (4) *fliers / billboards / pop-up ads* anymore.

8A Qualities of creative people

Match the correct words to complete the sentences.

1. Nora has the ____f____ to practice daily to achieve her dream of becoming an opera singer.

2. The director was _____ when he chose the actors for the cast. He chose quickly, and didn't ask anyone back for a second audition.

3. Ellie has been on several archeological digs in Asia and is _____ about ancient Chinese and Korean cultures.

4. Pablo is _____ to complete five paintings to enter in the art competition this spring.

5. Gino is _____ in his business; for example, he uses recycled materials to build homes.

6. Chad's science fiction stories are set 500 years in the future and show great _____.

a. decisive

b. resourceful

c. determined

d. knowledgeable

e. originality

f. discipline

8B Collocations for problem solving

Choose the correct words to complete the text.

Groupware

If you ever worked for a multinational company in the past, you know that sometimes it could take hours just to set up a meeting with your colleagues. To help improve productivity, technology companies explored various ways to (1) *find a mistake /* *find a solution* to the problem. They studied the way people worked and (2) *made a mistake / analyzed this information* to figure out how companies might work together more effectively and efficiently. Technological innovators (3) *explored the possibilities of /* *found problems for* using networked computers and digital office tools. Eventually, they were able to (4) *solve this problem / analyze the problem* by designing groupware, which is software that helps groups of people work together and share information on the Internet. With groupware, colleagues can set up a meeting quickly and have meetings via video, across several continents. And electronic file-sharing systems allow workers to (5) *find alternatives / organize information* and share documents instantly. Problem solved!

9A Expressions related to accepting or changing things

Choose the correct words to complete the conversation.

Amber: I just met your sister. She's so passionate about changing society! She really wants to (1) *follow the crowd* / (*make waves*) / *fit in.*

Becca: Oh yes, Olivia and I are pretty different. I tend to follow the rules and am much more (2) *conventional* / *rebellious* / *unconventional* than she is.

Amber: What was it like growing up in your family? Did your parents teach you to behave yourself and (3) *accept* / *stand up to* / *confront* society's rules?

Becca: Actually, our parents were pretty (4) *unconventional* / *amenable* / *conservative* in their attitudes. At a time when most of their friends were becoming bankers and lawyers, my parents helped set up food pantries to feed poor people in our town.

Amber: Well, that helps explain why Olivia is so active in organizing that free tutoring program at the community center. But why do you think you're so different from her?

Becca: I guess it's just my personality. I want to help people, but I'm kind of shy and don't like to (5) *fit in* / *follow the crowd* / *confront* people.

Amber: I think that's good! You're (6) *being your own person* / *being rebellious* / *making waves* after all.

9B Expressions with *keep* and *stay*

Replace the underlined words in each sentence with an expression from the box above that means the same thing.

keep in touch	keep out of trouble	keep things in perspective	stay awake

1. Sofia is moving to a new neighborhood, but her friends hope she will <u>stay connected</u>.

   Sofia is moving to a new neighborhood, but her friends hope she will _____*keep in touch*_____ .

2. When Pedro gets stressed out about his challenging new job, he tries to <u>remember what's truly important in life</u>.

   When Pedro gets stressed out about his challenging new job, he tries to

   _____ .

keep connected	keep up with	stay awake	stay out of trouble

3. Our economics class is difficult, and the professor assigns so many reports and research projects. How do you <u>get it all done</u>?

   How do you _____ it all?

4. Ever since Jack changed schools, he's been hanging out with the wrong crowd. I hope he can <u>avoid getting into a bad situation</u>.

   I hope he can _____ .

10A Expressions with *drive*, *get*, and *make*

Cross out the words that do <u>not</u> fit the meaning of the sentences.

> Hey, friends, I just returned from a wonderful trip to Bangkok! What amazing street life there! And the food was so spicy and delicious. But traveling there drove (1) *me crazy / ~~me down~~ / me mad*.
> My flight from Los Angeles was cancelled because of some bad storms. There were long lines to rebook flights, but what made (2) *my blood boil / me mad / on my nerves* was the airline's terrible customer service. It took an hour to get my ticket for a new flight, and then I had to wait two more hours to get through security. Standing in line always gets (3) *me sick / on my nerves / under my skin*. I got stuck behind a family with six noisy, spoiled kids. I was thinking to myself, "Excuse me, but I just used all of my savings for this ticket, and I have to board my flight in 10 minutes!" Talk about driving (4) *someone upset / someone up a wall / someone mad!*
>
> When I finally got on the plane, I ended up sitting next to a guy who kept talking about his big, important job. He bragged so much that it made (5) *my blood boil / me down / me mad*. To get him to stop talking, I pretended to fall asleep. I was so happy when our flight landed!

10B *-ed* words that describe feelings

Use words from each box to correct the underlined mistakes in the sentences.

baffled	infuriated	insulted

1. Max read over the instructions in his new computer manual several times, but he was still <u>stunned</u>. The instructions were not written very clearly. _____*baffled*_____

2. My boss is impatient and gets angry when she has to wait for things. She was <u>saddened</u> that she had to wait for six months to get a refund for a defective cell phone. _____

3. In some cultures, people feel <u>enraged</u> if new acquaintances refuse to shake hands. _____

frustrated	mystified	stunned

4. Julia was <u>confused</u> because her rent was due on the first of the month, but she wouldn't get her paycheck until the following week. _____

5. After the doctor disappeared, the detective conducted a thorough investigation. Even after analyzing all the evidence, he was still <u>demoralized</u> about what had actually happened. _____

6. Vicky didn't think her violin audition went very well, so she was <u>humiliated</u> to learn that the conductor had selected her for first chair in the orchestra. _____

11A Forming antonyms with prefixes

Choose the true statement for each sentence.

1. Nick thinks it's unethical to tell a white lie, even if it's to protect someone's feelings.
   - ☑ a. Nick thinks it's dishonest to tell a white lie.
   - ☐ b. Nick thinks it's irresponsible to tell a white lie.

2. Mai believes that making wishes is irrational, and that it gives people false hopes.
   - ☐ a. Mai thinks that making wishes is disagreeable.
   - ☐ b. Mai thinks that making wishes is illogical.

3. The accountant is scrupulous about tracking all of the company's profits.
   - ☐ a. The accountant is agreeable.
   - ☐ b. The accountant is responsible.

4. Most lawyers think the judge has a solid reputation for being trustworthy.
   - ☐ a. The judge's behavior is ethical.
   - ☐ b. The judge's behavior is unacceptable.

5. The investigator reported that the bank's lending practices may be unscrupulous.
   - ☐ a. The bank's lending practices may be illegal.
   - ☐ b. The bank's lending practices may be irrational.

6. It's unfair to copy test answers from another student.
   - ☐ a. It's illogical to copy test answers from another student.
   - ☐ b. It's unethical to copy test answers from another student.

11B Adjectives and nouns referring to personal values

Choose the correct words to complete the conversation.

Yoko: One quality I value in my friends is (1) *indifference / selfishness /* (*compassion*).

Omar: I agree! I also think it's important for friends to be (2) *honest / tender / generous* if they think I'm doing something wrong.

Yoko: It's helpful when my friends are truthful, but I also want them to be (3) *selfish / sensitive / resilient.* I don't want them to hurt my feelings.

Omar: Yeah, I guess that's important. You know, I wish some of my friends were better at keeping secrets! They need to show a little (4) *discretion / kindness / tolerance* when I share something personal.

Yoko: That's true! I expect my friends to have (5) *generosity / resilience / respect* for my privacy. I'm pretty open, but it's annoying when people ask too many questions.

Omar: Yeah, some people are too curious. But, I think overall, my friends are (6) *kind and generous / sensitive and selfish / resilient and indifferent,* and they make me happy!

12A Expressions ending with prepositions

Choose the correct words to complete the email.

Hi Jill,

I heard that you're moving to Tokyo soon to teach English. That's something to (1) *be scared of /* (*be excited about*)!

I remember that when I moved to Buenos Aires last year, it took a while to (2) *get accustomed to / look forward to* a new culture. I had to learn about the way people do business, make friends, and have fun. Luckily, I can speak Spanish, so I was able to (3) *be familiar with / participate in* meetings and conversations. I wanted to (4) *take advantage of / become aware of* cultural events, so I attended concerts, saw plays, and even learned to play guitar from an Argentinean musician!

My advice is to keep an open mind and give yourself time to (5) *adjust to / take advantage of* your new home. And don't (6) *be scared of / become aware of* trying new things.

I (7) *am familiar with / look forward to* hearing about your adventures in Japan!

Henry

12B Compound adjectives

Combine words from the boxes to make compound adjectives to complete the travel tips. Some words will be used more than once. Sometimes more than one answer is possible.

culturally	non	open	self

assured	aware	judgmental	minded	reliant	sensitive

Travel Tips

1. Be ____*open-minded*____ about trying new kinds of food. You may be captivated by a new cuisine!

2. Be _____ when it comes to exploring places on your own. You want people to think you're a confident, experienced traveler.

3. Be _____ when you experience new cultures. Consider all sides of an issue before forming an opinion.

4. People tolerate different levels of risk. Be _____ and assess your own tolerance for adventure, uncertainty, and possible danger when you plan your trips.

5. If you're traveling on business, learn about local customs and manners and try to be _____ when you meet with clients.

6. If you're going to hike in the mountains, prepare to be _____. Pack essentials such as water, food, rope, maps, a flashlight, and a first-aid kit.

Credits

Illustration credits

Photography credits

Text credits

Answers

Page 44, Exercise 1B: Story 3 is false.

Jack C. Richards & Chuck Sandy

Passages

Third Edition

Video Activity Worksheets

1

CAMBRIDGE
UNIVERSITY PRESS

Before you watch

A Choose three personality types that are difficult for you to deal with.

☐ calm   ☐ friendly   ☐ nervous

☐ cool   ☐ generous   ☐ reserved

☐ easily angered   ☐ independent   ☐ wild

B Pair work Compare your answers. Do you agree on which personality types are difficult? Why or why not? Discuss your opinions.

While you watch

A Which personality type would say each sentence? Choose the correct answers.

The Bully   *The Exploder*   *The Know-It-All*   *Mr. Negative*

	The Bully	The Exploder	The Know-It-All	Mr. Negative
1. I enjoy making other people feel bad.	☐	☐	☐	☐
2. I love to complain about how bad things are.	☐	☐	☐	☐
3. I can't stand not getting what I want.	☐	☐	☐	☐
4. I scream and yell a lot.	☐	☐	☐	☐
5. I insist on telling everyone else how to do things.	☐	☐	☐	☐
6. I feel better by making others feel upset.	☐	☐	☐	☐
7. I enjoy getting into arguments.	☐	☐	☐	☐
8. I love getting attention.	☐	☐	☐	☐

B Choose the correct answers according to the information in the video.

1. The worst thing about difficult people is that _____.

   a. you run into them so often   b. they can make life miserable   c. you may find them at work

2. You can learn to _____ to change the behavior of difficult people.

   a. give rewards   b. stop rewards   c. get rewards

3. People are difficult because they want to _____.

   a. get rewards   b. stop your reward   c. make you get emotional

4. The main point of the two-step process is to change _____.

   a. the reward   b. how you interact with the person   c. difficult behavior into rewards

5. An example of a reward for a Bully is _____ .

    a. getting you to leave the room   b. stopping an argument   c. winning an argument

6. Some people throw tantrums as a way to get _____ .

    a. everyone to focus on them   b. someone to stop talking   c. others in trouble

7. _____ difficult people is the best way to deal with them.

    a. Talking to   b. Avoiding interaction with   c. Using a two-step approach with

8. The two-step process will work with _____ .

    a. only Bullies and Exploders   b. only Mr. or Ms. Negatives   c. all difficult people

C Write the steps in the two-step process for dealing with difficult people. Then check your answers with a partner.

1. _____

2. _____

After you watch

A Pair work Discuss how you would use the two-step process to deal with these personality types. Then tell the class about your ideas.

The Know-It-All

Step 1: _____

Step 2: _____

Mr. or Ms. Negative

Step 1: _____

Step 2: _____

B Pair work Read the descriptions and choose a role. Take a few minutes to prepare some ideas. Then take turns role-playing the employee and the employer.

Role 1 – Employee

You have worked for a long time at a car rental company and are aware of many problems with the cars and the customers. Today you have a meeting to fill in your new boss about how things are running at the company. Act the part as Mr. or Ms. Negative, the Bully, the Exploder, or the Know-It-All.

Role 2 – Employer

You are the manager of a car rental company. You have not worked there for long, so you are having interviews with your employees. You want to get a report about how things in the company are, but the person has a difficult personality. How do you deal with him or her?

C Group work Discuss how the role play would be different if the employer were the difficult person. What would change? Would you use the two-step process differently? If so, how?

Before you watch

A Pair work Think about times when you had these experiences. Tell your partner what happened.

1. You did something by accident that turned out to be lucky.
2. You suspected something that turned out to be correct.
3. You experimented with something new.
4. You noticed something unusual that could be useful.

A: I was late for work last week because I forgot to set my alarm.

B: How did that turn out to be lucky?

A: Well, I missed a big traffic accident because I was late!

B Group work Which actions do you think accidentally resulted in these inventions? Write the letter of the invention next to the correct action. Discuss and explain your answers.

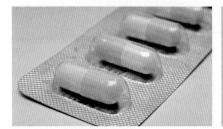  

a. a powerful medical treatment

b. a common household appliance

c. a special material for attaching things

1. taking a dog for a walk ____
2. forgetting to wash the dishes ____
3. bringing a snack to work ____

While you watch

A Write the letter of the correct word or phrase to complete each sentence. Were your answers in *Before you watch* part B correct?

a. the microwave	c. a magnetron	e. penicillin
b. hooks and loops	d. mold	f. Velcro

1. ____ was discovered in 1928.
   It started as ____ on some unwashed dishes.
2. In 1945, Percy Spencer was working with something called ____.
   It melted his chocolate and led to the creation of ____.
3. George de Mestral identified that burrs work by using ____.
   He had to try lots of prototypes to finally invent ____.

B Choose the correct answers according to the information in the video.

1. Alexander Fleming was _____ to help humans.

    a. studying bacteria   b. culturing molds   c. mixing powerful drugs

2. Because Fleming _____ , he noticed something interesting.

    a. was away on vacation   b. paid attention to an unusual change   c. was positive he could find a wonder drug

3. Percy Spencer was standing next to the machine that melted the chocolate because he

    _____ .

    a. wanted to make a snack   b. figured he could blow up eggs   c. was working with military radar technology

4. Spencer's idea of containing his invention in a box was _____ .

    a. suggested by his co-workers   b. the result of making a mess   c. done to make its effects stronger

5. While removing burrs, George de Mestral was _____ .

    a. thinking about making new hunting clothes   b. curious about what made them stick   c. looking for a solution to his dog's problem

6. George de Mestral was confident his invention would be _____ .

    a. very useful for astronauts   b. used as a prototype   c. very popular

C Take notes to answer the questions in your own words. Then compare answers with a partner.

1. What are two events that caused penicillin to be discovered?

    _____

    _____

2. What are two events that caused the microwave to be developed?

    _____

    _____

3. What are two events that caused Velcro to be invented?

    _____

    _____

After you watch

A Pair work Discuss these questions. Then share your ideas with the class.

1. What chain of decisions or steps led to each accidental discovery in the video?

2. What things could each inventor have done differently that might have changed the outcome?

B Think of an achievement in your life that may have been influenced by an accident. Trace the chain of events that led to it and draw conclusions about what happened.

Example: I learned to swim last year. I took the swimming class because a friend asked me to do it with her. I met her when I joined the gym. I joined the gym to get in shape again after I broke my leg. So if I had never broken my leg, I might not have learned to swim!

C Pair work Share your stories. Then ask and answer questions to get more information. Do you agree with your partner's conclusions? Can you think of any other possible scenarios?

Before you watch

A What do you know about these cities? Choose one box for each question. Then compare your responses with a partner.

Which city . . .	Dubai	Amsterdam	Pittsburgh	Tokyo
1. is a bicycling town?	☐	☐	☐	☐
2. is in the United States?	☐	☐	☐	☐
3. is on the Persian Gulf?	☐	☐	☐	☐
4. has some very small sleeping spaces?	☐	☐	☐	☐
5. is a Dutch tourist town?	☐	☐	☐	☐
6. has the world's tallest building?	☐	☐	☐	☐
7. used to be an industrial city?	☐	☐	☐	☐
8. has the world's largest population?	☐	☐	☐	☐
9. is famous for its canals?	☐	☐	☐	☐
10. has man-made islands?	☐	☐	☐	☐
11. is in Asia?	☐	☐	☐	☐
12. has more bridges than Venice?	☐	☐	☐	☐

B Pair work What is your area known for? Make a list of interesting things in your area. Share your list with the class.

While you watch

A Which cities are they? Write *D* for Dubai, *A* for Amsterdam, *P* for Pittsburgh, or *T* for Tokyo.

1. ____   2. ____   3. ____   4. ____

5. ____   6. ____   7. ____   8. ____

B Watch the video and check your answers to *Before you watch* part A. Were you correct? Did any answers surprise you? Why?

C Choose the correct answers according to the information in the video.

1. The world's tallest building is _____ .
   a. 828 stories high   b. 828 meters high   c. 160 meters high

2. The world-famous Burj al-Arab in Dubai calls itself the world's only _____ .
   a. seven-star hotel   b. indoor ski slope   c. man-made island

3. In Amsterdam, nearly _____ of all travel is done by bicycle.
   a. one quarter   b. half   c. all

4. Traveling _____ can take twice as long as by bicycle in Amsterdam.
   a. by car or bus   b. by train   c. on foot

5. The sparkling city of Pittsburgh is on _____ .
   a. a beachfront   b. a river   c. three rivers

6. The Tokyo metropolitan area has _____ .
   a. around 10 million people   b. about 25 million people   c. over 35 million people

After you watch

A Think about what you learned from the video. Then answer the questions.

Dubai	*Amsterdam*	*Pittsburgh*	*Tokyo*

1. Which city do you think is the greatest? Why?

_____

_____

_____

2. Which city would you most like to visit? Why?

_____

_____

_____

3. Which city would you most like to live in? Why?

_____

_____

_____

B Pair work Compare your opinions from part A. Remember to use words like *despite* and *however* and phrases to agree and disagree.

C Class activity Tell the class about your partner's city preferences.

Before you watch

A Do you do any of these activities 30 to 60 minutes before bedtime? Choose all that apply.

- ☐ watch TV
- ☐ check email
- ☐ play video games
- ☐ text friends
- ☐ surf the Internet
- ☐ study or work on a computer
- ☐ read electronic books
- ☐ catch up on social media
- ☐ videochat with friends or family

B Pair work Compare your answers. Then think about how much time you spend looking at electronic screens before bed. How might this affect your sleep? Discuss your ideas.

While you watch

A According to the video, what does lack of sleep affect negatively? Choose the correct answers.

- ☐ 1. performance on the Internet
- ☐ 2. social media relationships
- ☐ 3. regular sleep schedules
- ☐ 4. weight control
- ☐ 5. blood pressure
- ☐ 6. productivity
- ☐ 7. our "fight-or-flight" response
- ☐ 8. levels of melatonin
- ☐ 9. connections with friends and family

B Choose the statement that best summarizes the main idea presented at these points in the video.

1.
   a. A health consequence of using screens is heart attack.
   b. Looking at electronic screens before bed causes weight problems.
   c. The lack of sleep associated with electronic screens can increase the risk of stroke.

2.
   a. Video games can cause a stress response at night, but texting won't.
   b. A fight-or-flight response makes you dream of video games.
   c. Scientific studies prove that playing video games can cause tossing and turning at night.

3. Melatonin Levels
   a. The brightness of screens can reduce levels of melatonin.
   b. Reducing the light from an electronic screen can increase melatonin production.
   c. Using electronic screens in a dark room won't affect melatonin.

4.
   a. The backlit screen of a phone can be used before bedtime because it is small.
   b. Checking texts or email before bed may make you feel productive.
   c. Checking texts or email before bed can prevent you from relaxing.

C Take notes to answer the questions in your own words. Then compare answers with a partner.

1. What are three types of screen-related activities mentioned in the video?

_____

_____

_____

2. What are two ways electronic screens affect sleep?

_____

_____

_____

3. What are three suggestions to keep screens from affecting our sleep?

_____

_____

_____

After you watch

A Pair work Discuss these questions with a partner.

1. What effects mentioned in the video concern you most?
2. Have you experienced any of those effects? For example, health issues or a fight-or-flight response?
3. Do you think you need to reduce your screen time at night? Why or why not?

B Group work Brainstorm three or more additional suggestions for how to reduce screen time or improve sleep.

_____

_____

_____

C Writing Think of how personal and work screen-use habits negatively affect your sleep or the sleep of someone you know. Write a plan to change those bad habits and improve sleep.

Before you watch

A Select the behaviors that you think are impolite.

☐ asking someone for help with homework or a task

☐ interrupting someone

☐ leaning in closely to talk to someone

☐ making small talk with a stranger

☐ sitting next to someone when empty seats are available

☐ talking loudly on a cell phone in public

☐ telling people exactly what's on your mind

☐ telling someone if they are bothering you

☐ telling someone they are being rude

☐ videotaping someone and not telling them

B **Pair work** Compare your responses. Do you agree on which behaviors you think are impolite? Why or why not? Discuss your answers.

While you watch

A Who says each sentence? Choose the correct answers.

John *Jill* *Ethan* *Andrea*

	John	Jill	Ethan	Andrea
1. "I mean, it's unusual to sit so close to someone in an empty room, right?"	☐	☐	☐	☐
2. ". . . but I never like to be offensive, you know?"	☐	☐	☐	☐
3. "Then he got a phone call and explained to his mom that he had been to the doctor . . ."	☐	☐	☐	☐
4. "He warned me that it might be contagious."	☐	☐	☐	☐
5. ". . . you know, it's customary to take calls outside the library, right?"	☐	☐	☐	☐
6. "I think it's a good idea to say exactly what's on your mind."	☐	☐	☐	☐
7. "Is something wrong with you?"	☐	☐	☐	☐
8. "Why should a rude person get to ruin my day?"	☐	☐	☐	☐

B Write the letter of the correct phrase to complete each response.

a. it is bad form	d. it is better to leave than say something
b. it was kind of strange	e. he is planning on sitting there
c. he is invading her personal space	f. he is trying to study

1. What does Jill say about where John sat down? She claims ____ .
2. How does Jill say she usually handles an uncomfortable situation? She explains that ____ .
3. What does Ethan say about sitting right next to somebody? He says ____ .
4. What does Ethan say when John is on the phone? He tells John ____ .
5. What does Andrea say to John when he sits down? She asks if ____ .
6. What does Andrea say when John is too close? She warns him that ____ .

C Write *T* (true) or *F* (false). Then correct the false statements with a partner.

____ 1. The narrator is interviewing people to find out who was rude to John.

____ 2. Jill likes to confront people who are rude.

____ 3. Jill usually leaves uncomfortable situations.

____ 4. Ethan disapproves of John's loud personal phone call in the library.

____ 5. John apologizes to Ethan when he asks him to be quiet.

____ 6. Andrea can't believe it when John asks for help with his history homework.

____ 7. In the end, Andrea decides John isn't rude.

After you watch

A Pair work Which person in the video are you most like: Jill, Ethan, or Andrea? How would you react in each situation? Discuss your ideas.

Jill   *Ethan*   *Andrea*

1. Someone sits next to you when empty chairs are available.
2. Someone talks loudly on a cell phone in a quiet place.
3. Someone invades your personal space.

B Group work What other rude behaviors really bother you? Make a list of the top three annoying behaviors for your group. Then compare your list with the class. What rude behaviors are listed most often?

1. _____

2. _____

3. _____

C Pair work What would you do in each situation you listed in part B? Discuss possible reactions. Then share your ideas with the class.

Before you watch

A What types of stories do you like: science fiction, mysteries, love stories, suspense stories, dramas, comedies, or horror? List your three favorite types of stories. Then give examples of books, movies, or other stories you like.

	Type	Example
1.		
2.		
3.		

B Pair work Compare your answers to part A. Give reasons for your choices.

A: I love dramas, so I really liked the movie *The Great Gatsby*. I also liked it because I like movies based on books and stories set in the past.

B: Really? Not me. I like science fiction and movies set in the future. It's more fun to imagine what things will be like! *The Terminator* is the best movie ever, in my opinion.

While you watch

A Write *T* (true) or *F* (false). Then correct the false statements with a partner.

_____ 1. The video begins by talking about when people started writing stories down.

_____ 2. Larry told his friends a story about the hole so they wouldn't fall into it.

_____ 3. Professor Evans's classes were dull because he only engaged emotions, not the mind.

_____ 4. In the sentences "But lately, people have been telling you stories. And after a time, you have started to make sense of the world," the phrase *but lately* refers to the time when you are older.

_____ 5. The main point of all three stories is to show that humans tell stories to teach their children.

B Choose the correct answers according to the information in the video.

1. Early humans began to write stories down _____.
   a. when they were older and smarter
   b. to tell them over and over
   c. to tell people about their caves

2. The first stories may have been told to _____.
   a. record personal information
   b. entertain others
   c. help people live better

3. Professor Evans started telling stories _____.
   a. then switched to teaching formulas
   b. instead of just teaching formulas
   c. about the theories that scientists must learn

4. Professor Evans succeeded because he _____.
   a. could explain theories well
   b. engaged his students emotionally and intellectually
   c. explained the dangers of blast-offs

5. When humans get older, they _____.

    a. continue to make sense of the world using stories

    b. often read childhood stories again to understand more

    c. tell children stories to learn more about them

6. Humans will always tell stories because _____.

    a. it makes us who we are

    b. we will always need them to survive

    c. we want to find new ways to tell them

C Take notes to answer the questions in your own words. Then compare answers with a partner.

1. What do stories help humans do?

    _____

    _____

    _____

    _____

2. Why are stories the natural way for humans to learn things?

    _____

    _____

    _____

    _____

3. How does telling stories to children help them?

    _____

    _____

    _____

    _____

After you watch

A Pair work Think about the way stories help humans survive, learn, and organize their world. Then think of a story that does each of these things. Explain how you think each story helps people.

1. _____

2. _____

3. _____

B Group work Write or retell a story that helps people survive, learn, or organize their world. Be sure to state the main learning point of the story at the end.

C Class activity Read or retell your group's story to the class but don't read the main point. Can the class say what the main point of the story is?

7 UNAPPRECIATED TECHNOLOGIES

Before you watch

A Match the inventions with the pictures. Then check answers with a partner.

a. refrigerator   c. plumbing   e. barcode   g. credit card
b. zipper   d. shipping container   f. pocket calculator   h. ATM / cash machine

1. ____

2. ____

3. ____

4. ____

5. ____

6. ____

7. ____

8. ____

B Pair work When do you think people started using the inventions in part A? Complete the chart with the names of the inventions. Then compare answers with your partner.

Thousands of years ago	Early 1900s	1950s	1960s and 1970s	1990s

While you watch

A Select the summary that best describes this episode of *Tech Talk*. Then check your answers to *Before you watch* part B.

☐ 1. This episode of *Tech Talk* discusses household inventions that will make our lives easier in the future.

☐ 2. This episode of *Tech Talk* covers inventions that are so common that they aren't always listed as great inventions.

☐ 3. This episode of *Tech Talk* talks about the importance of inventions that people don't know that much about.

☐ 4. This episode of *Tech Talk* explains why email and the Internet were not thought to be important at first.

B Write *T* (true) or *F* (false). Then correct the false statements with a partner.

_____ 1. The inventions covered in this episode of *Tech Talk* are new.

_____ 2. Plumbing was not brought inside the home as soon as it was invented.

_____ 3. Because of shipping containers, products from abroad can be as affordable as local products.

_____ 4. Barcodes make things cheaper for stores because tracking, pricing, and selling are all done faster.

_____ 5. Both hosts of *Tech Talk* agree that the ATM is the most important invention in finance.

_____ 6. According to *Tech Talk*, the Internet is the best invention because it speeded up communication.

C Choose the item or action the video mentions as being improved or replaced by these inventions.

1. refrigerators
   a. shopping for food
   b. eating ice cream
   c. going to the store

2. zippers
   a. hooks and clasps
   b. buttons
   c. ties and laces

3. plumbing
   a. using bottled water
   b. going to a well
   c. carrying buckets

4. shipping containers
   a. loading and unloading boats
   b. cardboard boxes
   c. shipping by truck

5. barcodes
   a. finding products
   b. tracking products
   c. using money

6. pocket calculators
   a. doing homework
   b. doing taxes
   c. counting on your fingers

7. credit cards
   a. writing personal checks
   b. using cash
   c. carrying a handbag

8. ATMs
   a. bank clerks
   b. waiting in lines
   c. making deposits

9. email
   a. writing by hand
   b. time needed to communicate
   c. making phone calls

After you watch

A Think about what you learned from the video. Then answer the questions.

1. Which invention from *Tech Talk* do you think is the greatest? Why?

_____

_____

2. Which invention from *Tech Talk* do you think is the least important? Why?

_____

_____

3. Which invention from *Tech Talk* do you think is the most unappreciated by a majority of people? Why?

_____

_____

B **Pair work** Compare your answers from part A. Give reasons and examples to support your opinions.

C **Group work** Create a list of the top five most important inventions or technologies *not* mentioned in *Tech Talk*. Talk about how life has been changed or improved by each invention to support your choices.

8 PROFILE OF AN ACTOR

Before you watch

A In your opinion, which are the most important traits an actor needs? Choose the top 10 traits from the list.

☐ adventurous   ☐ expressive   ☐ organized

☐ creative   ☐ good-looking   ☐ passionate

☐ curious   ☐ innovative   ☐ patient

☐ determined   ☐ lucky   ☐ physically fit

☐ enjoys attention   ☐ motivated   ☐ a strong voice

B Pair work Compare your answers. For each trait, discuss why or why not an actor would need that trait.

While you watch

A Choose the topics the actor mentions in the video.

☐ 1. when he first knew he wanted to be an actor

☐ 2. what working as a child actor is like

☐ 3. what the schedule of an actor is like

☐ 4. how to deal with the audition process

☐ 5. how to handle tough competition

☐ 6. the top school for acting training

☐ 7. which kinds of acting work pay better

☐ 8. his least favorite acting job

☐ 9. the best costume he ever wore

☐ 10. his favorite acting job

☐ 11. what is best about being an actor

☐ 12. traits that an actor should have

☐ 13. how long an actor's career usually is

☐ 14. how many fans he has

B Complete the sentences with the correct words from the video.

1. "I needed an outlet . . . to have . . . to put out my _____ side."

2. "To become an actor, you have to have _____ for the work."

3. "You have to be really _____ to get yourself up . . . every day, to get out there every day, and . . . give it your all."

4. "To be an actor . . . you have to have a strong sense of _____ and a lot of _____."

5. "Someone who has a lot of _____ would be a good actor."

6. "Someone who has a really _____ would be a great actor."

7. "Someone who enjoys _____ would be a great actor."

C Choose the correct answers according to the information in the video.

1. The actor decided what he wanted to do for the rest of his life while performing
   _____ .
   a. at an amusement park   b. for the Cub Scouts   c. at the Boston Common

2. The real work of acting is _____ .
   a. dealing with auditions   b. performing in theaters   c. staying motivated

3. Because it pays more, _____ is a better way to support an acting career.
   a. theater work   b. film work   c. amusement park work

4. The actor really enjoyed a job where he _____ .
   a. was a comedian in Boston   b. did a Shakespeare play   c. worked on a big film

5. Patience is required to be an actor because _____ .
   a. it's a hard lifestyle   b. it takes a long time to develop job security   c. it takes a while before it is fun

6. The actor thinks he will always be an actor because he _____ .
   a. feels he is determined and passionate   b. wants to show his family he can be successful   c. can't see himself doing anything else

After you watch

A Pair work Discuss the questions.

1. Which of the traits from *Before you watch* part A does the actor in the video seem to have? Support and explain your answers.

2. Could you or someone you know be an actor? Think about the traits mentioned in the video and discuss why you feel this way.

B Other types of jobs might require different skills and traits. List five traits and the kinds of jobs in which they would be an advantage.

	Trait	Possible jobs
1.		
2.		
3.		
4.		
5.		

C Writing Choose a job you listed in part B. Write a paragraph about the job and include at least three additional traits that would make someone good at it. Explain why each trait would be necessary for the job.

Before you watch

A Select the qualities you think most employers are looking for when interviewing people for jobs.

☐ adaptable   ☐ has a sense of humor   ☐ thinks outside the box

☐ emotional   ☐ persistent   ☐ ultracompetitive

☐ fits in with others   ☐ playful   ☐ unconventional

B Pair work Compare your answers. Do you agree on what qualities most employers are looking for? Why or why not? Discuss your opinions.

While you watch

A Write *M* for Monica, *D* for David, or *A* for Ashley.

Monica

David

Ashley

1. Who saw the box as a platform? ____
2. Who worked on the same idea for nearly the entire five minutes? ____
3. Who tried to melt wax to stick the candle to the wall? ____
4. Who was unable to think of additional approaches due to stress? ____
5. Who playfully tried a bunch of solutions? ____
6. Who tried several approaches but still didn't find a solution? ____

B Write the letter of the correct phrase to complete each sentence according to information in the video.

a. being able to preserve a sense of humor	d. looking for other perspectives
b. fitting in with the company	e. thinking outside the box
c. thinking about the problem in new ways	f. being persistent

1. Before implementing hiring tests, companies used to hire people based on ____ .
2. Except when trying the wrong idea, ____ is a good thing.
3. If people get overly frustrated, they will have difficulty ____ .
4. A good problem-solving strategy is ____ .
5. Studies show an important part of problem solving is ____ .
6. The person who solved the problem did it by ____ .

C Take notes to answer the questions in your own words. Then compare answers with a partner.

1. How did Mark Hernandez's company change how they measure candidates?

_____

_____

2. What does the problem of the matchbook, candle, thumbtacks, and corkboard reveal about each candidate?

Monica: _____

David: _____

Ashley: _____

3. What are the three main points that Mark mentions about problem solving?

_____

_____

_____

After you watch

A Pair work Given what you know about the candidates from how they tried to solve the problem, what kinds of jobs do you think each person would be good at? Why?

Monica: _____

_____

David: _____

_____

Ashley: _____

_____

B Group work Compare your answers from part A. Then work together to decide upon the best job for each candidate. Share your group's answers with the class. Be specific about the job and why it is the best fit for that person.

C Writing How can Monica and David improve their interviewing skills? Write some advice for them about how to better interview for the jobs you chose for part A. Support your ideas with facts, reasons, and examples.

Before you watch

A Label the pictures with the words in the box. Then check your answers with a partner.

ambulance	chalkboard	cicada	wind chimes
angle grinder	chainsaw	crows	vuvuzela horn

1. _____

2. _____

3. _____

4. _____

5. _____

6. _____

7. _____

8. _____

B Pair work Think about the sounds the items in part A make. Which do you think are loud or annoying? Which don't bother you at all? Discuss your opinions.

While you watch

A Cross out the items that you do *not* see or hear for each sound category in the video. More than one item may be crossed out for each.

1. Loud:

   an ambulance siren / drums / a train / a chainsaw

2. Annoying:

   wind chimes / crows / chalk on a board / glass breaking

3. Loud and annoying:

   rock music / cheering / vuvuzela horns / race cars

4. The most annoying:

   nails on a chalkboard / fire trucks / a knife on glass / angle grinders

5. Sounds people say annoy them:

   loud TVs / loud phone conversations / a family member's laugh /

   loud motorcycles / loud music / elevator music /

   cicadas / helicopters / a fork on glass

B Choose the statement that best summarizes the main idea presented at these points in the video.

1.

    a. News reporters often have problems with noise.

    b. People in cities often complain about noise.

    c. There are many loud and annoying sounds in the city.

2.

    a. The World Cup in 2010 was louder than usual.

    b. South African soccer players complained that the fans were too loud.

    c. The horns used by fans at the World Cup were particularly loud and annoying.

3.

    a. Some sounds are annoying but not that loud.

    b. Some types of sounds can actually hurt our hearing.

    c. Certain types of sounds bother the most people.

4.

    a. A baby's cry is one of the most stressful sounds to humans.

    b. Babies cry when they are annoyed by noise.

    c. People begin crying and screaming when stressed at an early age.

C Write the letter of the correct phrase to complete each sentence.

a. elevator music	c. people talking loudly on their cell phones	e. a certain person's laugh
b. the sound of an insect	d. the sound of loud motorcycles	

1. Margaret Allen says she gets irritated by ____ .
2. Something that bugs James Williams is ____ .
3. Henry Snider and his son, Kyle, hate ____ .
4. Graciela Martinez feels sick from ____ .
5. Lisa Manap says what really gets under her skin is ____ .

After you watch

A Think about the sounds in the video. Make a list of the top five most annoying sounds for you. Give reasons for your choices. Then share your list with the class.

B Pair work Make a list of 10 other sounds, actions, or things that may be considered annoying. Rank them in order from *worst* (1) to *not so bad* (10).

C Group work Compare your lists from part B and make a final top 10 list of annoying sounds, actions, or things. Then share the list with the class.

Before you watch

A Which of the following behaviors do you think are typical of people from the United States? Choose all that apply based on your opinion.

☐ tend to be on time

☐ tend to be late

☐ don't express emotion

☐ express emotion openly

☐ value freedom for the individual

☐ prefer to fit in with the group

☐ embrace rebelliousness

☐ respect the elderly

☐ are obedient to family

☐ believe people are equal

☐ think fate is predetermined

☐ believe people make their own fate

B **Pair work** Compare and discuss your answers for part A. Then select six behaviors you both agree are typical of Americans. Share your opinions with the class and give reasons to support your choices.

While you watch

A Choose the six topics discussed in the video.

☐ 1. friendships

☐ 2. time

☐ 3. food

☐ 4. emotions

☐ 5. individuality

☐ 6. families/groups

☐ 7. customs

☐ 8. equality

☐ 9. jobs

☐ 10. rewards from hard work

B Who says each sentence? Write *O* for Olivia, *H* for Hikaru, *R* for Ranbir, or *E* for Enku.

Olivia, the U.S.   *Hikaru, Japan*   *Ranbir, India*   *Enku, Ethiopia*

_____ 1. "Americans would think it disrespectful to be late unless they have a very good reason."

_____ 2. "I often wish I could express my emotions with more freedom."

_____ 3. "I wish I had a dollar for every time Americans talked about freedom!"

_____ 4. "But then I realized: It's not about the freedom to do illegal things, but the freedom to be an individual."

_____ 5. "It's more about the family than the individual."

_____ 6. "But it's more about the group – fitting in with people at work, for example."

_____ 7. "If we had been better about it from the beginning, I think we could have avoided a lot of war and violence."

_____ 8. "I can't imagine not choosing the life I want to lead."

C Choose the correct answers according to the information in the video.

1. If you were in _____ , you might not worry about being late.
   a. Japan　　　　　　　　　　b. the U.S.　　　　　　　　　c. Ethiopia

2. As an American, you might think of someone who is late as _____ .
   a. insensitive　　　　　　　b. respectful　　　　　　　　c. important

3. In _____ , you would never yell at someone in public, even if you were very angry.
   a. Japan　　　　　　　　　　b. India　　　　　　　　　　c. Ethiopia

4. A young woman in _____ would do what her family wants.
   a. the U.S.　　　　　　　　b. India　　　　　　　　　　c. Ethiopia

5. Not everyone believes they can change their fate in _____ .
   a. Olivia's family　　　　　b. the U.S.　　　　　　　　　c. Ethiopia

6. A very uniquely American idea is that if you _____ .
   a. work hard, you can achieve whatever you want
   b. are born into a certain lot in life, you can't change it
   c. follow the path your parents choose, you will succeed

After you watch

A Make a list of the behaviors in *Before you watch* part A that are true about people in your culture.

B **Pair work** Compare your choices for part A and review the behaviors again. Which behaviors from part A do you agree are OK or normal in most cultures? Which are disrespectful in most cultures? Which depend on the culture a person is from? Complete the chart.

Acceptable	Disrespectful	Culturally dependent

C **Group work** Make lists of behaviors you think are generally acceptable or not acceptable in most cultures. Include at least three or four behaviors for each category. Present your lists to the class.

Generally acceptable	Generally not acceptable

Before you watch

A Imagine you are going to study in Germany for a year. Which five things would you have the most difficulty with? Number your choices from 1 (most difficult) to 5 (least difficult).

____ learning about a new city	____ learning a new language	____ different weather
____ getting around in a foreign country	____ homesickness	____ different food
____ taking classes in another language	____ making friends	____ different cultural ideas

B Pair work Compare your answers. How similar are your views? Discuss your choices and give reasons for your answers.

A: I think I'd have a difficult time eating different foods. I'm a picky eater.

B: Not me! I love to try new foods. I'll eat anything. But I can't stand being cold. I might have a hard time if the weather is cold.

While you watch

A Choose the statement that best summarizes the main idea presented at these points in the video.

1.

   a. Monica's classes are held in these old buildings.

   b. Monica has just arrived and she is excited.

   c. Monica feels Germany is very different from L.A.

2.

   a. Monica is excited to practice speaking with Germans.

   b. She enjoys relaxing with friends in her room every night.

   c. She has made new friends.

3.

   a. Monica cannot wait to go home for the winter holidays.

   b. She is enjoying her first cold weather and snow.

   c. Due to the weather, she finally had to figure out the trains.

4.

   a. Monica is sad to leave Berlin because she has met someone.

   b. She wants to stay another eight months.

   c. She likes the food and now feels more at home in Germany.

B Number the sentences from 1 to 7 in the order the topics are mentioned in the video.

_____ Monica hopes that before she goes home, she'll have figured out the trains.

_____ She is going to a holiday feast.

_____ She thinks that before the year ends she will have become fluent.

_____ She is surprised by how much she likes the food.

_____ She is afraid that by the end of the year she will have only gotten to know her room.

_____ She is beginning to feel connected to others, such as Julia and Annika.

_____ She wouldn't have discovered her favorite spot in the city if she hadn't gotten lost.

C Take notes to answer the questions in your own words. Then compare answers with a partner.

1. Why is Monica scared in October?

_____

_____

2. What is the most difficult thing about December for her?

_____

_____

3. Why is April 16 an important day for Monica?

_____

_____

After you watch

A **Pair work** Discuss how Monica's attitude and experiences changed over the eight months she was abroad. What conclusions might one draw from this?

B **Group work** Compare your conclusions from part A with another pair. Discuss how they are the same or different.

C **Writing** Write a paragraph explaining how you feel about new and challenging experiences, such as studying abroad. Are these types of experiences fun, exciting, challenging, or frustrating for you? How do you handle these types of situations?

Video Activity Worksheets Credits

Video credits

Video screen grabs courtesy of Steadman Productions, Boston, MA: 200, 201, 206, 207, 208, 209, 211 (*top, center top*), 212, 213, 214, 215

Photography credits

192 (*left to right*) ©motion.pi/Shutterstock, Inc., ©Johan Larson/Shutterstock, Inc., ©Pressmaster/Shutterstock, Inc., ©Alexander Kirch/Shutterstock, Inc; **193** (*clockwise*) ©Johan Larson/Shutterstock Inc., ©motion.pi/Shutterstock Inc., ©Alexander Kirch/Shutterstock, Inc., ©Pressmaster/Shutterstock, Inc.; **194** (*top left to right*) ©Denis Dryashkin/Shutterstock, ©maggee/Shutterstock, ©Video supplied by Oxford Scientific/Getty Images; **195** ©wavebreakmedia/Shutterstock, Inc.; **196** (*top left to right*) ©Tidepool Stock/Shutterstock Inc., ©picture.uk/Shutterstock Inc., ©Gavin Hellier/Shutterstock Inc., ©OrlowskiDesigns/Shutterstock Inc., (*bottom left to right*) ©OrlowskiDesigns/Shutterstock Inc., ©dubassy/Shutterstock Inc., ©Holger Mette/Shutterstock Inc., ©Geoff Tompkinson/Getty Images; **197** (*left to right*) ©Hellier/Shutterstock Inc., ©Tidepool Stock/Shutterstock Inc., ©FootageFirm Inc., ©skyearth/Shutterstock Inc.; **198** (*top to bottom*) ©Neustock Media/Shutterstock Inc., ©footagefirst/Shutterstock Inc., ©wavebreakmedia/ Shutterstock, Inc., ©freeonestock/Shutterstock Inc.; **199** ©motion.pl/Shutterstock, Inc.; **203** (*center, bottom*) ©ReeldealHD/Shutterstock Inc., ©Dualstock/ Shutterstock, Inc.; **204** (*top left to right*) ©Wiktoria Pawlak/Shutterstock, ©Pixel Embargo/Shutterstock, ©Illin Sergey/Shutterstock, ©qingqing/Shutterstock; (*bottom left to right*) ©MJTH/Shutterstock, ©Todd Taulman/Shutterstock, ©cretolamna/Shutterstock, ©gualtiero boffi/Shutterstock; **210** (*top left to right*) ©Francois Arseneault/Shutterstock Inc., ©jim Barber/Shutterstock Inc., ©one_clear_vision/Shutterstock Inc., ©Dr. Michael Gellner/Shutterstock Inc., (*bottom left*) ©eFOOTAGE.com, (*bottom center left*) ©Sky News/Getty Images, (*bottom center right*) ©Alice Day/Shutterstock Inc.; (*bottom right*) ©Smit/Shutterstock Inc.; **211** (*bottom, center bottom*) ©Film Footage courtesy of Shutterstock Inc., ©Derek Thomas/Shutterstock, Inc.

Jack C. Richards & Chuck Sandy

Passages
Third Edition

Workbook 1

CAMBRIDGE
UNIVERSITY PRESS

Contents

Credits

Illustration credits

Kim Johnson: 4, 28, 45, 66, 67
Dan McGeehan: 7, 54
Paul Hostetler: 8, 27, 56, 60, 64
Koren Shadmi: 33, 52, 62
James Yamasaki: 22, 35, 61

Photography credits

1 ©Chris Bennett/Aurora/Getty Images; **3** (*clockwise from top center*) ©Keith Levit/Design Pics/Corbis, ©iStock/Thinkstock, ©Iconica/Commercial Eye/Getty Images; **6** ©Barry Austin Photography/Getty Images; **9** ©iStock/Thinkstock; **10** ©dieKleinert/Alamy; **11** ©Holger Hollemann/dpa/picture-alliance/Newscom; **12** ©Christian Guy/Getty Images; **13** ©iStock/Thinkstock; **14** ©iStock/Thinkstock; **15** ©iStock/Thinkstock; **16** ©John W Banagan/Photographer's Choice/Getty Images; **18** (*top left to right*) ©trekandshoot/Shutterstock, ©iStock/Thinkstock, ©iStock.com/wdstock, ©A. T. Willett/Alamy; (*bottom*) ©Rudolf Balasko/Thinkstock; **20** ©Media Bakery; **23** ©Blue Jean Images/Alamy; **24** ©andresrimaging/iStockphoto; **26** ©Pulp Photography/The Image Bank/Getty Images; **29** ©iStock/Thinkstock; **30** ©Clover/SuperStock; **31** ©Eric Isselee/Shutterstock; **34** ©Elke Meitzel/age fotostock; **36** (*top to bottom*) ©assalave/iStockphoto, ©Antonio Balaguer soler/Thinkstock; **38** ©iStock/Thinkstock; **40** ©Wavebreak Media/Thinkstock; **41** ©iStock.com/DSGpro; **44** (*left to right*) ©Jodi/Jake/Media Bakery, ©Masterfile Royalty Free, ©Andresr/age fotostock; **46** ©Caspar Benson/fstop/Corbis; **47** (*left to right*) ©wavebreakmedia/Shutterstock, ©Juanmonino/E+/Getty Images, ©iStock.com/pressureUA, ©homydesign/Shutterstock; **48** (*top*) Janos Levente/Shutterstock, (*center*) Sofi photo/Shutterstock; **49** ©Masterfile Royalty Free; **50** (*clockwise from top left*) Suprijono Suharjoto/Thinkstock, Blend Images/SuperStock, Jack Hollingsworth/Thinkstock, Jupiterimages/Thinkstock; **53** ©Mitchell Funk/Photographer's Choice/Getty Images; **56** ©Stockbyte/Thinkstock; **59** (*left to right*) ©Enrique Algarra/age fotostock, ©Dan Brownsword/Cultura/Getty Images, ©Masterfile Royalty Free; **63** ©Vicki Reid/E+/Getty Images; **68** ©Iakov Kalinin/Shutterstock; **70** Arvind Balaraman/Thinkstock; **71** (*left to right*) ©Greg Epperson/Shutterstock, ©Image Source/age fotostock; **Back cover:** (*clockwise from top*) ©Leszek Bogdewicz/Shutterstock, ©Wavebreak Media/Thinkstock, ©Blend Images/Alamy, ©limpido/Shutterstock

Text credits

The authors and publishers acknowledge the following sources of copyright material and are grateful for the permissions granted. While every effort has been made, it has not always been possible to identify the sources of all the material used, or to trace all copyright holders. If any omissions are brought to our notice, we will be happy to include the appropriate acknowledgments on reprinting.

48 Adapted from "Everyday Creativity," by Carlin Flora, *Psychology Today,* November 1, 2009. Psychology Today © Copyright 2005, www.Psychologytoday.com; **54** Adapted from "Why We Dream: Real Reasons Revealed," by Rachael Rettner, *LiveScience,* June 27, 2010. Reproduced with permission of LiveScience; **60** Adapted from "The Survival Guide for Dealing with Chronic Complainers," by Guy Winch, PhD, *Psychology Today*, July 15, 2011. Reproduced with permission of Guy Winch, www.guywinch.com; **66** Adapted from "Internet On, Inhibitions Off: Why We Tell All," by Matt Ridley, *The Wall Street Journal,* February 18, 2012. Reproduced with permission of The Wall Street Journal. Copyright © 2012 Dow Jones & Company, Inc. All Rights Reserved Worldwide; **72** Adapted from "International Careers: A World of Opportunity: Battling Culture Shock Starts with Trip to Local Bookstores, Seminars: Advance preparation is critical in adjusting to the challenges of life in a foreign country," by Karen E. Klein, *Los Angeles Times*, September 11, 1995. Copyright © 1995. Los Angeles Times. Reprinted with permission.

1 FRIENDS AND FAMILY

LESSON A ▸ *What kind of person are you?*

 GRAMMAR

Which verbs and expressions can complete the sentences?
Write the correct numbers of the sentences next to the verbs.

1. I _____ spending time outdoors.

2. I _____ to spend time outdoors.

a. __*1*__ am afraid of   g. _____ feel like

b. _____ am into   h. _____ hate

c. _____ avoid   i. _____ insist on

d. _____ can't stand   j. __*1, 2*__ love

e. _____ don't mind   k. _____ prefer

f. _____ enjoy   l. _____ worry about

2 GRAMMAR

Read the conversations and complete the sentences using the gerund or infinitive form of
the verb. If the two forms are possible, write both of them.

1. Ada: Sam isn't happy when he has nothing to do.

   Gary: I know. It really bothers him.

   Sam can't stand _*having nothing to do / to have nothing to do.*_

2. Vic: I hardly ever go to school parties anymore.

   Joon: Me neither. They're not as much fun as they used to be.

   Vic and Joon avoid _____

3. Tina: You visit your parents on the weekends, don't you?

   Leo: Yes, I visit them on Sundays so I can spend the whole day with them.

   Leo prefers _____

4. Tom: Are you going to take an Italian class this summer?

   Ivy: Yes, I am. I love to learn new languages.

   Ivy is into _____

5. Ang: Do you want to go rock climbing with me this weekend?

   Sue: I don't know. Rock climbing sounds dangerous!

   Sue is worried about _____

6. Josh: What sort of volunteer work do you do for the library, Celia?

   Celia: I love to read to kids, so I volunteer as a storyteller on Saturdays.

   Celia enjoys _____

3 GRAMMAR

Write sentences about yourself using the verbs and expressions in the box.
Use the gerund of the verbs in the phrases below.

am afraid of	avoid	don't mind	hate	love
am into	can't stand	enjoy	insist on	prefer

1. go shopping on the weekend

   I love going shopping on the weekend.

2. try different types of food

3. learn new sports or hobbies

4. meet new people

5. work on the weekend

6. clean and organize my room

4 VOCABULARY

A Match the words to make logical sentences.

1. Angelina volunteers at a hospital. She's very __b__.
2. Stan drives too fast and stays out late. He's _____.
3. Anna never gets angry. She's always _____.
4. Don hates a messy room. He likes being _____.
5. Tad avoids speaking out in class. He's _____.
6. Neil loves throwing parties and making his guests feel welcome. He's _____.
7. City life is crazy! In the country, I feel more _____.
8. Julia insists on doing things her way. She's _____.
9. Mei never hides her true feelings. She's always _____.

a. wild and crazy
b. kind and generous
c. shy and reserved
d. friendly and outgoing
e. calm and cool
f. neat and tidy
g. honest and sincere
h. laid-back and relaxed
i. strong and independent

B Use the vocabulary above to write sentences about people you know.

1. *My sister is shy and reserved. She avoids meeting new people.*
2. _____
3. _____
4. _____
5. _____
6. _____

5 WRITING

A Choose the main idea for each paragraph, and write it in the blank below.

My mother loves speaking Chinese.

My mother is very adventurous.

I really admire my mother.

I am not like my mother at all.

1. _____. She enjoys doing unusual things and pushing herself to the limit. Last year, for example, she insisted on visiting China. She enrolled in Chinese language classes, planned her trip, and then took off across China with a friend. She loves exploring new places, and she doesn't hesitate to start conversations with locals wherever she goes.

I have a friend named John.

My friend John and I are in the same class.

My friend John is the kind of person who loves to talk.

My friend John always says what is on his mind.

2. _____. He's probably the most outspoken person I know. Last week after class, for example, he said to our English teacher, "Some of the students are a little confused by this week's class, but I have some ideas to help explain it to them. Do you want to hear my suggestions?" John was saying what he thought, and luckily our teacher was willing to listen to him.

B Complete these two sentences. Then choose one of them, and write a paragraph to support it.

1. My friend _____ is the kind of person who _____

   _____

2. _____ is the most _____ person I know.

   _____

   _____

   _____

   _____

   _____

1 GRAMMAR

Read the blog entry. Then underline the noun clauses.

May 15, 2014

I love my family so much, and I really get along with everyone – my parents and my four brothers and sisters. However, sometimes they drive me crazy. There are both good and bad things about coming from a large family. One of the best things about coming from a large family is <u>that I always have someone to talk to.</u> Unfortunately, one of the disadvantages is that I never have any privacy. And of course, the trouble with not having any privacy is that I never have any space I can call my own. Our house is big, but sometimes not big enough!

2 GRAMMAR

Combine each pair of sentences into one sentence using noun clauses.

1. I'm the youngest in my family. The best thing is I'm the center of attention.

   The best thing about being the youngest is that I'm the center of attention.

2. I have a lot of kids. The disadvantage is I can't give each of them the individual attention they want.

   _____

   _____

3. I live with my father-in-law. The problem is we disagree about everything.

   _____

   _____

4. I have two younger sisters. The worst thing is they always want to know all about my personal life.

   _____

   _____

5. I have an identical twin. The trouble is no one can ever tell us apart.

   _____

   _____

3 GRAMMAR

Use noun clauses and your own ideas to complete these sentences.

1. A disadvantage of having siblings who are successful is *that my parents expect me to be successful, too.*

2. The problem with having a large family is _____

3. The best thing about having grandparents is _____

4. The trouble with being part of a two-income family is _____

5. One benefit of living far away from your family is _____

6. The worst thing about taking a family vacation is _____

7. An advantage of living with siblings is _____

4 VOCABULARY

Are the statements true or false? Choose the correct answer.

	True	False
Sylvia's mother has a great-uncle named Martin.		
1. Sylvia is Martin's great-granddaughter.	☐	☑
2. Sylvia's mother is Martin's grandniece.	☐	☐
Hal's wife, Nikki, has a sister named Joanne.		
3. Joanne is Hal's sister-in-law.	☐	☐
4. Joanne is Hal's grandmother.	☐	☐
Hugo's niece Diana has a son-in-law named Jason.		
5. Jason's wife is Hugo's granddaughter.	☐	☐
6. Diana is Jason's mother-in-law.	☐	☐
Molly's nephew Tom has a daughter named Jennifer.		
7. Molly is Tom's aunt.	☐	☐
8. Molly is Jennifer's great-aunt.	☐	☐
Irene's father, Roberto, has a grandfather named Eduardo.		
9. Eduardo is Roberto's grandson.	☐	☐
10. Eduardo is Irene's great-grandfather.	☐	☐

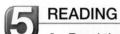

A Read the article. Then choose the main idea of each paragraph.

Is it Better or Worse to Be an Only Child?

If you are an only child – someone with no brothers or sisters – you have probably been the object of both sympathy and suspicion. "Oh, you poor thing!" some people say. "You must have been so lonely!" Other people might not say much, but you know they are thinking that you are selfish, spoiled, and have no idea how to get along with others. People assume that only children are somehow at a disadvantage because of their lack of siblings, and this idea has probably been around as long as only children have.

Recent studies, however, have shown that the stereotype of the only child is really just a myth. Only children show very little difference from children with siblings, and as adults they are just as likely to be well adjusted. One slight difference they show from children with multiple siblings is that they often score higher on intelligence and achievement tests. But first-born children and those with only one sibling have similar results, so we can't really say this is a characteristic of the only child, either. The one undeniable difference is that only children get more of their parents' time and

attention for the simple reason that there are fewer demands on the parents. The same goes for educational opportunities – there tend to be more resources available in single-child households. However, there is little evidence that this has long-term benefits for only children.

For some reason, though, popular opinion and culture seem to have a hard time accepting the fact that only children are just like everyone else. Movies and TV shows still portray "onlies" as socially awkward and expecting to get whatever they ask for. What keeps the stereotype alive? Could it be that most of us have wished – at one point or another – to be an only child? At least we wouldn't have had to deal with siblings playing with our toys, borrowing our clothes, and eating that last piece of cake we had saved for later.

1. First paragraph:
   ☐ a. Only children all wish they had siblings.
   ☐ b. Only children think other children are selfish.
   ☐ c. Many people make assumptions about only children.

2. Second paragraph:
   ☐ a. Only children really are different from children with siblings.
   ☐ b. Only children are basically the same as those with siblings.
   ☐ c. No one has really studied only children.

3. Third paragraph:
   ☐ a. The popular view of only children seems difficult to change.
   ☐ b. The popular view of only children has changed recently.
   ☐ c. The popular view of only children is based on facts.

B Are the statements true or false? Choose the correct answer. Then rewrite the false statements to make them true.

	True	False
1. Some people feel sorry for only children.	☐	☐
2. When only children grow up, they are less sociable than children with siblings.	☐	☐
3. Only children are more intelligent than children with siblings.	☐	☐
4. According to the author, people's ideas about only children need to change.	☐	☐

2 MISTAKES AND MYSTERIES

LESSON A ► Life lessons

1 VOCABULARY

Correct the underlined mistakes in each sentence. Write the correct form of a verb from the box after each sentence. Sometimes more than one answer is possible.

aggravate	avoid	cause	deal with	identify	ignore	run into	solve

1. Jim said I <u>solved</u> the problem with my tablet when I spilled water on it.
   _____caused_____

2. Grace didn't pay her credit card bill last month. When she didn't pay it again this month, she only <u>ran into</u> her debt problem. _____

3. I always ask Kate for help with math. She can <u>ignore</u> any problem.
   _____

4. Tim's report was late. He <u>aggravated</u> problems with his computer that he didn't expect. _____

5. John <u>caused</u> his weight problem for years. Now he can't fit into any of his clothes! _____

6. Mike has many problems with his projects at work, so he often stays late to <u>identify</u> them. _____

7. My brother is an amazing auto mechanic. He can look at a car's engine and <u>ignore</u> what is causing problems. _____

8. Pedro <u>identifies</u> problems with computer viruses by updating his antivirus software every week. _____

2 GRAMMAR

Choose the past modal or phrasal modal of obligation that best completes each sentence.

1. I *wasn't supposed to* /⟨*had to*⟩give Mr. Lee my phone when he caught me texting in class.

2. Eve was worried that she *needed to* / *didn't have to* pass her exam to graduate.

3. Frank *didn't have to* / *was supposed to* take his grandmother to the store, but he wanted to.

4. I *needed to buy* / *shouldn't have bought* these boots, but they were on sale!

5. Bob *was supposed to* / *didn't need to* bring dessert to the party, but he brought an appetizer instead.

6. I *didn't need to* / *was supposed to* clean my apartment before my friend arrived, but I didn't have time.

3 GRAMMAR

Complete the email with the past modals and phrasal modals of obligation in the box. Use each modal only once.

didn't have to	had to	needed to	should have	shouldn't have	was supposed to

New Message

Hey Ally,

I (1) **_was supposed to_** pick up my brother at practice yesterday, but I forgot. Well, I didn't forget . . . I went to the café instead.

I (2) _____ go, but I wanted to see you guys.

I (3) _____ thought about my brother, but I didn't. When my mom discovered that my brother (4) _____ walk home alone, she got upset with me. She said I (5) _____ forgotten about my brother. So now she doesn't trust me. She said I (6) _____ think about my responsibilities and behave more responsibly to regain her trust. Anyway, this means I won't be able to go on the trip with you guys this weekend. I'm so frustrated!

Gigi

4 GRAMMAR

Use past modals and phrasal modals of obligation to write a sentence for each situation.

1. make a left turn instead of a right turn
I should have made a left turn
instead of a right turn.

2. hand in a research paper today
_____
_____

3. pick up a friend from the airport
_____
_____

4. not eat a big lunch
_____
_____

WRITING

A Look at the brainstorming notes and add two more ideas to each category.

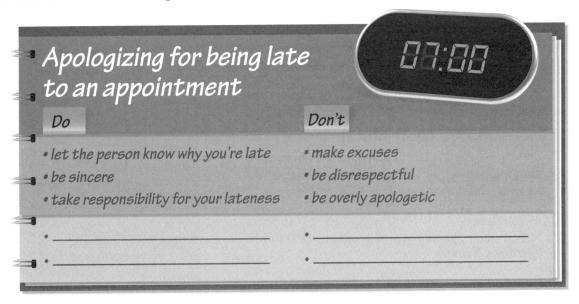

Apologizing for being late to an appointment

07:00

Do	Don't
• let the person know why you're late	• make excuses
• be sincere	• be disrespectful
• take responsibility for your lateness	• be overly apologetic
• _____	• _____
• _____	• _____

B Complete the sentences with ideas from your brainstorming notes.

1. You need to _____ when you apologize.
2. You shouldn't _____ when you apologize.

C Choose one of the sentences you completed above and brainstorm supporting ideas for its topic. Then write a paragraph based on your brainstorming notes.

You shouldn't make excuses when you apologize. You have to simply say you are sorry. For example, if you are late for an appointment, you should never say you were confused about the meeting time. Next, you shouldn't say your directions were bad. In addition, you shouldn't blame public transportation for your lateness. . . .

_____

_____

_____

_____

_____

_____

_____

_____

_____

_____

_____

1 GRAMMAR

Underline the modals in the sentences. Then write *C* for modals expressing degrees of certainty or *O* for modals expressing obligation, advice, or opinion.

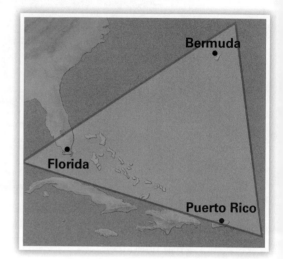

_**C**_ 1. Some people are certain the boats and airplanes that have disappeared in the Bermuda Triangle <u>must have</u> vanished due to human error.

_____ 2. Others believe the boats and airplanes that disappeared in the Bermuda Triangle could have been affected by supernatural forces.

_____ 3. The people who vanished should have planned their route more carefully to avoid entering the Bermuda Triangle.

_____ 4. Experts say the people who got lost in the Bermuda Triangle must not have been prepared for strong water currents and changing weather patterns.

_____ 5. While many people have successfully navigated through the Bermuda Triangle, there are others who shouldn't have tried, as they are now missing.

2 GRAMMAR

Choose the phrase that best completes each sentence.

THE **BLOG** SPACE

August 31

I just watched a documentary about the princess who died in a mysterious car accident. It was so interesting – everyone (1) (*should watch*) / *should have been watching* it. The princess was too young and smart to die in such an awful accident. Many people feel that she (2) *shouldn't have gone* / *may not have been going* in the car that night. Anyway, the documentary said there are many theories about how the car accident happened. Some people think the car's brakes (3) *might have been tampered* / *should have tampered* with. Others believe that the princess's driver (4) *should have caused* / *could have caused* the accident. Some even think the princess (5) *could have been kidnapped* / *could have kidnapped*. The police never figured out what really happened. I'm not sure what to believe, but there (6) *shouldn't have been* / *must have been* a way to solve this mystery!

Comments (4)

GRAMMAR

Use modals expressing degrees of certainty and your own ideas to write about
the following situations.

1. Your friend got the highest grade on a difficult English exam.

   He must have studied really hard. It's also possible the test may have been too easy.

   _____

2. You don't hear from your best friend for several days.

   _____

   _____

3. Your favorite jacket isn't in your closet.

   _____

   _____

4. You see some very large footprints while walking in the park.

   _____

   _____

VOCABULARY

Use the verbs of belief in the box to write a sentence about each topic.

assume	be sure	figure	know for a fact
be certain	bet	guess	suppose
be positive	doubt	have a hunch	suspect

1. Elephants are the world's smartest animals.

   I am sure that elephants are the world's

   smartest animals.

2. There is a monster that lives in Loch Ness in Scotland.

   _____

   _____

3. Global warming is causing changes in worldwide weather patterns.

   _____

4. People eat bananas more than any other fruit in the world.

   _____

5. Some pyramids were built more than 2,000 years ago.

   _____

6. Dinosaurs were wiped out by an asteroid that caused changes in the climate.

   _____

5 READING

A Read the article quickly to find the answers to the questions.

1. When did the British couple go on vacation? _____

2. Who gave the couple directions to Spain? _____

Hotel Time Warp

The idea of traveling backward or forward through time has long been a favorite subject of books, movies, and TV shows. Although some scientists suspect that it may actually be possible, no one has invented a way to make it happen. However, many people have reported traveling in time.

One famous story is about a British couple who were vacationing in France in 1979. They were looking for a place to stay for the night and noticed a sign for an old circus. They found a hotel nearby and discovered that almost everything inside the hotel was made of heavy wood and there were no modern conveniences such as telephones or TVs. Furthermore, their room doors did not have locks, and the windows had wooden shutters instead of glass. In the morning, two police officers entered the hotel wearing old-fashioned uniforms with capes. After getting confusing directions from the officers to Spain, the couple paid their amazingly inexpensive hotel bill and left.

Two weeks later, the couple returned to France and decided to stay at the odd, but very cheap, hotel again. This time, however, the hotel was nowhere to be found. Positive that they were in the exact same spot because of the circus posters, the couple realized that the hotel had completely vanished. Even more confusing, they found that the photographs they had taken inside the hotel did not develop. Later, their research uncovered that the French officers had been wearing uniforms dating from before 1905.

Researchers analyzing these events call them "time slips" and believe that they must happen randomly and spontaneously. However, researchers cannot explain why, when, or how they occur. But when they do occur, people are so bewildered and confused that they can barely explain what happened to them, even though they are sure they have experienced some sort of time travel.

B Read the article again. Choose the statements you think the author would agree with.

☐ 1. Time travel is not a favorite subject of books, movies, and television shows.

☐ 2. Few people have reported traveling through time.

☐ 3. Scientists have invented a way to make time travel happen.

☐ 4. People who experience time slips do not remember the experience afterwards.

☐ 5. It is not known why, when, or how time slips occur.

☐ 6. Many people believe they have traveled through time.

3 EXPLORING NEW CITIES

LESSON **A** ▶ *Popular destinations*

 GRAMMAR

Underline the relative clauses in the postcard. Then add commas where necessary.

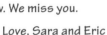

July 15

Dear Mom and Dad,

Greetings from Maine where the water is too cold for us to go swimming, but the scenery is beautiful. We're having a great time, and we've enjoyed every place that we've visited. This week we're in Bar Harbor which is a lovely island town. The place is absolutely full of tourists! Tonight we're going for a ride on a boat that will take us to one of the nearby islands. Our friend James who lives here has already taken us hiking and to the Bar Harbor Music Festival. It's been fun! That's it for now. We miss you.

Love, Sara and Eric

 GRAMMAR

Join the following sentences using non-defining relative clauses.

1. Many tourists enjoy seeing the Kuala Lumpur skyline in Malaysia. It includes some of the tallest skyscrapers in the world.

   Many tourists enjoy seeing the Kuala Lumpur skyline in Malaysia,

   which includes some of the tallest skyscrapers in the world.

2. People visit Washington, D.C., in the spring. They can see the cherry trees in bloom then.

   _____

   _____

3. The cherry trees in Washington, D.C., were a gift from the Japanese government to the U.S. They are admired by everyone.

   _____

   _____

4. Thousands of years ago, people in Mexico began to grow corn. Corn continues to be a very important food in Mexico today.

   _____

   _____

5. The tortilla is typically eaten in Mexico. It is a thin, flat bread.

   _____

VOCABULARY

Choose the correct words to complete the sentences.

1. When preparing to host the 2012 Olympics, London updated its *hotels /
   climate /* (*transportation system*) with improvements to its subway.

2. New York City has hundreds of restaurants offering a wide variety of
   climates / cuisines / green spaces, including Italian, Chinese, and Indian.

3. Many people are moving from bigger cities to smaller towns because
   the *cost of living / landmark / climate* is more affordable.

4. If you enjoy *neighborhoods / shopping / nightlife*, you'll love the music
   and live shows in Rio de Janeiro.

5. Some people think Reykjavik, Iceland, is cold in the wintertime, but
   surprisingly, it has a very mild *climate / cuisine / transportation system*
   during the winter months.

6. Some famous *green spaces / neighborhoods / landmarks* in Paris
   include the Eiffel Tower and the Louvre Museum.

7. Many cities are preserving *green spaces / hotels / cuisines* in their
   downtown areas for people to have picnics, walk their dogs, and
   enjoy outdoor concerts.

GRAMMAR

Use defining or non-defining relative clauses to write sentences about these topics.

- a popular tourist activity in your city
- a town with many historical attractions
- a place with a good climate
- an excellent city for shopping

1. *Tourists in Rome like to visit the famous*
   squares, which have many beautiful
   statues and fountains.
   _____

2. _____
   _____
   _____
   _____

3. _____
   _____

4. _____
   _____

WRITING

A Look at the words and phrases in the box about Chiang Mai, Thailand. Choose the main idea and write it in the center of the mind map. Then write the supporting details in the mind map.

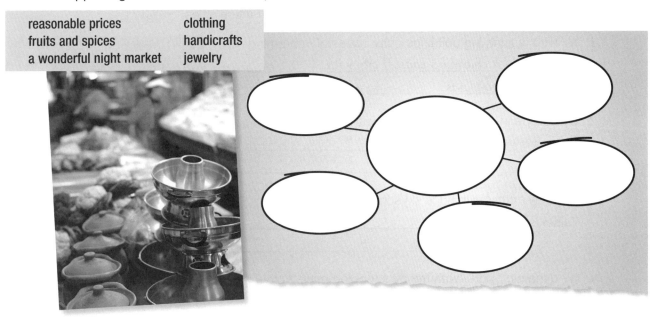

reasonable prices
fruits and spices
a wonderful night market

clothing
handicrafts
jewelry

B Now read the paragraph about Chiang Mai. Answer the questions.

Chiang Mai is a city in northern Thailand that has a wonderful night market. In the evening, the main street is lined with small stands and shops that sell almost anything you can imagine. Some stands sell jewelry or clothing, others sell traditional Thai handicrafts, and still others sell fresh fruit and spices. I love spicy Thai food. It's easy to spend an entire evening just looking at everything. If you decide to buy something, you won't be disappointed. The prices are very reasonable. There are a lot of wonderful attractions in Chiang Mai, but the night market is a favorite for many people.

1. What is this paragraph about? _____

2. What is the topic sentence of the paragraph? _____
   _____

3. Which sentence does not support the main idea? Cross it out.

C Write a paragraph about one of the places you mentioned in Exercise 4 on page 14. Include a topic sentence with the main idea and several supporting ideas.

_____
_____
_____
_____
_____

1 GRAMMAR

Unscramble the words to complete the sentences about these cities.

1. a / with fascinating buildings / city / coastal / charming
   Salvador is _a charming coastal city with_
   fascinating buildings.

2. a / European / city / quaint / old / with a lovely castle
   Prague is _____
   _____

3. a / lively / city / with huge skyscrapers / modern
   Taipei is _____
   _____

4. a / dynamic / port / with trendy shopping malls / city
   Singapore is _____
   _____

5. a / industrial / modern / large / city / with a beautiful lakeshore
   Chicago is _____

6. an / with world-famous theme parks / tourist / exciting / destination
   Orlando is _____

2 VOCABULARY

Choose the word that best completes each sentence.

| border | coastal | college | mountain | port | rural | tourist |

1. Ana lives in a _____rural_____ town. The nearest big city is more than two hours away.

2. The local university employs most of the people living in this _____ town.

3. _____ towns are near an ocean, a lake, or a river where ships unload cargo.

4. People traveling from the U.S. to Mexico through _____ towns must stop and show their passports or other identification.

5. I work in a small _____ town with great beaches and seafood places.

6. We stopped in a crowded _____ town full of overpriced souvenir shops.

7. Nick lives in a _____ town that is nearly 3,000 meters above sea level.

3 GRAMMAR

Rewrite the sentences using the words in parentheses.

1. The streets are well lit, but it's best to be careful at night. (in spite of)
   In spite of the well-lit streets, it's best to be careful at night.

2. There is a crime problem, but it's still a wonderful place to visit. (despite)
   _____

3. The shopping malls are crowded, but people aren't buying much. (although)
   _____

4. It snows a lot, but I still like living here. (even though)
   _____

5. My city is on the ocean, but the water here is too polluted for people to go swimming. (however)
   _____

6. The city center is very picturesque, but there's not much to do. (nevertheless)
   _____

7. There's a lot to do here at night, but it's a very noisy neighborhood. (on the other hand)
   _____

4 GRAMMAR

Complete the sentences with your own opinions about cities you know.

1. The worst thing about ____Los Angeles____ is ____the heavy traffic____.
   In spite of that, _it is an ideal place to live_____.

2. The worst thing about _____ is _____.
   Nevertheless, _____.

3. The best thing about _____ is _____.
   However, _____.

4. Even though _____ has a lot of _____,
   _____.

5. The weather in _____ is _____.
   On the other hand, _____.

6. _____ would be a great place to live. However, _____
   _____.

7. Although _____ is a favorite tourist destination for many, it also has its problems. For example, _____.

A Match the words in the box with the photos. Then read two articles about megacities.

| auto emissions | carpooling | a landfill | public transportation |

1. _carpooling_ 2. _____ 3. _____ 4. _____

MEGACITIES: TWO VIEWS

1 The world's population is not only growing, it is also becoming more urbanized. An increasing number of people are moving to cities in the hope of having a better life. The cities promise steady work and higher salaries. With more money, people think they can provide for their families more easily.

As the population becomes more urbanized, megacities are created. Yes, there are more jobs in urban areas, but is the quality of life better in these megacities? A quick survey of several major cities reveals some of their problems: Pollution from auto emissions is poisoning the air; landfills are overflowing with garbage. With declining resources and growing competition, sometimes there is not enough food. These are all very serious problems.

We cannot get rid of megacities – they are here to stay. What we should concentrate on, however, is building "villages" inside the cities. These "urban villages" could be self-sufficient and grow their own food. The members of these villages would recycle more and do less damage to the environment. The villages would serve the needs of the local people, not big business. We need to limit large-scale development, not encourage it.

2 It's true that megacities have problems, but these have been exaggerated. The truth of the matter is that people move to cities to escape their hard life in the country. Urban areas, even with their problems, offer people a better life than rural areas. The old ways of life in rural areas have broken down, and it is now very difficult to make a living as a farmer.

People live longer in the cities. Medical care is better. And, of course, employment opportunities can be found more easily in the city. We should continue to develop city services so that people can enjoy their lives in the world's urban centers.

Rather than limiting development, we should encourage it. Public transportation systems need to be developed so that people can travel to and from work and school easily. Carpooling should be encouraged to cut down on pollution. The more we clean up and develop our megacities, the more life will improve for the residents.

megacity
a city with a population of 10 million or more

B Match the statements with the articles that support them.

	1	2	1 & 2
1. "Megacities have problems."	☐	☐	☐
2. "Life in rural areas is hard."	☐	☐	☐
3. "We should recreate village life in the cities."	☐	☐	☐
4. "There are more chances to work in the cities."	☐	☐	☐
5. "Continued development will hurt the quality of life."	☐	☐	☐
6. "Continued development can improve the quality of life."	☐	☐	☐

4 EARLY BIRDS AND NIGHT OWLS

LESSON A ► *It's about time!*

1 GRAMMAR

Combine the sentences using the words in parentheses. Use reduced time clauses wherever possible.

1. Classes are over for the day. I often go out with my friends. (after)
   After classes are over for the day, I often go out with my friends.

2. I lost my watch. I've been late for all my appointments. (ever since)
   _____

3. You should relax and count to 10. You start to feel stressed. (as soon as)
   _____

4. I go for a run. I stretch for at least 15 minutes. (right before)
   _____

5. She shouldn't listen to music. She is studying for a big test. (while)
   _____

6. I watch TV. I fall asleep. (until)
   _____

7. I get to the office. I start planning what I need to do that day. (from the moment)
   _____

2 GRAMMAR

Read the statements. Are they true for you? Choose true or false. Then rewrite the false statements to make them true.

	True	False
1. Whenever I get stressed out, I take a walk and try to relax.	☐	☑

   I usually eat a lot of snacks whenever I get stressed out.

| 2. As soon as I wake up, I check my email and phone messages. | ☐ | ☐ |

   _____

| 3. Ever since I started studying English, I've spoken more confidently. | ☐ | ☐ |

   _____

| 4. I like to read the news while I'm eating lunch. | ☐ | ☐ |

   _____

| 5. After I fall asleep, nothing can wake me up. | ☐ | ☐ |

   _____

③ VOCABULARY

Use the phrasal verbs from the box to complete the conversations.

| burn out |
| calm down |
| chill out |
| doze off |
| perk up |
| turn in |

1. A: I lost my car keys! I'm going to be late for my doctor's appointment!
   B: You need to ___*calm down*___. Relax. Maybe you can reschedule.

2. A: You look tired. You need to _____ before our meeting.
   B: Yeah, you're right. Maybe I should have a cup of coffee.

3. A: Poor Jenny. She has two papers to write and a final exam to study for.
   B: That's a lot of work. I hope she doesn't _____ before graduation.

4. A: My flight leaves tomorrow morning at six o'clock.
   B: You should _____ early tonight so you'll wake up on time.

5. A: What a day! I had three meetings and a business lunch. I'm so tired.
   B: Let's have some dinner. Then let's _____ and watch TV.

6. A: Oh, sorry! I guess I fell asleep.
   B: You should go to bed earlier. Then you wouldn't _____ in class.

④ GRAMMAR

Use time clauses to complete the sentences so they are true for you.

1. __*As soon as*__ I get home from work, I *change into some comfortable clothes and make dinner.*

2. _____ I have the chance to chill out, I _____

3. _____ I met my best friend, we _____

4. _____ I started riding a bike, I _____

5. _____ eating a large meal, I _____

WRITING

5

A Read the paragraph and choose the best topic sentence. Is each topic sentence too general, too specific, or just right? Choose the correct answer.

1. _____

We experience a gradual rise of energy in the morning, peaking around noon. There is a slow decline in energy in the midafternoon with a second peak early in the evening. This is followed by a steady decline in energy until bedtime. Everyone experiences these energy patterns. They are a part of daily life.

	Too general	Too specific	Just right
a. People need energy to get through the day.	☐	☐	☐
b. People's energy patterns change according to the time of day.	☐	☐	☐
c. Everyone's energy peaks around noon.	☐	☐	☐

2. _____

Newborn babies sleep an average of 15 to 18 hours a day, but as children grow older, they sleep less. However, as teenagers, they seem to need a lot of sleep again. It is not unusual for teens to sleep until noon on weekends if their parents let them. As people age beyond their thirties, they tend to sleep less and less and for shorter periods of time.

	Too general	Too specific	Just right
a. People's sleep needs change as they go through life.	☐	☐	☐
b. Babies sleep more than elderly people.	☐	☐	☐
c. Everyone needs sleep.	☐	☐	☐

3. _____

In fact, Americans now spend close to $30 billion a year on vitamins and food supplements. Vitamin companies supply an almost endless variety of vitamins. There are multivitamins for adults, special vitamins for women, flavored vitamins for children, and even vitamins to help students study better. New types of vitamins come out regularly, and at least one store in every shopping mall sells vitamins.

	Too general	Too specific	Just right
a. Vitamins supplement a healthy diet.	☐	☐	☐
b. Vitamins are popular with women.	☐	☐	☐
c. In the U.S., vitamins are big business.	☐	☐	☐

B Write a topic sentence about how to keep your energy up or sleep well. Then write a paragraph that supports your main idea.

_____

_____

VOCABULARY

Rewrite the sentences by replacing the underlined words with phrases from the box.
Sometimes more than one answer is possible.

be fast asleep
be sound asleep
be wide awake
drift off
feel drowsy
have a sleepless night
nod off
sleep like a log
take a power nap
toss and turn

1. If Elisa is worried when she goes to bed, she is <u>unable to sleep</u>.
   If Elisa is worried when she goes to bed, she tosses and turns.
   If Elisa is worried when she goes to bed, she has a sleepless night.

2. My father always <u>falls asleep</u> after eating a heavy meal.
   _____

3. Simon often <u>sleeps for a few minutes</u> to boost his creativity at work.
   _____

4. The loud music didn't wake Sue. She must <u>be in a deep sleep</u>.
   _____

5. Liz is lucky she <u>sleeps heavily</u> because her roommate snores so loudly!
   _____

6. Marina isn't tired at all. In fact, she <u>is completely alert</u>!
   _____

7. Kenji often <u>begins to feel sleepy</u> when he reads on the train or in a car.
   _____

GRAMMAR

Choose the word or phrase that best completes each sentence.

1. *Considering that / Just in case /* (*Unless*) I'm really worried, I usually sleep well.
2. *Even if / Just in case / Only if* I have bad dreams, I don't recall the details later.
3. *Even if / As long as / Unless* I sleep well, I wake up feeling rested.
4. *Considering that / Only if / Unless* I didn't sleep last night, I feel pretty good.
5. Bring an umbrella with you *only if / as long as / just in case* it rains later.

3 GRAMMAR

Use the information in the box and the expressions in parentheses to write new sentences.

> I drink too much caffeine during the day.
> I forget to set my alarm clock.
> I get thirsty in the middle of the night.
> I sleep deeply.
> I'm completely exhausted.
> I've slept well the night before.

1. I always feel great in the morning. (as long as)

   I always feel great in the morning as long as I've slept well the night before.

2. Sometimes I have trouble drifting off. (even if)

   _____

3. My neighbors listen to loud music every night. (considering that)

   _____

4. I never oversleep in the morning. (unless)

   _____

5. I keep a glass of water by my bed. (just in case)

   _____

6. I have trouble falling asleep. (only . . . if)

   _____

4 GRAMMAR

Answer these questions using clauses with *as long as, considering that, even if, (just) in case, only . . . if,* or *unless.*

1. Do you stay awake thinking, or do you fall asleep as soon as you lie down?

   I only stay awake thinking if I'm having a problem at work.

2. Are you usually alert or still sleepy when you first get up in the morning?

   _____

3. Do you ever take naps during the day, or do you wait until bedtime to sleep?

   _____

4. Do you sleep like a log all night, or do you toss and turn?

   _____

5. Do you always need eight hours of sleep a night, or can you survive on less?

   _____

A Read the article quickly. Which three sleep theories are mentioned?

_____

Why Sleep?

For some people, sleep is a great pleasure that they look forward to after a long day. For others, sleep is just a necessity, almost a waste of time. Regardless of where you stand, there's no denying that, at some point, everyone needs sleep. Without it, you'll find yourself irritable, confused, and lacking in energy. And the fact is that humans can survive longer without food than they can without sleep. But why is sleep necessary?

There are several theories that try to explain why sleep is so important. One of them, the energy conservation theory, suggests that a period of inactivity gives the body a chance to save energy. Basically, most mammals sleep through the night because instinct tells them it is less practical and more dangerous to hunt for or gather food in the dark. Another possible explanation is the restorative theory. According to this theory, the body needs time to repair itself after the physical efforts of the day, and certain repair functions can only happen during sleep. One of the most fascinating discoveries about sleep is that it is not a period of total inactivity, as scientists previously believed. While we sleep, things are happening in the brain that researchers are only beginning to understand. The brain plasticity theory states that sleep is necessary to allow the brain to adjust to new experiences and information, and that a reorganization of the information in the brain takes place during sleep. Experts say that plenty of sleep the first night after learning a new skill or a new set of facts is crucial for improving memory and performance.

Dr. Robert Stickgold, a cognitive neuroscientist, says, "There's an old joke that the function of sleep is to cure sleepiness." Since there is no real agreement on a single reason for sleep, that may be the best explanation we have. Not to mention the fact that, after an exhausting day, it just feels good.

B Are the statements true or false? Choose the correct answer. Then rewrite the false statements to make them true.

	True	False
1. Humans need food more than they need sleep.	☐	☐
2. The conservation and restorative theories are concerned more with physical than mental processes.	☐	☐
3. Scientists have always believed there is brain activity during sleep.	☐	☐
4. Scientists have a complete understanding of what happens in the brain during sleep.	☐	☐
5. According to the brain plasticity theory, sleeping well after learning something new will help you remember it.	☐	☐

_____

_____

_____

_____

_____

5 COMMUNICATION

LESSON A ▶ *Making conversation*

1 GRAMMAR

Are these customs similar to or different from customs in your culture? Choose your answer.
For the customs that are different, write an explanation.

	Similar	Different
1. It's customary in India to take your shoes off when entering a home.	☐	☐

In my culture, _____

_____

2. In Greece, it's not unusual to kiss friends and relatives on both   ☐   ☐
cheeks when meeting them.

_____

_____

3. In some countries, owning a pet like a dog, a cat, or a bird is   ☐   ☐
considered inappropriate.

_____

_____

4. In the U.S., arriving 30 minutes early to a dinner party isn't a   ☐   ☐
good idea.

_____

_____

2 VOCABULARY

Choose the word or phrase that best describes how each situation is viewed in your culture.
Then write a sentence about the custom.

1. saying hello to strangers (appropriate / inappropriate / (normal))
   Saying hello to strangers in my culture is considered normal.

2. opening a door for someone (bad form / polite / strange)

   _____

3. splitting a restaurant bill with a friend (a compliment / an insult / typical)

   _____

4. offering your seat on a bus to a child (normal / offensive / unusual)

   _____

5. chewing with your mouth open (polite / rude / typical)

   _____

3 GRAMMAR

Use the information in the chart to make sentences about the dos and don'ts of customs in the U.S. Use the infinitive form of the verb in your answers.

Customs in the U.S.	
Dos	Don'ts
Acceptable: Use hand gestures while speaking.	Inappropriate: Talk about religion or politics.
Not unusual: Ask people how they feel.	Not a good idea: Ask about someone's salary.
Customary: Ask what someone does for a living.	Rude: Tell someone he or she has gained weight.

1. *It's acceptable to use hand gestures while speaking.*
2. _____
3. _____
4. _____
5. _____
6. _____

4 GRAMMAR

Use gerunds to rewrite the sentences you wrote above.

1. *Using hand gestures while speaking is acceptable.*
2. _____
3. _____
4. _____
5. _____
6. _____

5 GRAMMAR

What should people know about your customs? Write sentences with infinitive phrases or gerunds.

1. meeting business associates

   When you meet business associates in my culture,
   it's typical to exchange business cards.
   When you meet business associates in my culture,
   exchanging business cards is typical.

2. getting married

   _____
   _____
   _____
   _____

3. eating out _____

   _____

WRITING

A Read the parts of a paragraph about small talk. They have been mixed up. Put them in the correct order according to the outline.

1. _____ Topic sentence
2. _____ Supporting sentences: General example
3. _____ Supporting sentences: Personal example
4. _____ Concluding sentence

a For example, personal income is seen as too private to be a suitable topic for small talk in the U.S. People in the U.S. normally avoid asking other people how much they make, and they rarely offer information about their own salary.

b Small talk is common in every culture, but the topics that are considered suitable or unsuitable vary from country to country.

c In conclusion, when dealing with people from other cultures, it's a good idea to be aware of which topics are considered suitable and avoid those that aren't – in that way, you can avoid creating the kind of awkwardness that small talk is meant to reduce.

d I remember being very taken aback when, at a party, a person from another country asked me what I did for a living and then asked me how much money I made. My inability to answer right away made me realize that this really is a taboo topic in our culture, if not in others. After some hesitation, and hoping I didn't sound rude, my answer was, "Oh, enough to support myself."

B Think of a topic of small talk that is avoided in your country or a country you know well. Write notes for a short paragraph about the topic using the outline below.

1. Topic sentence: _____

2. Supporting sentences:

　2.1　General example: _____

　2.2　Personal example: _____

3. Concluding sentence: _____

C Write a paragraph about the topic using the outline and your notes above.

_____
_____
_____
_____
_____
_____
_____

GRAMMAR

Read Victoria and Alicia's conversation about a movie star. Then read the sentences below. One mistake is underlined in each sentence. Rewrite the sentences with the correct verb tenses.

Victoria: Did you see the new *Star Monthly*? Jenny Roberts bought an amazing new house!

Alicia: When did she buy it?

Victoria: She moved in last week.

Alicia: Lucky Jenny. Is she happy?

Victoria: Actually, she's not. That's what it says here in *Star Monthly*.

Alicia: Really? Let me see that.

Victoria: Yeah. She found out the closets are too small!

1. Victoria told Alicia that Jenny Roberts <u>did buy</u> a new house.

   Victoria told Alicia that Jenny Roberts had bought a new house.

2. Alicia asked Victoria when she <u>was buying</u> it.

   _____

3. Victoria told Alicia that she <u>was moving in</u> last week.

   _____

4. Alicia asked Victoria if Jenny <u>is</u> happy.

   _____

5. Victoria told Alicia that Jenny <u>will not be</u> happy.

   _____

6. Victoria told Alicia that Jenny <u>has found out</u> the closets were too small.

   _____

GRAMMAR

Read the conversation. Use reported speech to complete the sentences.

Mark: Sandra, sit down. Did you hear about Paul Alvaro?

Sandra: No, I didn't. What happened?

Mark: He got a promotion.

Sandra: When did it happen?

Mark: Yesterday. The official announcement will be made soon.

1. Mark told Sandra *to sit down.* _____

2. He asked her _____

3. She said that _____

4. She asked Mark _____

5. Mark said that Paul _____

6. Sandra asked Mark _____

7. Mark said that it _____

8. He said that the official announcement _____

VOCABULARY

Use the expressions in the box to complete the blog entry. Sometimes more than one answer is possible.

she claimed that	she explained that	she warned me not to
she encouraged me to	she told us that	she wondered

November 10

My technology teacher gave us a difficult assignment today. (1) _____*She told us that*_____ we had to prepare a 10-minute oral presentation for Friday. I can't stand speaking in front of the class. Anyway, I asked my teacher if I could do a different assignment – like a written report. (2) _____ why I didn't want to do the presentation, so I told her how nervous I get when I have to speak in class.

(3) _____ she couldn't change the assignment for me. But she did have some advice. (4) _____ put off the assignment. Then (5) _____ practice my presentation with a friend. (6) _____ if I practiced my presentation ahead of time, I would feel more comfortable on the day I actually had to give it. So, I hope Rita can come over tomorrow and listen to my presentation. Are you reading this, Rita? Please say "yes"!

💬 COMMENTS (12)   🔗 SHARE THIS

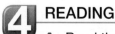

4 READING

A Read the article. Find the boldfaced words that match the definitions.

1. problems ___*pitfalls*___   4. concern for others _____

2. increase _____   5. talking too proudly about yourself _____

3. unclear _____   6. not thinking you are better than others _____

How nice of you to say so ...

Everyone appreciates a compliment. They are expressions of admiration, acceptance, and affection that make the recipient of the compliment feel good and **boost** positive feelings in the giver of the compliment as well. Friendships and good working relationships alike can develop out of a well-worded and appropriately timed compliment. As in most areas of social interaction, though, giving and receiving compliments can present problems. What's meant to be positive can turn out to be offensive unless you're aware of the possible **pitfalls**.

One point that many of us forget – or perhaps never realized – is that the best compliments are specific. Instead of a quick "Good job!" to a colleague or classmate, mentioning how well organized their presentation was, or how it taught you something new, will have the greatest effect. Similarly, try to avoid **vague** language like, "Wow, you got a new haircut!" If the recipient of your intended compliment is feeling unsure about this new look, they might think: ". . . and it looks terrible!" Explain what's good about it or why it's an improvement so there is no misunderstanding.

Sincerity is also important when it comes to compliments. When salespeople tell you how great you look or how smart you seem, you can often tell if they really mean it or if they are just trying to get you to buy something. Similarly, other people, especially those close to us, can usually tell if a compliment is automatic or insincere. And a compliment that sounds forced can actually make the recipient feel worse than if we had said nothing at all.

How you receive a compliment can also determine if the exchange will be a positive or a negative one. Many people reject compliments by saying, "Oh, it was nothing," or "It wasn't me – Tom did all the work." This may seem like the right, and **humble**, thing to do. Accepting a compliment with no argument can feel like **boasting** to many people and in many cultures. However, in the U.S. and most Western cultures, graciously accepting a positive statement with a simple thank-you shows the other person that you respect their judgment and appreciate their **thoughtfulness**. So the next time someone comments on your new outfit, try to resist saying you bought it for next to nothing, it doesn't fit well and, anyway, your sister picked it out. Just smile, say thank you, and accept it as a positive moment for both of you.

B Read the article again. Choose the correct answers.

1. The author believes that giving compliments . . .
   - ☐ a. always has a positive effect.
   - ☐ b. can present problems.
   - ☐ c. isn't complicated.

2. According to the article, an unclear compliment . . .
   - ☐ a. is as good as a specific one.
   - ☐ b. always causes offense.
   - ☐ c. can be misunderstood.

3. According to the article, some salespeople might use compliments in order to . . .
   - ☐ a. make themselves feel better.
   - ☐ b. influence your decision.
   - ☐ c. appear humble.

4. In the U.S., rejecting a compliment gives the impression that . . .
   - ☐ a. you don't respect the giver.
   - ☐ b. you are boasting.
   - ☐ c. you feel insecure.

6 WHAT'S THE REAL STORY?

LESSON A ▶ *That's some story!*

1 GRAMMAR

Choose the sentences with grammatical mistakes. Rewrite them using the correct verb forms.

☑ 1. A government spokesperson has announced new economic policies yesterday.

    A government spokesperson announced new economic policies yesterday.

☐ 2. Unusual weather events have been happening across the country.

_____

☐ 3. Police arrested several identity thieves so far this year.

_____

☐ 4. Burglars have stolen two paintings on Monday night.

_____

☐ 5. Several observers saw a rare butterfly in Central Park over the past week.

_____

☐ 6. Jazz pianist Jacqueline Gray gave a concert at the Civic Center last night.

_____

☐ 7. The stock market has fallen sharply the other day.

_____

2 GRAMMAR

Choose the verbs that best complete this update about an ongoing news story.

> UPDATED 8:12 A.M.
>
> The County Municipal Airport (1) ⟨*has delayed*⟩ / *has been delaying* a flight to London. The delay (2) *has occurred* / *has been occurring* because airline personnel (3) *have been trying* / *tried* to locate a snake inside the plane. While information is incomplete at this time, we do know a few things. As flight attendants were preparing for takeoff, several passengers saw a snake under their seats. The pilot alerted the flight control tower, and the flight was delayed in order to find the snake. Crew members (4) *have searched* / *have been searching* the plane ever since. They still (5) *haven't been locating* / *haven't located* the snake, and no one (6) *has come up* / *has been coming up* with an explanation as to how it got there. Technicians (7) *have removed* / *have been removing* a section of the cabin floor to see if it may have hidden there. All the passengers (8) *have left* / *have been leaving* the plane already. They (9) *have sat* / *have been sitting* inside the terminal enjoying free soft drinks and snacks.

VOCABULARY

Match these headlines with the news events in the box.

epidemic	kidnapping	political crisis	recession	scandal
hijacking	natural disaster	rebellion	robbery	

Millions Found in Director's Secret Bank Account

1. _____scandal_____

$1.5 Million Stolen!

2. _____

Airline Passengers Still Being Held Captive

3. _____

Earthquake Destroys Houses Downtown

4. _____

Prime Minister Resigns!

5. _____

Virus Sickens Thousands

6. _____

Hundreds of Inmates Take Over Prison

7. _____

Millionaire's Wife Held for Ransom

8. _____

Stocks and Employment Numbers Fall

9. _____

GRAMMAR

Complete these sentences about some of the headlines above with your own ideas. Use the present perfect or present perfect continuous form of the verbs in parentheses.

1. Officials say the director (withdraw) _has been withdrawing hundreds of thousands of dollars from the company account for the past three years._

   The director (deny) _has denied stealing any money._

2. A bank robber (steal) _____

   _____

   The bank robber (hide) _____

3. Passengers on Flight 200 (hold) _____

   _____

   The hijackers (demand) _____

4. The earthquake (destroy) _____

   _____

   Many people (volunteer) _____

WRITING

A Read the news story. Then number the pictures in the correct order.

a. 4

b.

c.

d.

Trapped Cat Rescued

After spending 14 days trapped inside the walls of a 157-year-old building in New York City last April, Molly briefly became a world-famous cat. Attempting to save the black cat, rescuers set traps and used special cameras and a raw fish to try to lure Molly out from between the walls. They even tried using kittens to appeal to the cat's motherly side so she would come out, but Molly would not budge.

Finally, after they removed bricks and drilled holes into the walls, someone was able to pull the curious cat out of the tiny space.

The bricks have now been replaced, but Molly has been getting visits from tourists daily since she was rescued. Even so, Molly's adventures may not be over. Her owners say that at least once they have caught her looking inside a similar hole in the building.

B Read the story again. Underline the present perfect and present perfect continuous verbs.

C Write a news story about an interesting recent event. Use the present perfect, present perfect continuous, and simple past.

_____
_____
_____
_____
_____
_____
_____

GRAMMAR

Choose the correct expressions to complete the sentences.

1. She was amazed when she won the competition. *The moment / The next day / (Until that time)*, she had never won anything.

2. I felt awful about breaking my friend's phone. *Afterwards / When / Until that time*, I offered to replace it.

3. Despite my fear, I loved flying. *The moment / Up until then / Later*, I had never been on an airplane.

4. On Saturday, my mother left an urgent message on my voice mail. *Until that time / Later / As soon as* I got it, I called her back.

5. I had a delicious meal at a restaurant on Sunday. *The next day / When / Up until then*, however, I woke up with a serious case of food poisoning.

6. When I walked into the room, everyone yelled "Happy birthday!" *As soon as / Before that / Afterwards*, I'd never had a surprise party.

7. I got a big promotion at work. *Until that time / When / Later*, while I was telling my family, I felt really proud.

GRAMMAR

Complete the sentences. Use the past perfect or the simple past of the verbs in parentheses.

1. I couldn't figure out why she looked so familiar. Later, I ___*realized*___ (realize) she was my sixth-grade teacher.

2. I knew it was the delivery person knocking on my door. As soon as I _____ (open) the door, he _____ (give) me a big package.

3. While hiking, we suddenly realized we were lost and didn't have a compass or GPS. Up until then, we _____ (not be) worried.

4. I had never experienced anything so exciting. Until that time, my life _____ (be) very uneventful.

5. I went to the airport and booked the next flight. Afterwards, I _____ (wait) for the announcement to board the plane.

6. It was my first time running a marathon. When I _____ (see) the finish line in front of me, I _____ (feel) relieved.

7. I finally passed my driving test. The moment I _____ (receive) my driver's license in the mail, I _____ (begin) to dance.

8. My father was moved by the performance. Before that, I _____ (never see) him cry.

③ VOCABULARY

Use the expressions from the boxes to complete the conversation.

it all started when	the next thing we knew	the thing you have to know is

Mia: Hi, Ben. I heard you and Luke got lost on your way to the big game.

Ben: Yeah. (1) ___*It all started when*___ we began singing along with this cool song.

Mia: What happened?

Ben: Well, we were having such a good time that, (2) _____, we'd missed the turn for the stadium.

Mia: How did you do that?

Ben: (3) _____, when I'm singing a song I really like, I don't pay attention to anything around me.

I forgot to mention that	meanwhile	the other thing was

Mia: So you were having such a good time you didn't notice you'd gone past your turn?

Ben: That's about right. (4) _____, we'd driven about 40 miles too far!

Mia: Forty miles? Wow!

Ben: And (5) _____, we ran out of gas.

Mia: You ran out of gas? On the highway?

Ben: No, not on the highway. (6) _____ we'd decided to take a shortcut.

I forgot to mention that	to make a long story short

Mia: Did you make it to the game?

Ben: Yes. But it took us about three hours to get there!

Mia: Are you kidding?

Ben: (7) _____ we also stopped for pizza.

Mia: Seriously?

Ben: Well, getting lost made us hungry! So, (8) _____, we only saw the last half hour of the game.

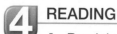
A Read the anecdotes about strange weather events. Then write brief summaries.

Susan's strange weather event was _____

_____

Elena's strange weather event was _____

_____

WACKY *Weather Stories*

Last summer, I was working at home on a sunny day. For some reason, I had gone around to the front of the house to get something. As I did, I felt some drops on my face, which soon developed into a very heavy shower. A few seconds later, I went to the back of the house and realized that it was totally dry there. The shower was only at the front of the house and not at the back. I stood in the hallway and looked one way – pouring – and the other way – sunny and dry. After a few minutes, the downpour stopped entirely. Up until then, I'd never seen such strange weather.

— Susan, United States

One spring day, I was sitting in the living room of my farmhouse in Uruguay watching TV and having lunch. I had just finished eating and was about to get up from the sofa to take my plate to the kitchen when suddenly a ball of fire the size of a soccer ball flew through the open kitchen window. About two seconds later, it disappeared under the front door and there was a terrible smell in the air. The TV and many electrical outlets in the house were burned, and a huge crack opened up in the kitchen wall. I didn't know what had happened until someone told me that the house had been hit by a *centella*, which is the Spanish word for lightning bolt. It was terrifying!

— Elena, Uruguay

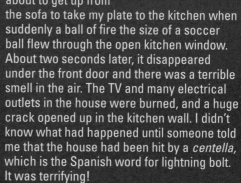

B Choose true or false. Then rewrite the false statements to make them true.

	True	False
1. It was already pouring when Susan went to the front of the house.	☐	☐
2. Susan witnessed two kinds of weather at the same time.	☐	☐
3. The rain soon spread to both sides of Susan's house.	☐	☐
4. The fireball caused actual damage to Elena's house.	☐	☐
5. Elena understood immediately what had happened.	☐	☐

7 THE INFORMATION AGE

LESSON A ▶ *A weird, wired world*

1 VOCABULARY

Use the words and phrases in the box to complete the sentences.

app	the cloud	podcasts	text
blog	download	spyware	virus

1. This _____ *app* _____ lets me find the lowest price for gasoline from my phone.

2. Do you have Wi-Fi here? I need to _____ some files for work.

3. Now that I store everything in _____, I can access my data from anywhere.

4. If your device is running really slowly, it probably has a _____.

5. Cal writes opinion pieces about music and posts them on his _____.

6. Even though I moved abroad, I still listen to _____ of shows from my favorite hometown radio station online.

7. Many people find it's more convenient to _____ than to talk to people on the phone.

8. Some programs use _____ to gather private information without your knowledge.

2 GRAMMAR

One of the underlined words in each sentence is a mistake. Circle it and write the correct word in the blank.

1. In the near future, more cars will (been) driven by computers than by people. _____ *be* _____

2. More tablets are being using in the classroom all the time. _____

3. Medical data has going to be accessed online by both doctors and patients. _____

4. More songs have be downloaded this year than ever before. _____

5. All laptops in the store have being priced to sell quickly. _____

6. More and more TV shows having been made available through apps. _____

7. Increasingly, shopping and banking will be do on portable devices. _____

8. Smartphones are going to been designed with even more features. _____

VOCABULARY

Choose the connector that best completes each sentence.

1. Nat dropped his phone on the sidewalk yesterday. *Nevertheless /* (*As a result*), it doesn't work anymore.

2. Parents should monitor the websites their children visit. *Additionally / On the other hand*, they need to talk to their children about Internet safety.

3. Cell phones are becoming more advanced. Some, *for instance / likewise*, have many of the capabilities of a computer.

4. Penny switched Internet service providers to save money. *Furthermore / In fact*, she's now spending $15 less each month.

5. I really don't like having a TV in my apartment. *Similarly / On the other hand*, it's useful to have one when I have friends over.

6. Higher education has become much more common due to technology. *For example / Therefore*, my cousin completed her degree online while living in another country.

GRAMMAR

Use the passive of the present continuous and your own information to complete the sentences.

1. Blogs *are being written by just about everybody these days!*

2. An increasing number of devices _____

3. Many online classes _____

4. Some spyware _____

5. More and more apps _____

WRITING

A Read the review of an online course. Underline and number the passages where the author of the review does the following things.

1. names and explains the service
2. explains where the service is offered
3. mentions positive features
4. suggests how it could be improved
5. states who would find it useful and why

Saturday, August 10

Curious about app creation?

Creating Mobile Apps is an online course that gives students the chance to explore a variety of app-building programs, to learn about the various uses of apps, and to develop their own app. Offered by Kelly Community College, it's an excellent source of information and hands-on experience for beginners while providing exposure to the latest programs for those who already have some experience.

K C C
CREATING MOBILE APPS

As someone already familiar with building apps, I was not very impressed with some of the material. However, I found the section on the possible uses of apps for everything – from shopping to home security – really eye-opening. Additionally, being able to create an app under the guidance of an expert made the whole process seem much simpler than expected. Overall, it provided a flexible learning experience, and I found that the biggest advantage of an online class is that you can move at your own pace. On the other hand, there's the obvious lack of real time spent with the instructor and fellow students.

I would definitely recommend this course to anyone looking to build an app. My only suggestion is that the college should offer better networking tools so that the discussions and brainstorming sessions are more efficient.

B Use one of these topics or your own idea to write a product or service review.

• a course you took   • a social networking site   • software you tried

_____

_____

_____

_____

_____

_____

_____

_____

_____

_____

1 VOCABULARY

Use the words and phrases in the box to complete the sentences.

banner ads	bumper sticker	infomercial	spam	text messages
billboard	crawl	pop-up ads	telemarketing	voice mail

1. Have you seen that funny ad for a tablet on a huge _____*billboard*_____ on the highway?

2. A(n) _____ is a long commercial that looks like a TV show.

3. I'm not sure how effective _____ is. I never answer calls from numbers I don't recognize.

4. The _____ at the bottom of the TV screen said a storm was coming.

5. If I don't answer my phone, just leave me a _____.

6. I rarely see _____ on my computer because my browser blocks them really well.

7. I find _____ really annoying when they appear everywhere on a blog I'm reading.

8. All _____ email I receive is sent to a separate folder that gets automatically cleared once a week.

9. I'm uncomfortable talking on my phone in public, so I prefer to send _____.

10. The car in front of me had a _____ that said, "I'm not driving too fast – I sure hope you aren't!"

2 GRAMMAR

Complete these negative questions or tag questions with *doesn't, don't, isn't, shouldn't,* or *wouldn't.*

1. _____*Don't*_____ you think that there are lots of great cooking sites online?

2. _____ it be terrific if Wi-Fi were free for everyone?

3. Sam's probably in a meeting. It's better to leave him a voice mail, _____ it?

4. _____ Sheila register for classes online before they fill up?

5. _____ it seem like it's impossible to keep up with your social networking accounts at times?

6. Computer viruses are getting more sophisticated, _____ you think?

7. _____ it strange that no one has sent me any email today?

8. Banner ads get really annoying when they take up too much of the screen, _____ they?

GRAMMAR

Rewrite the sentences in two ways using negative questions and tag questions and the words in parentheses.

1. It's amazing how much time someone can waste online. (isn't)

   Isn't it amazing how much time someone can waste online?

   It's amazing how much time someone can waste online, isn't it?

2. It would be great to get a bus wrap to advertise our business. (wouldn't)

   _____

   _____

3. Students should try to avoid sending text messages during class. (shouldn't)

   _____

   _____

4. It seems like new technologies are being invented every day. (doesn't)

   _____

   _____

5. It's annoying that some ads move all over the computer screen. (isn't)

   _____

   _____

6. It's amazing how some people can watch infomercials for hours. (don't you think)

   _____

   _____

GRAMMAR

Write negative questions or tag questions about things you can do online.
Choose from the items in the box or use your own ideas.

shopping
reading the news
watching videos
planning a vacation
making new friends
looking for a job

1. *It's so convenient to shop online nowadays, isn't it?*
2. _____
3. _____
4. _____
5. _____
6. _____

A Read the blog post. Find the boldfaced words that match these definitions.

1. prepared; having no objection ___willing___
2. someone you know, but not well _____
3. invited to connect on a social network _____
4. accidents _____
5. are grateful for _____
6. at the same time _____

Are You **Tech** Obsessed?

Tuesday, February 2

Most of us **appreciate** the convenience of our tech devices, but for some people, it goes beyond a healthy appreciation. Take this quiz about tech obsession. How many of these are true for you?

1. Do you ever have **mishaps** because you are using your device while walking?

2. Are you **willing** to wait in line for more than 12 hours to get the latest version of a device?

3. Do you wake up in the middle of the night to check all your social networking accounts?

4. Do you text your friends even when they are in the same room?

5. Do you ever watch different shows on your phone, tablet, and TV **simultaneously**?

6. Do you check your phone continuously when you're out with friends or family at a movie, a sporting event, or a restaurant?

7. Do you change your device covers all the time? Are you one of the millions who love choosing new "fashions" for their devices?

8. Do you use online slang when you're offline? For example, you might say about a new **acquaintance**, "I **friended** him in English class last week."

This quiz was pretty funny, don't you think? Unfortunately, I answered "yes" to seven of the questions! How about you? Are you tech obsessed like me?

Posted by Walker White at 5:36 p.m.

B Read the statements. Do you think the author of the blog post would say these behaviors are obsessive or not obsessive? Choose the correct answer.

	Obsessive	Not obsessive
1. You have to be reminded to check your device for calls and messages.	☐	☑
2. People don't always understand you because you use a lot of online slang.	☐	☐
3. You often trip and fall in the street because you're checking email on your phone.	☐	☐
4. You have been using the same version of your device for several years.	☐	☐
5. You have a huge collection of colorful covers for your devices.	☐	☐
6. You turn off your device when you're with friends.	☐	☐

8 PUTTING THE MIND TO WORK
LESSON A ▶ *Exploring creativity*

1 GRAMMAR

Rewrite the sentences by making the reduced clauses into full clauses.

1. A person with great cooking and business skills would make a good restaurant owner.
   A person who has great cooking and business skills would make a
   good restaurant owner.

2. Those able to think creatively are the best team leaders.
   _____

3. A person opening a new business should try unusual marketing methods.
   _____

4. People with musical skills should share their talent with others.
   _____

5. People hoping to succeed in the arts should be prepared for financial challenges.
   _____

2 GRAMMAR

Reduce each relative clause. Then complete the sentences with your own ideas.

1. A person who is living on a tight budget . . .
   A person living on a tight budget shouldn't eat out too often.

2. Anyone who is interested in becoming a doctor . . .
   _____

3. Someone who is considering an artistic career . . .
   _____

4. People who are able to work at home . . .
   _____

5. A supervisor who has too much work to do . . .
   _____

6. A person who is required to take a foreign language in school . . .
   _____

7. People who are becoming bored with their jobs . . .
   _____

3 VOCABULARY

A Write the nouns that relate to the adjectives.

1. curious _____*curiosity*_____
2. decisive _____
3. determined _____
4. disciplined _____
5. innovative _____
6. knowledgeable _____

7. motivated _____
8. original _____
9. passionate _____
10. patient _____
11. perceptive _____
12. resourceful _____

B Now write sentences about these people using adjectives and nouns from above.

1. business executive *A knowledgeable person who has innovative ideas*
   might make a good business executive.

2. web designer _____
   _____

3. journalist _____
   _____

4. lawyer _____
   _____

4 GRAMMAR

What qualities are needed to do these jobs? Use reduced relative clauses in your answers.

singer

1. *A person considering*
   becoming a singer needs
   to be _____
   _____
   _____
   _____

landscaper

2. _____
   _____
   _____
   _____
   _____

architect

3. _____
   _____
   _____
   _____
   _____

5 WRITING

A Read Erica's story. Choose the word or words you would use to describe her.

☐ curious ☐ determined ☐ original ☐ resourceful

If you've ever planned a big event, something like this may have happened to you, but I certainly never thought it would happen to me! My fiancé and I were planning to get married in six months when his company decided to transfer him overseas – in two weeks! He wouldn't be able to return to the U.S. for some time, which meant we couldn't get married as planned. I told a friend about this, and she said, "So get married now!" I reminded her that there was no time to plan anything. She responded, "Then get creative." So I did. First, I designed and sent out email invitations. Then, as there was no time to book a venue, we decided to have both the ceremony and reception in my parents' backyard. My mother put together the decorations, which were flowering plants in pots. A friend of mine who's a chef prepared the food, and we had lots of cupcakes instead of a big cake. The clothes were the biggest challenge; there wasn't any time to make a new dress as I had planned. Luckily, I remembered the dress I'd made for a project in college. With a few alterations, it was perfect. I asked my three bridesmaids to wear dresses they already had – in any color. In the end, the wedding was fantastic thanks to everyone putting their creativity to work.

B Read the story again. Write a *P* where you think each new paragraph should begin.

C Write a three-paragraph composition about a problem you actually had or imagine you might have. How did you or would you solve the problem?

If you _____, something like this may have happened to you, but I certainly never thought it would happen to me. _____

_____

_____

_____

_____

_____

_____

_____

_____

VOCABULARY

Choose the word that best completes each sentence.

1. Seat belts alone did not protect car passengers enough, which is why researchers (found) / made / solved a safer solution: air bags for cars.

2. You need to *explore / organize / solve* your information before you present it to other people. Otherwise, they won't understand it.

3. Our report *explored / made / solved* several possibilities for increasing the car's efficiency.

4. The board of directors *analyzed / found / organized* the alternatives carefully when they chose a new location for the research facility.

5. It's important to consider many solutions when you are *making / organizing / solving* a problem.

6. Our science experiment didn't work. We *explored / made / solved* a mistake in the calculations.

4305OZ02

GRAMMAR

Read the conversation. Find the mistakes in the underlined sentences, and rewrite them so that they are correct. The mistake might be use of commas.

A: Why are we leaving so early? The meeting doesn't start for another 30 minutes!

B: At this time of day, the traffic is terrible! (1) It moves at only about 20 miles an hour, that means we need to leave now.

A: Why don't we take public transportation?

B: (2) The buses are even slower which is why people avoid using them.

A: Then how about walking? (3) The office is a short distance from here, which it means that it shouldn't take long.

B: True. (4) And we can get some exercise, too, it is great!

1. *It moves at only about 20 miles an hour, which means (that) we need to leave now.*

2. _____

3. _____

4. _____

3 GRAMMAR

Write sentences about these topics. Use non-defining relative clauses beginning with *which is why* or *which means (that)*.

the common cold   *ATM*   *video chatting*   *pollution*

1. There is no cure for the common cold, *which is why researchers are working to* *find one.*

2. ATMs are available everywhere, _____
   _____

3. Video chatting is easy for almost everyone, _____
   _____

4. Pollution has become less of a problem in many cities, _____
   _____

4 GRAMMAR

Combine the sentences with non-defining relative clauses beginning with *which is why, which means (that),* or *which is* + adjective.

1. People feel the need to keep in touch. Social networking sites are popular.
   People feel the need to keep in touch, which is why social networking sites *are popular.*

2. New diseases are being discovered all the time. Researchers have to work even harder.
   _____

3. Some people like listening to music on vinyl records. It's strange to me.
   _____

4. Traffic congestion is becoming a major problem in cities. New types of public transportation will have to be developed.
   _____

5. Reality TV shows are cheap and easy to produce. There are so many of them now.
   _____

5 READING

A Read the article quickly. Choose the best title for the article.

☐ Some People Will Never Be Creative   ☐ How to Become an Artist

☐ What Everyday Creativity Means

When we think of creativity, we think of Mozart, Picasso, Einstein – people with a combination of talent and opportunity. But the truth is that all sorts of people are capable of engaging in creative processes. Just because you don't plan to be a famous actor or choreographer doesn't mean that you can't use your natural creativity and make your life your own masterpiece.

Zorana Ivcevic, a psychologist who studies creativity, has found that while some people fit into more traditional creative roles, as dancers or scientists, many others express their creativity through more routine acts. She also found that certain personality traits are shared by the "officially" creative and those who practice everyday creativity. Both groups tend to be open-minded and curious, and they are persistent, positive, energetic, and motivated by their chosen activities. And while 30 percent of the people studied showed no signs of creativity, they shouldn't lose hope. Other studies show that taking up creative pursuits actually makes people more flexible and less judgmental.

Experts at the Harvard Medical School define everyday creativity as expressions of originality and meaningfulness. Rebecca Whitlinger provided an example of this when she decided to make use of her seemingly useless collection of bridesmaid dresses. She resolved to wear them everywhere and asked friends to take snapshots of her wearing them in many unlikely situations, even while parasailing. Then it occurred to her to turn this idea into a fundraising event for a charity she worked for. Guests were asked to wear outfits they would be unable to wear again (such as a bridesmaid dress). Creative? Yes. Meaningful? Well, the fundraiser made $90,000 in its first few years.

"It's too bad that, when considering what endeavors may be creative, people immediately think of the arts," says Michele Root-Bernstein, co-author of *Sparks of Genius*. "It's the problem-solving processes they exhibit rather than the content or craft that make them so. Just about anything we do can be addressed in a creative manner, from housecleaning to personal hobbies to work."

B Read the article again. Choose the answers that best reflect the ideas in the article.

1. According to Zorana Ivcevic, how many people naturally show signs of creativity?

   ☐ a. everyone   ☐ b. more people than most of us think   ☐ c. very few people

2. According to the article, which of these personality traits is not as commonly linked to creativity?

   ☐ a. impatience   ☐ b. optimism   ☐ c. curiosity

3. Rebecca Whitlinger had the idea for a fundraising event when she . . .

   ☐ a. joined a charity.   ☐ b. took up photography.   ☐ c. creatively reused some clothes.

4. Michele Root-Bernstein believes that creativity can be . . .

   ☐ a. found in everything we do.   ☐ b. found only in the arts.   ☐ c. hard to define.

 **GENERALLY SPEAKING**

LESSON A ▶ *How typical are you?*

 GRAMMAR

Choose the expression that best completes each sentence.

1. (Unlike)/ *While* many Americans, people in my country do not watch a lot of TV.

2. *In contrast to / While* many of my friends eat meat, I'm a vegetarian.

3. Monica is a typical teenager, *unlike / except for the fact that* she likes to get up early in the morning.

4. *Unlike / While* lots of my friends, I spend very little time on my phone.

5. I'm similar to people my age, *while / except that* I don't live at home.

6. *Unlike / While* most of my classmates, I prefer walking home to taking the bus.

7. Students in my country are just like other teens, *unlike / except that* we sometimes have to go to school on Saturdays.

8. I like all kinds of music, *except that / except for* jazz.

 VOCABULARY

Use the words and phrases in the box to complete the sentences.

amenable
conform to
conservative
fits in
follows the crowd
make waves
rebellious
unconventional

1. Emma _____*fits in*_____ easily with the other girls in her college.

2. I don't mind working overtime. I'm actually quite _____ to it.

3. Neil likes to do his own thing. He doesn't _____ other people's ideas.

4. Sam does the opposite of what people tell him to do. He's very _____.

5. My town is very resistant to change. It's quite _____.

6. Sadie always goes along with her friends' plans. She doesn't like to _____.

7. Jake has _____ ideas about his work. He tries to be original.

8. My cousin usually _____ when it comes to fashion. She likes to dress exactly like her friends.

Read these descriptions of people. Who are you similar to or different from?
Write sentences using *unlike, while, in contrast to, except that, except for,*
and *except for the fact that.*

What are you like ?

I am a college sophomore, and my major is
English literature. My interests include tennis,
reading, and travel. I enjoy exploring new
places – especially places few people visit.

—KIM

Hi! I love music of all kinds, and I play guitar
in a band. I love loud music – the louder the
better. I'm interested in musical instruments,
and I enjoy collecting them.

—MARIA

I am a 25-year-old computer science
student. I am very interested in technology
and soccer. I love building computers in my
spare time.

—DONALD

Do you like visiting historical sites? Do you
enjoy reading books about history? I do. I am
23 and an accountant, but my real passion is
history. I also enjoy collecting rare coins.

—LUIS

1. _I have a lot in common with Kim, except that I don't like sports._

2. _____

3. _____

4. _____

A Read these paragraphs and answer the questions.

> More and more Americans are living alone nowadays. While an increasing number of people end up living alone because of varying life circumstances, such as a change in marital status, more people are choosing to live alone today than in the past. According to a recent U.S. census, 28 percent of all households in the United States are made up of just one person. This is a dramatic change from the extended families of just a couple of generations ago.

1. What is the topic sentence?

   _____

2. What reasons are given to support the topic sentence?

   _____

   _____

3. What fact is given to support the topic sentence?

   _____

> The typical American living alone is neither old nor lonely. In fact, about 5 million people between the ages of 18 and 34 live alone, and the majority of them have chosen to do so. They are acting on a desire to be more independent, and they often have a more varied social life.

4. What is the topic sentence?

   _____

5. What fact is given to support the topic sentence?

   _____

6. What reasons are given to support the topic sentence?

   _____

   _____

B Choose the topic sentence below that you like best. Then add at least four supporting statements to make a complete paragraph.

- It is *unusual / typical* for young people in my country to live alone.
- It is *easy / difficult* to get into college in my country.

_____

_____

_____

_____

_____

_____

LESSON **B** ▶ *Problems and solutions*

1 GRAMMAR

Complete the blog post with *used to* or *would* and the words in the box. Sometimes more than one answer is possible.

| like | listen | not be | not turn on | play | save | watch |

---

http://blogs.cup.org/ryansreflections

Sunday, March 14

I had a funny conversation with my grandfather the other day. He was telling me what things were like when he was a kid. First of all, there (1) ____*didn't use to be*____ any technology like tablets, smartphones, or handheld game consoles to entertain him. When he wanted to hear music, he (2) _____ to the radio, or he (3) _____ a record on a record player. He did have a TV, but he (4) _____ it only at night. He (5) _____ the TV during the day because there were only four channels, and the programs were boring in the daytime. He also said he (6) _____ reading mystery and suspense novels. He (7) _____ his allowance to buy his favorite books. I feel kind of bad for my granddad – it doesn't sound like the most exciting childhood.

2 VOCABULARY

Complete the conversation with *keep* or *stay*. Sometimes more than one answer is possible.

Lola: Mrs. Wu's class is so difficult! I'm always up late studying for her class, so I can barely (1) ____*stay*____ awake the next morning. I don't know how I'll survive the semester!

Max: Yeah, I remember how demanding Mrs. Wu can be. My best advice is to (2) _____ up with the work you need to do each day. And don't procrastinate!

Lola: That's good advice. Her assignments are long and complicated. I always worry I won't be able to (3) _____ my grades up in her class!

Max: Even though you're stressed out, try to (4) _____ things in perspective. Also, if you let her know that you'll do what it takes to get good grades, maybe she'll help you (5) _____ out of trouble.

Lola: That's a good idea. I'll talk to Mrs. Wu tomorrow. And I'll (6) _____ in touch with you to let you know how things go.

3 GRAMMAR

Rewrite each sentence using the past habitual with *used to* or *would*. If there are two possibilities, write them both.

1. James was a very good chess player when he was younger.

   James used to be a very good chess player when he was younger.

2. In college, my friends and I studied for our tests together at the library.

   _____

3. I always asked my older sister for help with my science homework.

   _____

4. My English teacher didn't assign work over holidays or long weekends.

   _____

5. Rowan lived in an apartment near the university.

   _____

6. Carrie emailed her mom every day when she went away to school.

   _____

4 GRAMMAR

Complete the sentences with *used to* or *would* and information that is true for you.

1. Three years ago, I _____*used to*_____ live
   in a very noisy apartment on a noisy
   city street.

2. Last summer, my friends and I _____
   _____
   _____
   _____

3. When I was younger, I _____ go to
   _____
   _____
   _____

4. A friend of mine _____ have trouble in _____
   class because _____

5. My favorite teacher was _____. He/She _____
   _____

6. When I was first learning English, I _____
   _____

A Read the article quickly. What is Deirdre Barrett's main theory on dreaming?

YOUR **DREAMS** CAN HELP SOLVE YOUR DAY'S **PROBLEMS**

The slumbering mind might not seem like the best tool for critical thinking, but according to recent research, humans can actually solve problems while asleep. In fact, one purpose for dreaming may be to help us find solutions to puzzles that bother us while we're awake. Dreams are highly visual and often illogical, which makes them useful for the type of "out-of-the-box" thinking that some problem solving requires, explained Deirdre Barrett, a psychologist at Harvard University. Barrett's theory on dreaming boils down to this: Dreaming is really just thinking, but in a slightly different state from when our eyes are open.

Barrett has studied problem solving in dreams for more than 10 years and has documented many examples of the phenomenon in this time. In one experiment, Barrett asked college students to pick a homework problem to try to solve while sleeping. Students focused on the problem each night before they went to bed. At the end of a week, about half of the students had dreamed about the problem, and about a quarter had had a dream that contained the answer.

Having extensively reviewed scientific and historical literature for examples of problems solved in dreams, Barrett also found almost every type of problem being solved, from the mathematical to the artistic. Many were problems that required the individual to visualize something in his or her mind, such as an inventor picturing a new device. The other major category of problems solved included "ones where the conventional wisdom is just wrong about how to approach the problem," Barrett said. She added that dreams might have developed to be particularly good at allowing us to work out puzzles that fall into these two categories. "It's just extra thinking time," she stressed – though it's time that allows us to think in more flexible and creative ways.

$$e = mc^2 \qquad dS \geq 0$$
$$a^2 + b^2 = c^2$$
$$\pi = c/d$$

B Read the article again. Are the statements true or false? Choose the correct answer. Then rewrite the false statements to make them true.

	True	False
1. The creative thinking associated with dreams makes them good for some types of problem solving.	☐	☐
2. Barrett has only recently begun studying dreams.	☐	☐
3. The students in Barrett's experiment all solved their problems while asleep.	☐	☐
4. According to Barrett, only certain kinds of problems can be solved while dreaming.	☐	☐
5. Inventors may find dreams particularly useful.	☐	☐

10 THE ART OF COMPLAINING

LESSON A ▶ *That really bugs me!*

1 GRAMMAR

Use the clauses in the box to complete the sentences.

> how quickly the battery runs down
> people who make noise when they eat
> waiting a long time to be seated
> water dripping in the sink
>
> when my favorite show is interrupted by a news bulletin
> who honk their horns all the time
> why people push in front of me in line

1. The thing that really bothers me at the dinner table is . . .

   The thing that really bothers me at the dinner table is people who make
   noise when they eat.

2. When I'm trying to sleep at night, something that irks me is . . .

   _____

3. One thing I can't understand in the supermarket is . . .

   _____

4. The thing that really irritates me when I go to a restaurant is . . .

   _____

5. Something I can't stand is drivers . . .

   _____

6. Something that bothers me about my new cell phone is . . .

   _____

7. When I'm watching TV, one thing that bugs me is . . .

   _____

2 GRAMMAR

Write sentences about things that irritate you. Use relative clauses and noun clauses, and your own ideas.

1. *The thing that bothers me at the dinner table is when people talk*
   with their mouths full.

2. _____

   _____

3. _____

   _____

4. _____

   _____

3 GRAMMAR

Use relative clauses and noun clauses to write about everyday annoyances in these places.

on the road   *in the park*   *in the library*   *on the subway*

1. *The thing that annoys me on the road is when other drivers follow too closely.*

2. _____

3. _____

4. _____

4 VOCABULARY

Choose the word that best completes each sentence. Sometimes more than one answer is possible.

1. One thing that *drives /*(gets)*/ makes* me down is when it rains on the weekend.

2. Something that *drives / gets / makes* me up the wall is when I have to wait on a long line to buy one or two items.

3. The thing that *drives / gets / makes* my blood boil is when my sister borrows my clothes.

4. One thing that *drives / gets / makes* me upset is when people are rude to store clerks for no reason.

5. The one thing that *drives / gets / makes* under my skin is when someone's cell phone rings during a movie or play.

6. When I'm talking to someone, the thing that *drives / gets / makes* on my nerves is when he or she keeps interrupting me.

7. My sister sending text messages during dinner *drives / gets / makes* me crazy.

8. One thing my brother does that *drives / gets / makes* me sick is when he leaves piles of dirty dishes in the kitchen sink.

WRITING

A Read the email complaining about a service. Number the four paragraphs in a logical order.

To: customerservice@bestgym.cup.com

Subject: Complaint about personal training service

To whom it may concern:

☐ My trainer, Dan, has not arrived on time for a single 6:00 a.m. session. The earliest he has arrived is 6:15, and several times he has come at 6:30. I am paying extra for his services, and I am certainly not getting my money's worth. Dan also tends to wander off while I am exercising, getting involved in conversations with other gym employees. My understanding was that he would carefully supervise my training, which he has not done.

☐ When I signed up for the program, the head trainer and I sat down, discussed my problems and needs, and drew up a plan, which was signed by both of us. This will show clearly what my expectations were in case you need to see this in writing. However, I hope it's clear by now that my needs have not been met.

☐ I would like you to assign me a new trainer or refund my fee for the personal training service. If you can't do this by next week, I will take my business to another gym.

☐ I am writing to complain about the personal trainer who was recently assigned to me at your gym. I signed up for six weeks of the intensive training program, including an individual fitness evaluation, and I am extremely dissatisfied.

Sincerely,
Elizabeth Smith
212-555-0199

B Use the numbers you wrote for the paragraphs above to answer these questions. In which paragraph does the writer . . .

a. explain the problem in detail? ____

b. explain what she wants? ____

c. describe the type of service clearly? ____

d. mention evidence of a service contract? ____

C Write an email complaining about a problem regarding a service or product you are not satisfied with.

To whom it may concern:

_____

_____

_____

_____

_____

_____

_____

GRAMMAR

Write *S* for a simple indirect question and *C* for a complex indirect question.

__S__ 1. I want to find out how to use less fat in my cooking.

____ 2. Why people aren't concerned about the crime rate is a mystery to me.

____ 3. I wonder if other people are concerned about the pollution problems in our city.

____ 4. The thing I don't get is why food prices are so high.

____ 5. One of my concerns is whether I will be able to afford a new car.

____ 6. I'd like to know if the weather will be nice this weekend.

____ 7. How some people can listen to such loud music is something I can't understand.

____ 8. I want to know when a cure for the common cold will be discovered.

GRAMMAR

Use the phrases in parentheses to rewrite the questions.

1. Why are the trains running so slowly? (. . . is a mystery to me.)
   Why the trains are running so slowly is a mystery to me.
   _____

2. Will there be cheaper health care for employees? (One of my concerns . . .)
   _____

3. Why do I get so much junk mail? (. . . is something I can't understand.)
   _____

4. How can you eat so much and not feel sick? (What I don't get . . .)
   _____

5. Who should I call if I don't get my passport on time? (I wonder . . .)
   _____

6. Will politicians do more to help the environment? (I'd like to know . . .)
   _____

7. Why don't people turn off their cell phones when they're at the movies?
   (. . . is beyond me.)
   _____

8. Why can't James get to work on time? (. . . is the thing that concerns me.)
   _____

9. Why do I get a cold every summer? (. . . is a mystery to me.)
   _____

10. Did someone use my tablet while I was out of the room? (I want to find out . . .)
    _____

3 VOCABULARY

Choose the word that best completes each sentence.

1. Lena was (infuriated)/ insulted when she missed her flight due to the traffic jam.
2. John was very irritated / saddened to hear about the house that had been damaged by the storm.
3. Vicky was depressed / mystified when the forecast called for rain on her wedding day.
4. The players on the football team were humiliated / insulted when they lost the championship game by 22 points.
5. We were absolutely demoralized / stunned when we found out we had won the prize.
6. Chiang was totally baffled / discouraged when a complete stranger started talking to him as if they were old friends.
7. Joan was enraged / discouraged when she saw that someone had damaged her car and not even left a note for her.
8. June became pretty insulted / annoyed when her Wi-Fi kept disconnecting.

4 GRAMMAR

Write sentences about each urban problem below or about ideas of your own.

transportation   sanitation   parking

1. I don't know _why bus service is so infrequent. It's almost impossible_
   to get to work on time.

2. It's beyond me _____
   _____

3. I wonder _____
   _____

4. My big concern _____
   _____

A Read the article quickly. Write the number of each section next to its title.

_____ a. Understanding What Chronic Complainers Want

_____ b. Understanding What Chronic Complainers Don't Want

_____ c. Understanding How Chronic Complainers Think

The Survival Guide For Dealing With Chronic Complainers

*Optimists see a glass half full. Pessimists see a glass half empty. Chronic complainers see a glass that is slightly **chipped**, holding water that isn't cold enough, probably because it's tap water when they asked for bottled.*

The constant negativity of chronic complainers presents a challenge for those around them. Trying to remain positive and productive when there's a constant stream of complaints can try anyone's patience. And trying to be helpful will only **backfire**. So here are some essential tips to help those who deal with chronic complainers on a daily basis.

1 Despite the **gloom**, complainers don't see themselves as negative people. They see *the world* as negative and themselves as responding to the unfortunate circumstances of their lives.

Survival Tip #1 Never try to convince complainers that things are "not as bad" as they seem. This will only encourage them to come up with 10 additional **misfortunes** that might help you understand how terrible their lives actually are.

2 Chronic complainers are looking for sympathy and emotional **validation**. All they really want is for you to tell them that, yes, they've gotten a bad deal, and you feel their pain – just not as much as they do.

Survival Tip #2 The quickest way to get away from a complainer is to express sympathy and then change the subject. For example, "The printer jammed on you again? Sorry! I know it's hard, but I hope you can be a trooper because we really have to get back to work."

3 The idea that chronic complainers' lives are filled with tragedy is a big part of their **sense of identity**. Therefore, even good advice is a threat, because what complainers really want is for you to know they are suffering. They will often tell you why your solution won't work or might even become upset because you don't understand how unsolvable their problems are.

Survival Tip #3 You should avoid offering advice or solutions and stick to sympathy. However, there are situations where a problem is obviously very real. In this case, offer sympathy followed by brief but clear advice, and it will probably be accepted and appreciated.

B Read the article. Find the boldfaced word that matches each definition.

1. lack of hope ___*gloom*___

2. bad things that happen _____

3. your idea of who you are _____

4. have the opposite effect to what was intended _____

5. damaged because a small piece has broken off _____

6. proof that something is true or real _____

11 VALUES

LESSON A ▶ *How honest are you?*

1 GRAMMAR

Complete the sentences with *even if, only if,* or *unless*.

1. I wouldn't interrupt a lesson _____*unless*_____ I had an important question.

2. I would leave the scene of a car accident _____ I knew for sure that no one was injured.

3. _____ I were really hungry, I still wouldn't take food that wasn't mine.

4. I would ask my neighbors to be more quiet in the morning _____ we had a good relationship.

5. I wouldn't ask to borrow a friend's phone _____ I knew he or she wouldn't mind.

6. _____ I didn't like my brother's new wife, I'd still be nice to her.

2 VOCABULARY

Choose the correct words to complete the sentences.

1. Steph won't mind if we rewrite parts of her article. She's very (agreeable) / *rational* to change.

2. It's *disapproving / unfair* that Mrs. Moore only blamed Lydia for the accident. Terry was responsible for the accident, too.

3. I'm sure Mark wasn't being *honest / irresponsible* when he said he liked my new shoes.

4. I can't believe Brianna wasn't fired from her job. Her *trustworthy / unscrupulous* business practices have cost this company thousands of dollars.

5. Min-hee is a good choice for club treasurer. She's good with money, and she's quite *unethical / responsible*.

6. In many places, it's *illegal / logical* to use a cell phone and drive at the same time.

3 GRAMMAR

Respond to what the first speaker says in each of these conversations.

1. **A:** If I found a friend's diary, I'd read it.

   B: Really? I wouldn't read it, even if _I were_
   really curious, because diaries are
   supposed to be private.

2. **A:** You should never give a friend your email password.

   B: I would give a friend my email password only if _____

3. **A:** If I heard someone spreading false information about a good friend, I wouldn't tell that friend about it.

   B: I wouldn't tell my friend about the false information unless _____

4. **A:** I would lend my best friend money if she needed it.

   B: I wouldn't lend my best friend a lot of money unless _____

4 GRAMMAR

How do you feel about these situations? Write sentences about them using *unless*, *only if*, or *even if*.

- recommending a friend's restaurant you don't consider very good
- lending money to someone you barely know
- giving fashion advice to a friend whose clothes you consider inappropriate
- saying you like a gift that you really don't like just to be nice

1. _I would never recommend a friend's restaurant that I don't consider very good_
   unless I knew he/she was trying to improve it.

2. _____

   _____

3. _____

   _____

4. _____

   _____

WRITING

A Read this composition and choose the best thesis statement.

☐ I am glad that I learned the importance of being responsible when I was young.

☐ I am thankful that I learned the importance of saving money when I was a child.

☐ I feel fortunate to have learned as a child how important family is.

_____ I grew up on a farm. My family had to care for the animals morning and evening, seven days a week. Even during school vacations and on weekends, there was work to be done, and each of my brothers and sisters had jobs that our parents depended on us to do.

For example, when I was 12, my parents entrusted me with the care of the young animals. That meant that if an animal was sick or injured, I had to take charge, giving the animal its medication and generally making sure it had a chance to get well. Most farmers had problems with their calves frequently getting sick. I was proud that my calves were usually healthy. That fact alone proved to me that I was doing a good job and making the right decisions.

Another way I learned responsibility is that, from the age of 12, I was paid for my work. Because I was working hard for my own money, I learned how to budget and save. When I was 14, I was able to buy a 10-speed bicycle with my savings. And because I demonstrated how responsible I was, by the time I was 16, my parents trusted me enough to help with the farm accounts.

In conclusion, being allowed to make important decisions and take charge of my own finances at an early age taught me what being responsible really means. Now, in my working life, I know that if I take care of the jobs that are given to me, my colleagues will see they can trust me with even more challenging tasks in the future.

B Now write a composition about something you learned as a child that is useful to you now. Begin the paragraphs as indicated below.

I'm glad that I learned _____

_____

_____

For example, _____

_____

_____

Another way I learned _____

_____

_____

In conclusion, _____

_____

_____

1 GRAMMAR

Complete the sentences with the correct form of the verbs in parentheses.

1. Jay: I'm taking a French class at the community college.

    Meryl: I wish I _____*had*_____ (have) more time to learn a second language.

2. Diego: I have to study tonight.

    Jim: If you _____ (study) yesterday, you would have been able to
    go to the concert with me tonight!

3. Camila: If only our neighbor _____ (play) his music more softly at night!

    Derek: I know. I haven't had a good night's sleep since he moved in!

4. Rohan: Our boss is going to be upset when he sees what you've done.

    Julie: It's true. If I had been careful, I _____ (not spill) my drink on
    my computer.

5. Albin: You look exhausted. Why don't you stop working for a few minutes?

    Lily: I wish I _____ (take) a break, but I have too much to do!

6. Hiroto: I'm so glad you didn't get caught in that snowstorm!

    Kay: If you _____ (not warn) me, I probably would have gotten
    stuck on the road.

2 GRAMMAR

Complete the sentences with wishes and regrets about the illustration.
Use the phrases from the box.

| forget my umbrella | check the weather forecast |
| wear my raincoat | find a taxi |

1. I wish *I hadn't forgotten my umbrella.* _____

   _____

2. If only _____

   _____

3. I wish _____

   _____

4. If only _____

   _____

3 VOCABULARY

Use the words in the box to complete the sentences.

| compassionate | generous | resilient | selfish |
| discreet | indifference | respect | tolerance |

1. Even though Mr. Soto gave a _____*generous*_____ donation to the library fund, he wishes he could have given more.

2. If I had been more _____, Jenny wouldn't have found out about her surprise birthday party.

3. Make sure to be on time for your appointment with Ms. Benson. She doesn't have much _____ for lateness.

4. We lost all _____ for Ben when he lied about what happened to the computer.

5. I think it's important to teach children to be _____ toward others.

6. Gina is pretty _____. Even though she lost the singing competition, she'll be ready to sing again tomorrow.

7. _____ to global warming really bothers me.

8. Brad is so _____. He only thinks about how things affect him.

4 GRAMMAR

Read each situation. Then write one sentence with a wish about the present or future and one sentence with a regret about the past.

1. Tim stopped at a store to get a soda. He put his wallet down on the counter. When he went to pick it up, the wallet was gone! His ID and credit cards were in the wallet.
   Tim wishes he could find his wallet.
   If Tim hadn't set his wallet down, he wouldn't have lost his credit cards.

2. Laura had a 5:00 flight. She planned to take the 3:45 bus to the airport. Unfortunately, the bus was late. She missed her flight.
   _____
   _____

3. Charles was planning to study for four hours for his driver's test the next day. He went to the movies with his friend instead and studied for only 20 minutes. He failed the test.
   _____
   _____

4. Maxine quit going to college in her junior year. She planned to take one year off to travel and then go back to school. That was five years ago.
   _____
   _____

A Read the article quickly. Decades ago, what was the assumption about how the Internet would affect people's honesty?

Internet On, Inhibitions Off:
Why We Tell All On The Net

It is now well known that people are generally accurate and (sometimes embarrassingly) honest about their personalities when profiling themselves on social networking sites. Patients are willing to be more open about psychiatric symptoms to an automated online doctor than a real one. Pollsters find that people give more honest answers to an online survey than to one conducted by phone.

But online honesty cuts both ways. Bloggers find that readers who comment on their posts are often harshly frank, but that these same rude critics become polite if contacted directly. . . .

Why is this? Why do we become more honest the less we have to face each other? Posing the question may make the answer seem obvious – that we feel uncomfortable about confessing to or challenging others when face to face with them – but that begs the question: Why? This is one of those cases where it is helpful to compare human beings with other species, to set our behavior in context.

In many monkeys and apes, face-to-face contact is essentially antagonistic. Staring is a threat. . . . Put two monkey strangers in a cage and they keep well apart, avoid eye contact, and generally do their utmost to avoid triggering a fight. Put two people in an elevator and the same thing happens. . . .

For many primates, face-to-face contact carries a threat. When we're online, we're essentially faceless. Deep in our psyches, the act of writing a furious online critique of someone's views does not feel like a confrontation, whereas telling them the same thing over the phone or face to face does. All the cues are missing that would warn us not to risk a revenge attack by being too frank. . . .

Internet flaming and its benign equivalent, online honesty, are a surprise. Two decades ago, most people thought the anonymity of the online world would cause an epidemic of dishonesty, just as they thought it would lead to geeky social isolation. Then along came social networking, and the Internet not only turned social but became embarrassingly honest. . . .

B Read the article again. Choose the correct answers.

1. What do social networking sites and automated online doctors have in common?
   - ☐ a. They make people more honest.
   - ☐ b. They make people less trustworthy.
   - ☐ c. They make people more ethical.

2. A monkey that stands face-to-face with another monkey probably . . .
   - ☐ a. wants to be agreeable.
   - ☐ b. is showing respect.
   - ☐ c. is looking for a fight.

3. Why does the writer talk about monkeys and apes in the article?
   - ☐ a. To make a contrast with human behavior.
   - ☐ b. To help explain human behavior.
   - ☐ c. To point out animals are capable of dishonesty.

4. What does the author suggest is the cause of online frankness?
   - ☐ a. People have become less sociable.
   - ☐ b. It's human nature to confront others.
   - ☐ c. We don't feel threatened for saying what we think.

LESSON A ▶ *Culture shock*

1 GRAMMAR

Look at the timeline that a mother has envisioned for her twins' lives. Are the sentences true or false? Choose the correct answer. Then rewrite the false sentences to make them true.

Max and Ava's Timeline

January 2010
born

September 2015
go to school for the first time

June 2032
graduate from college

August 2032
leave on a trip around the world

July 2035
return home from trip

October 2035
start their careers

	True	False
1. By September 2026, Max and Ava will have been going to school for 10 years.	☐	☑

By September 2026, Max and Ava will have been going to
school for 11 years.

	True	False
2. By July 2032, they will already have graduated from college.	☐	☐

	True	False
3. By September 2033, they will be leaving on a trip around the world.	☐	☐

	True	False
4. By August 2035, they will have been traveling for three years.	☐	☐

	True	False
5. It's now October 2034. By this time next year, they will have started their careers.	☐	☐

	True	False
6. By October 2037, they will have been working for one year.	☐	☐

2 GRAMMAR

Complete the email. Use the future perfect or future perfect continuous of the verbs in parentheses.

To: Julie
Cc:
Subject: Paris!

Hi Julie,

By this time tomorrow, I (1) _____ *will have arrived* _____ (arrive) in France! I can't believe I get to study there! I'm nervous, but I hope by next week I (2) _____ (learn) my way around. I'm sure I (3) _____ (get) lost several times by then, too.

I (4) _____ (meet) my roommate by this time next week, too. I hope she's nice. I'm nervous about meeting my new classmates. They're all from different parts of the world. I hope in six month's time I (5) _____ (have) the opportunity to get to know each of them.

I can't wait for you to visit. Maybe you can come in December. That should give you some time to save money since you (6) _____ (work) for a few months by then. And also by then, I'm sure I (7) _____ (find) some great restaurants to eat at. I know how much you love French food!

I already miss you, so write to me as soon as you can!

Isabella

3 VOCABULARY

Complete the sentences with *about*, *in*, *of*, *to*, or *with*. Sometimes more than one answer is possible.

1. Kenji can't wait for his trip to the United States. He's looking forward _____ *to* _____ visiting California and New York.

2. Before Nicole left to work in her company's branch in Spain, she participated _____ a special training program.

3. If you have the opportunity to work in another country, don't be scared _____ taking it.

4. Michelle made friends easily after she adjusted _____ the new culture.

5. Jack was very excited _____ meeting his colleagues from China.

6. If you want to take advantage _____ your school's study abroad programs, you should talk to your adviser.

7. She wasn't familiar _____ the customs in her host country, but she soon adapted to life there.

8. As soon as he became aware _____ his company's policy allowing employees to work in another country for a year, he decided to apply.

WRITING

A Read the three conclusions about the experience of working abroad. Write the letters of all the methods used in each conclusion.

a. looks to the future   c. summarizes the main points
b. concludes with the main idea   d. makes recommendations

b, c, d **1.**   In conclusion, those who decide to live abroad gain experience of other cultures, understanding of others' work practices, and a deeper empathy for people of other countries. Working abroad widens your view of the world, and that will be of lasting benefit in both your work and personal life. Definitely do it if you can.

_____ **2.**   To sum up, people who decide to work abroad will have the opportunity to change their lives in several ways. First, they will develop a deep understanding of another culture. Second, they will gain first-hand experience of work practices that can give them a new perspective on their own work. Last, they will broaden their knowledge of the world in ways that will stay with them for the rest of their lives.

_____ **3.**   In brief, whether you decide to work abroad on a short-term basis or for an extended period, it is an experience that is educational, pleasurable, and practical. The experience allows you to flourish in all aspects of your life long after the experience is over and is highly recommended for anyone who has the chance to do it.

B Underline the words or phrases in each conclusion above that helped you decide which methods were used.

C Write a short essay about what people should expect to experience if they come to work or study in your country. Your conclusion should contain at least one of the methods listed above.

_____
_____
_____
_____
_____
_____
_____
_____
_____
_____
_____
_____
_____
_____
_____
_____
_____

GRAMMAR

Use the verbs in parentheses to complete the email. Use mixed conditionals.

Dear Elena,

Well, I'm halfway through my tour of Peru. I'd like to say that everything is going well, but unfortunately, that isn't the case. I think if I (1) _____ ***had prepared*** _____ (prepare) a little more thoroughly, I (2) _____ (enjoy) myself a lot more right now. I guess if I (3) _____ (take) more time to research where I was going to stay, I (4) _____ (have) a better time in this beautiful country.

My biggest mistake is that I didn't bring the right clothes. I brought all my summer clothes, and it is absolutely freezing! If I (5) _____ (bring) the right clothes, I (6) _____ (feel) more comfortable right now. Instead, I've been staying indoors as much as possible and have a terrible cold. I went to a local pharmacy to get some cold medicine, but I had some trouble reading the labels. I think I bought the wrong medicine. If I (7) _____ (buy) the right medicine, I (8) _____ (not sneeze) all the time! If I (9) _____ (follow) your advice about the weather and accommodations, I (10)_____ (not have) so many problems right now!

Anyway, I'll remember next time. I miss you!

Love,
Sophia
Attached: perutrip014.jpg

GRAMMAR

Match the clauses to make conditional sentences. Write the correct letter.

1. If I had packed more carefully, _____

2. If I hadn't chosen a discount airline, _____

3. If I had studied English more often, _____

4. If I had left for the airport earlier, _____

5. If I hadn't forgotten my novel, _____

a. I wouldn't be afraid to ask people for directions.

b. I wouldn't be reading a boring magazine right now.

c. I wouldn't be searching my bags for my passport.

d. I would have a free movie to look forward to on board.

e. I wouldn't be worried about missing my flight!

3 VOCABULARY

What characteristics do you think would be most important for these people?
Write sentences about each picture using the adjectives from the box.

culturally aware	nonconforming	open-minded	self-motivated
culturally sensitive	nonjudgmental	self-assured	self-reliant

mountain climber

businessperson abroad

1. The mountain climber has to be ____*self-reliant*____ because *she could be left* _____
   on her own in an emergency. _____

2. If the mountain climber weren't _____, she _____
   _____

3. The businessperson abroad should be _____
   _____

4. If the businessperson abroad weren't _____
   _____

4 GRAMMAR

Complete the sentences so they are true for you.

1. If I had been open-minded about *studying abroad in college, I would have* _____
   much more international experience on my résumé. _____

2. If I had been more self-assured when _____,
   I _____

3. If I had been more culturally aware when I was younger, I _____
   _____

4. If I hadn't been open-minded about _____,
   I _____

A Read the article quickly. Choose the tips that are mentioned.

☐ call your friends at home   ☐ spend a lot of time alone

☐ take a course in anthropology   ☐ prepare for culture shock

☐ take a class for people going abroad   ☐ visit a doctor regularly

BEATING CULTURE SHOCK

You have a chance to live and work overseas, to get to know another culture from the inside. It's a wonderful opportunity, but don't be surprised if you experience at least some culture shock. "When you're put into a new culture, even simple things will throw you. You become like a child again, unable to handle everyday life without help," says L. Robert Kohls, an expert on culture shock.

Taking an intercultural studies or anthropology course at a university or attending one of the many classes offered for people going abroad is an important way to reduce the stress of culture shock, says Elsie Purnell, the founder of a counseling agency. She advises people going overseas to expect culture shock and to try to be prepared for it.

Someone living in a new culture typically goes through four stages of adjustment. Initial euphoria, or the honeymoon stage, is characterized by high expectations, a focus on similarities in the new culture, and a tendency to attach positive values to any differences that are noticed.

Culture shock, the second stage, begins very suddenly. The symptoms of culture shock include homesickness, feelings of anxiety, depression, fatigue, and inadequacy. Some people going through culture shock try to withdraw from the new culture, spending most of their free time reading about home, sleeping 12 hours a night, and associating only with others from their own country. Others eat too much, feel irritable, and display hostility or even aggression.

A period of gradual adjustment is the third stage. Once you realize you're adjusting, life gets more hopeful. "You've been watching what's been going on, interpreting things, and you're starting to recognize the patterns and learn the underlying values of the culture," says Kohls. It feels more natural, and you feel more self-assured.

The fourth stage, full adjustment, can take several years, and not everyone achieves it. According to Kohls, a lot depends on people's personalities – how rigid or how easygoing they are – and how seriously they try to understand the new culture.

B Read the article again. At what stage would someone make the following statements?

	Stage 1	Stage 2	Stage 3	Stage 4
1. "I just want to sleep all the time."	☐	☑	☐	☐
2. "The customs here are different, but they are so wonderful and sophisticated!"	☐	☐	☐	☐
3. "I've lived here for so many years that it feels like home."	☐	☐	☐	☐
4. "Everyone has been so helpful and friendly since I've arrived. The people here are so polite!"	☐	☐	☐	☐
5. "I'm starting to understand the culture and feel more self-assured here."	☐	☐	☐	☐
6. "I only spend time with people from my own country."	☐	☐	☐	☐